Projects for Woodworkers
Volume 2

Projects for Woodworkers
Volume 2

The Editors of *The Woodworker's Journal*

Madrigal Publishing Company

Printed in the United States of America.

Fifth Printing: June 1994

Library of Congress Cataloging-in-Publication Data:
(Revised for vol. 2)

Projects for woodworkers.

Includes index.
Contents: v. 1. [without special title] —
v. 2. 60 project plans for furniture, toys, and
accessories.
1. Woodworking. I. Woodworker's journal.
TT185.P76   1987   684'.08   87-15414
ISBN 0-9617098-2-0 (pbk. : v.2)

Madrigal Publishing Company
517 Litchfield Road
P.O. Box 1629
New Milford, CT 06776

Contents

(continued on next page)

Acknowledgment

Our thanks to the following individuals who contributed material to this book:

Sam Allen, Rough-Sawn Cedar Clock, Laminated Shoehorn, and Old-Time Radio Case; Jon W. Arno, Candle Box; Steve Benjamin, Early American Wall Cupboard; Bob Boxess, Band Saw Boxes; Donald E. Cornue, Country Kitchen Cabinet; G.T. Kirsch, Jr., Butcher Block Knife Rack; Paul Levine, Flip-Top Box, Tambour Desk, Geodesic Lighting Fixture, Cider Press Lamp, Toy Tool Box, and Woodpile Trivet; Robert C. Lewis, 18th Century Lawyer's Case; C.J. Maginley, Toy Helicopter and Toy Jeep; Patrick D. Mahaney, Swinging Cradle; Robert A. McCoy, Veneered End Table and Candle Holder; Donald McLean, Dishtowel Holder; Walter Miles, Contemporary Writing Desk; Joseph Oliveri, Early American Chest; Roger E. Schroeder, Stepped-Back Hutch, Empire Footstool, Buckboard Seat, Hutch Clock, Cheese Cutting Board, Mahogany Tripod Table, Ship's Wheel Weather Station, Chess Table, and Lyre Clock; James R. Spence, Jr., Dovetailed Footstool; Clarence D. Stallman, Collector's Plate Frame; Donald Tyson, Pine Footstool; Joe Walker, Artist's Easel; Ted Wheeler, Oak Hanging Light Fixture; John M. Wilson, Blanket Chest.

Also, our thanks to Armor Products for the Willie and Tuna Toy; Cherry Tree Toys for the Frog Pull Toy and the Whale Toy; Joe Gluse who did the technical art for the Early American Chest, Swinging Cradle, Veneered End Table, and Oak Hanging Light Fixture; Gene Marino III who did the technical art for the 19th Century Step-Chair, 19th Century Danish Washstand, and Early American Wall Cupboard; and John Kane of Silver Sun Studios for the cover photo and many of the project photos.

The Editors

Introduction

Whether you're starting a project that will take one hour or a hundred hours to complete, the first thing you'll need is a plan from which to work. This book contains 60 plans for projects selected from the 1982 issues of *The Woodworker's Journal* magazine. Although these issues are now out of print, the plans remain appropriate for today's woodworkers.

The projects range in complexity from the little spaghetti measuring paddle to the massive oak double-tambour desk. Also, the designs cover a period of roughly 200 years, from the quaint 18th century lawyer's file case to the contemporary geodesic lighting fixture.

We've tried to include enough projects to appeal to a wide variety of tastes, skill levels and ambitions, and it is our sincere hope that this book will become well shopworn while providing you with many interesting ideas and techniques. May it also provide the incentive to continue developing your woodworking skills and sense of craftsmanship.

The Editors

This reproduction of an antique hutch is so simple in design that it can be made with a minimum of tools. Since it's made of number 2 common pine with no elaborate hardware, it can be built at a cost appreciably under $100.00 and will be an attractive addition to any Early American setting.

Begin by gluing up 1″ pine lumber (actually ¾″ thick) to make the sides (A). A 7¼″ wide board slightly longer than 6 feet is glued and clamped to a 7½″ wide x 36½″ long board. If both boards are carefully jointed and glued, no dowels should be necessary to reinforce the joint. Make up two sides (A) and trim them to finish width and length. The dadoes for the shelves and rabbet for the top (C) can be cut with the radial arm, table saw or portable router and straight bit.

After completing the sides cut the shelves to size (parts B, D and E) and the top (C). Note that parts B and D have grooves for plates. These are made by running the lumber over a table saw blade set at 45 degrees and then at 90 degrees. The grooves need only be about ¼″ deep.

The two shelves (E), differ in that one has a 20½″ long by ¼″ deep notch cut into it and the other has a ¼″ x ¼″ rabbet. These modifications follow the original while all else is ¾″ thick with the exception of the ⅜″ door panel.

The door is next. The stiles, parts K, L, and M, are cut from full 1 inch thick pine and joined together with mortises and tenons. The panel for the door, part N, is glued up from ½″ thick stock and planed down to ⅜″. An alternate door assembly would use ¾″ thick (actual) pine for the stiles and rails and, if available, pine veneered plywood of ¼″ thickness could be used for the door panel. If this method is used, the rail tenons and corresponding grooves should be cut ¼″ wide rather than ⅜″.

The original door panel molding was shaped with a molding plane but most lumberyards carry a suitable small panel molding similar to the molding P shown in the detail. This molding is mitered and attached to the door rails and, stiles with glue and small brads. Do not glue the molding to a door panel made from solid stock. The back of the panel may be left as is or dressed up with a small quarter-round molding.

Secure the shelves with counterbored 1″ x #10 fh wood screws that are plugged with ⅜″ dia. dowels before sanding the assembled hutch. The top (C) is secured with finishing nails.

The hutch back consists of three wide ¾″ thick boards joined together with tongues and grooves or a ship lap joint. The back boards are held to the sides and shelves with finishing nails. If sufficiently wide boards cannot be secured, narrower boards can be used to avoid gluing up wide boards. The matching tongues and grooves can be

Stepped-Back Hutch

Bill of Materials (All Dimensions Actual)							
Part	Description	Size	No. Req'd	Part	Description	Size	No. Req'd
A	Side	¾ x 14¾ x 72	2	I	Bottom Stile	¾ x 8 x 33	2
B	Counter	¾ x 15¼ x 37½	1	J	Back Board	¾ x as req'd x 71¼	As Req'd
C	Top	¾ x 7 x 35¾	1	K	Door Stile	1 x 3¼ x 33	2
D	Upper Shelf	¾ x 6¼ x 35½	2	L	Upper Door Rail	1 x 3¼ x 14¾	1
E	Lower Shelf	¾ x 14 x 35½	2	M	Lower Door Rail	1 x 5¾ x 14¾	1
F	Top Rail	¾ x 5¼ x 36½	1	N	Door Panel	⅜ x 14⅝ x 24⅝	1
G	Top Stile	¾ x 4½ x 29¾	2	O	Top Molding	(See Detail)	5 Ft.
H	Bottom Rail	¾ x 3¼ x 36½	1	P	Door Molding	(See Detail)	7 Ft.

safely cut with a portable router.

Parts F, G, H and I are next cut to size and attached to the sides and shelves with couterbored and plugged 1″ x #10 fh screws.

The door hinges, brass or black steel, are mortised into the door. Black, flush-mounted "H" hinges can be substituted and will also look authentic. The turnbutton, or latch is cut from a piece of scrap and mounted with a 1″ x #10 black round-head wood screw. The 1¼″ diameter door knob is of the standard turned wood type found in most hardware stores.

The upper molding, part O, consists of two pieces of ¼″ pine and ¾″ cove.

These pieces can be individually mitered and fastened with small finishing nails.

Before putting on the finish, plug all screw holes with ⅜″ dowel plugs and sand them flush. Screws may also be covered with plugs cut from face grain of pine scrap using a ⅜″ plug cutter in an electric drill. Plugs of this type will not be very noticeable which you may or may not prefer. They do sand down flush easier than birch dowel plugs.

After sanding, the choice of stains to be used will depend on your individual preferences. The choices are all attractive and include light and dark browns, reddish browns or honey tones.

Pigmented oil stains are readily available and easy to apply evenly with brush and rag.

Two or three coats of a satin finish varnish should be applied to all visible surfaces. The final coat is rubbed down with 4/0 steel wool to achieve a uniform low sheen. To minimize warping, don't forget to varnish both sides of all parts including the shelves. An easier finishing method is to apply a number of coats of one of the modern penetrating oils such as Watco Danish Oil. Initial coats penetrate and help stabilize the wood. Additional coats will enhance the color and build up an attractive low luster surface finish.

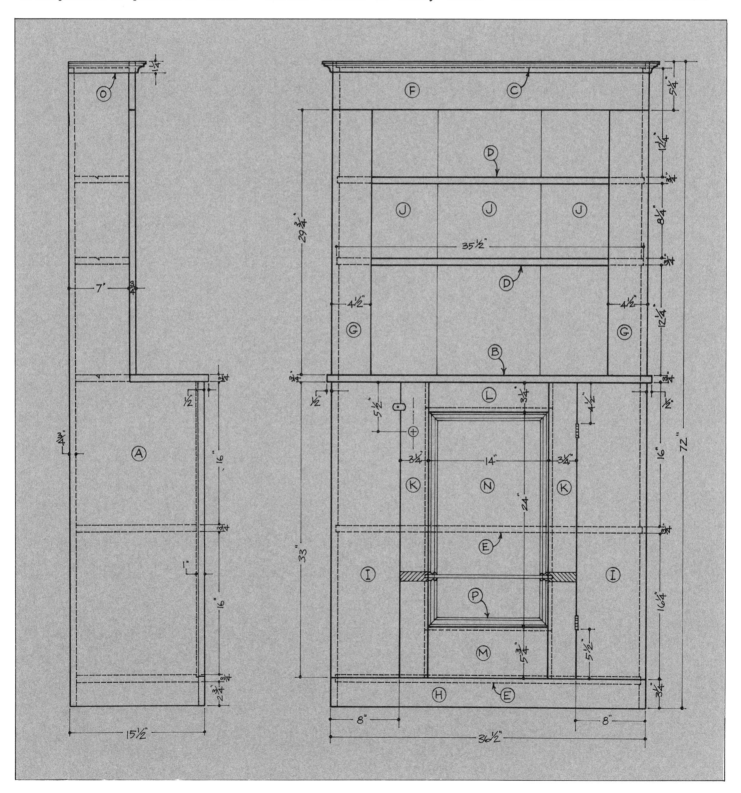

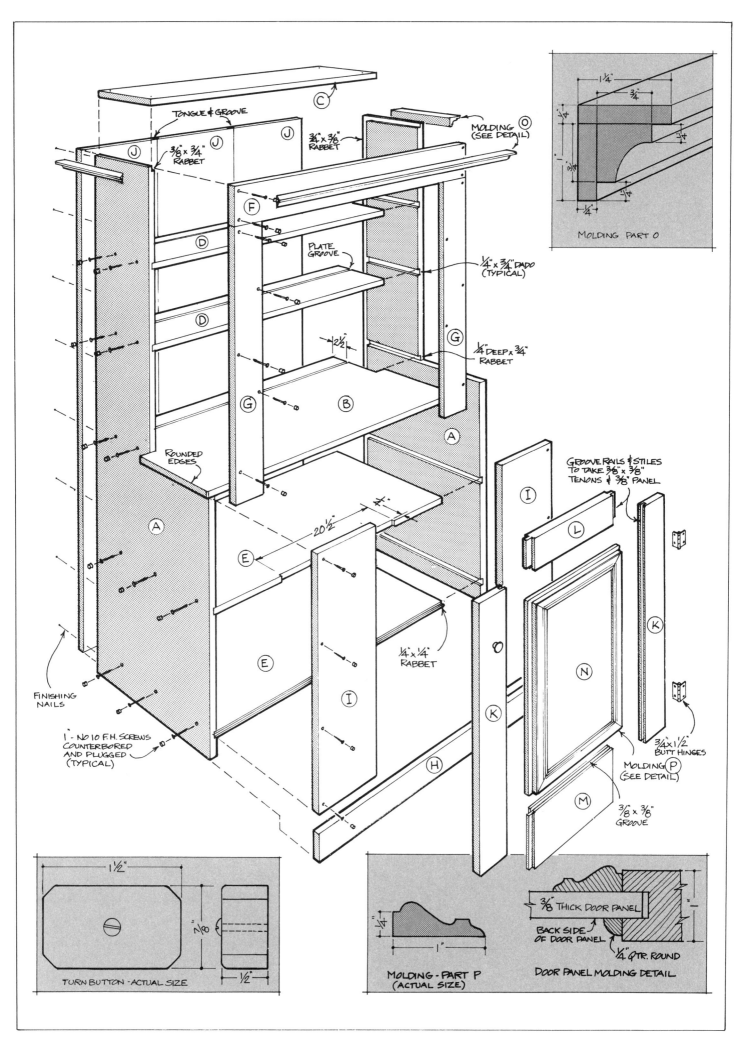

Butcher Block Knife Rack

A free-standing knife rack is an attractive kitchen accessory that can be put to good use in most any household. This one is made from pine, although maple would be an even better choice. It's designed to handle most of the common knife sizes, but before starting it's best to check your knives for blade length, width, and thickness. If necessary, it's an easy matter to change dimensions to suit.

Here's how to make it:

Step 1: Cut stock to length and width.

Step 2: Set sawblade to a depth of ⅝-inch. Locate rip-fence to cut a groove ¾-inch from the fence. Cut groove A along entire workpiece, then place opposite edge against fence and cut groove B.

Step 3: Locate rip-fence to cut a groove 2⅛ inches from the fence. Cut groove C along entire workpiece, then place opposite edge against fence and cut groove D.

Step 4: Crosscut workpiece into two 23-inch lengths. Flip over as shown, align the grooves and glue and clamp together. Avoid getting glue in the grooves. Before gluing, drive several short brads, then clip off the heads so that about ⅛-inch is exposed. This will keep the two halves from sliding when clamped. Make sure you don't locate the brads along the cutting lines shown in Step 5.

Step 5: Crosscut as shown. Note a little extra stock is provided.

Step 6: Glue and clamp as shown, again using headless brads.

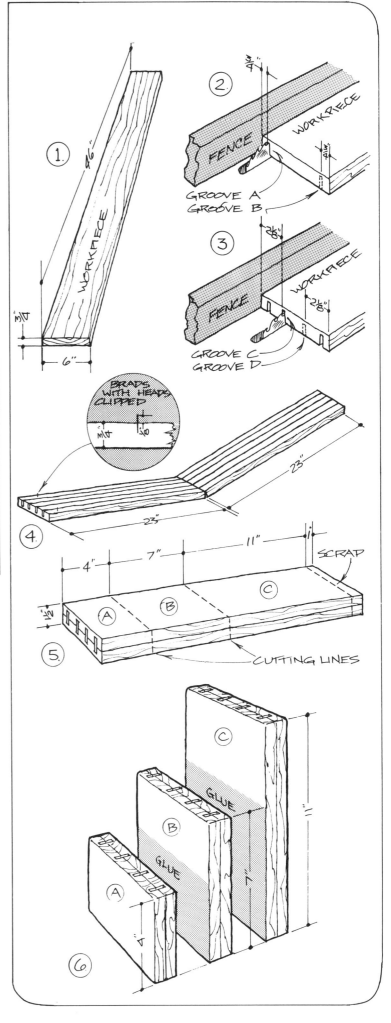

Artist's Easel

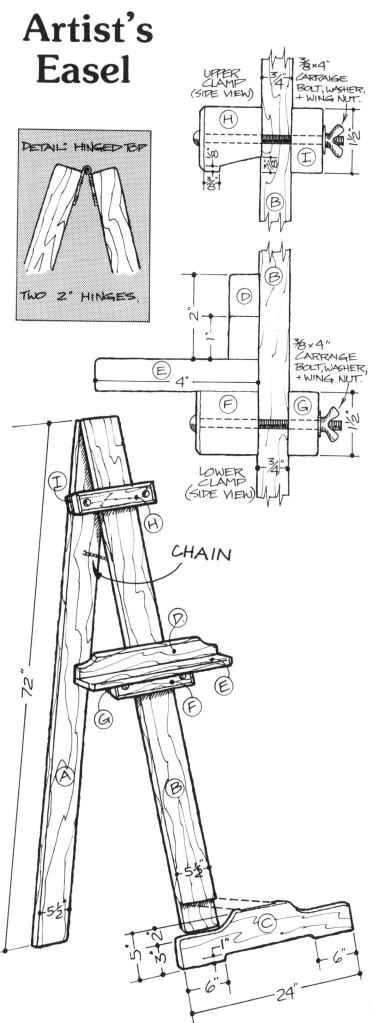

DETAIL: HINGED TOP

TWO 2" HINGES.

UPPER CLAMP (SIDE VIEW)

3/8 × 4" CARRAIGE BOLT, WASHER, + WING NUT.

3/8 × 4" CARRAIGE BOLT, WASHER, + WING NUT.

LOWER CLAMP (SIDE VIEW)

CHAIN

With a design that's simple yet functional, this lightweight easel can be built by devoting just a few evenings in the workshop. An upper clamp serves to hold the canvas in place when painting outdoors on breezy days. To keep weight to a minimum, this one's made from pine, but if weight isn't a consideration you can use just about any hardwood. Oak would be an excellent choice.

The back leg (A) is made from ¾ inch (actual) by 5½ inch wide by 72 inch long stock. Choose a piece that's free of any large knots that can reduce strength.

The front leg (B) is cut to ¾ x 5½ x 71. A ⅜ inch deep by 4 inch wide half lap is cut to accept part C. The half-lap can be cut on the table or radial arm saw equipped with a dado head cutter.

Make the foot (C) from ¾ x 5 x 24 stock. A ⅜ inch deep x 4 inch wide dado is cut to accept part B. The shape of the curves is not critical. Make a cardboard template of one-half of the foot and transfer the shape to the stock, then flip the template over to mark the other side. Cut to shape with a band or saber saw.

Cut part D (¾ x 2 x 20), part E (¾ x 4 x 20), part F (1½ x 1½ x 8½), part G (¾ x 1½ x 8½), part H (1½ x 1½ x 9), and part I (¾ x 1½ x 9). Note that the lower edge of part H is tapered to add holding strength to the upper clamp. Assemble as shown. Parts D, E, and F are secured with glue. A pair of 2 inch butt hinges joins the two legs. A short chain is also added. Final finish consists of two coats of polyurethane varnish.

Flip-Top Box

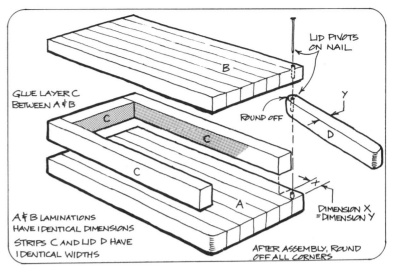

GLUE LAYER C
BETWEEN A & B

LID PIVOTS
ON NAIL

ROUND OFF

Y

D

A & B LAMINATIONS
HAVE IDENTICAL DIMENSIONS
STRIPS C AND LID D HAVE
IDENTICAL WIDTHS

DIMENSION X
= DIMENSION Y

AFTER ASSEMBLY, ROUND
OFF ALL CORNERS

This striking small box is simplicity itself to make and provides another way to use up your scraps of exotic woods. The box shown is 1⅛″ x 2⅛″ x 3¾″ but you can make them in any handy small size. A & B are made by gluing together strips of contrasting wood to form a lamination long enough which when cut in half, forms the two sides. Parts C and D are all cut from one strip. Glue and clamp parts C between A & B, then place the lid D in position and drill through for a pivot nail. Sand the box, rounding all corners and finish with penetrating oil.

Candle Box

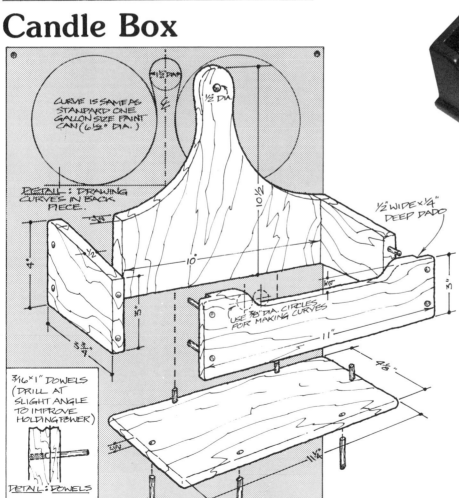

CURVE IS SAME AS STANDARD ONE GALLON SIZE PAINT CAN (6½″ DIA.)

DETAIL: DRAWING CURVES IN BACK PIECE.

1½ DIA

½ DIA

10½

½″ WIDE x ¼″ DEEP DADO

USE ⅜″ DIA. CIRCLES FOR MAKING CURVES

10

11

3″

3/16″ x 1″ DOWELS (DRILL AT SLIGHT ANGLE TO IMPROVE HOLDING POWER)

DETAIL: DOWELS

11¼″

Thanks to Thomas Edison, the candle box has been obsolete in most American homes for the better part of a century. But by "obsolete", we mean that it is no longer needed for its original purpose. It is still a very handy and attractive accent piece, a perfect place to store the electric bill and other incoming mail until we have the time and money to respond.

The candlebox shown here is not a reproduction of any surviving, colonial original; rather, it has been designed and sized for its modern use. But, at a glance, an 18th century American would certainly experience a sense of familiarity.

Assemble as shown using glue and pegs. Stain to suit and final finish with two coats of polyurethane varnish.

Infinity Mirror

It's nearly impossible to fully describe the visual effect that results when this mirror's lights are turned on. Looking into it, you see what appears to be a rectangular tunnel of small white lights, with the tunnel gradually getting smaller in size and fading into darkness — or more precisely, into infinity. It's not magic though, the effect comes from a set of 50 G.E. (General Electric) Miniature "String Along" clear bulbs installed between a regular mirror and a two-way mirror. Any equivalent lights can be substituted. When the lights are turned off the Infinity Mirror can be used as a regular mirror.

The inner frame (parts C & D) can be made first. If you can't get ½ inch pine, most millwork shops will surface plane 1 inch (¾″ actual) stock down to ½ inch. After parts C & D are cut to length and width, use the table or radial arm saw to cut a ⅛ inch deep by ¼ inch wide rabbet along the back inside edge. The rabbet won't show so it's not necessary that it be stopped along part C, just run it through. Next the light holes can be drilled, using the spacing detail as a guide. The closest standard drill size is 11/32 inch. This is okay although the lights will fit-up a little sloppy and require epoxy glue. To make ours a good snug fit, we filed down an old ⅜″ spade bit so that it would drill a near perfect size hole. After drilling, parts C & D can be butt joined as shown. Each joint is secured with glue and two finishing nails driven through pilot holes in part C. Before setting aside to dry, make sure the frame is dead square, or you'll have problems later when the mirror is installed.

Before attaching the lights, test the string to make sure they all work, then remove each bulb. The G.E. Christmas tree lights we've specified will operate even if a light burns out. Starting with the first hole in the lower part D (see detail drawing) insert the first light (it's the first of two starter lights on the string). Insert the socket until it's just flush with the inside surface of part D. Continue adding lights until all 50 are inserted. A small dab of epoxy glue will secure any that are loose. To keep sawdust out of the sockets, temporarily cover them with strips of masking tape.

The ½ inch thick oak outer frame (parts A & B) is made as shown. Note that the miters are reinforced with splines. Like the inner frame, this outer frame must also be square.

To make the hardboard frame front (E), cut a piece of ⅛ inch hardboard slightly larger than the outside frame dimensions. Using ¾″ wire nails and glue, attach this piece (rough side in) to the frame so that it slightly overhangs the outer frame on all four sides. When dry, plane the hardboard perfectly flush with the outside frame.

Make four ¾ inch thick by 1¼ inch wide by 4 inch long spacer blocks (not shown). Lay the frame (hardboard side down) on a flat surface, then place a spacer block (1¼″ face down) at the center of each outer frame side. If all cuts have been made accurately the inner frame should just fit inside the four spacer blocks — if not, make adjustments.

With the inner frame sitting between the blocks, use the inside of the inner frame as a template and scribe a pencil line around all four sides. After drilling a few starter holes, use a saber saw to cut out this rectangle, taking care to stay about ⅛ inch on the waste side of the pencil line. The spacer blocks can now be glued in place.

Apply a coat of glue to the front edge of the inner frame, then fit it in place between the spacer blocks. Holding it in place, flip the entire assembly over, then secure with ¾ inch wire nails. When dry, use a file or Stanley Surform to shave the hardboard flush with the inside of the inner frame.

To work effectively the mirror needs a light absorbing surface on the front of parts E and on the inner surface of parts C and D. Black velvet will work just fine, but it is somewhat fussy to apply because it must be glued in place. An easier approach, we found, is to use Con-Tact brand, black Cushion-All, a felt-like material with a self-adhesive back that's covered by peel-off paper. It can be ordered at most hardware stores. If not available however, another acceptable option is to apply a couple of coats of flat black paint.

Note that part I covers the vertical frame leg and part J the horizontal leg. The basic shape and dimensions are

Part	Description	Size	No. Req'd
	Bill of Materials **All Dimensions Actual**		
A	Vertical Outer Frame	½ x 2½ x 20½	2
B	Horizontal Outer Frame	½ x 2½ x 15½	2
C	Vertical Inner Frame	½ x 2½ x 17	2
D	Horizontal Inner Frame	½ x 2½ x 11	2
E	Hardboard Frame Front	⅛ x 15½ x 20½	1
F	Two-Way Mirror	¼ x 15¼ x 20¼	1
G	Glass Mirror	⅛ x 11⅜ x 16⅜	1
H	Hardboard Back	⅛ x 15½ x 20½	1
I	Vertical Cushion-All	See Detail	2
J	Horizontal Cushion-All	See Detail	2
K	Molding	See Detail	6½ feet

shown on the grid pattern; however, if your frame is slightly bigger or smaller, adjust the patterns accordingly. It's a good idea to first cut a paper pattern and try it out.

To wrap the frame, begin with part I. First remove the paper backing from the Cushion-All, then starting at the front corners, press the material in place, working in both directions toward the edges (see Detail). Smooth it out as you go along. The extra length can be folded over or trimmed off. Part J is applied in the same manner. Make sure the Cushion-All covers all wood surfaces.

With a sharp knife, cut a small hole where the Cushion-All covers the sockets, then insert the bulbs. Again make sure the wood surface does not show. Now use the knife to slit the Cushion-All at the inside frame rabbet, then insert the mirror. Tuck excess Christmas light cord into the space between the frames, then connect to the female plug of an extension cord of adequate length. Note that the extension cord female plug is also tucked between the frames. Cut out the 1/8 inch hardboard back (H) and join to the frame with 5/8" x #4 FH wood screws. To keep the edge of the hardboard from showing, we beveled it at 45 degrees. Also, note a corner is nipped off to permit entry of the cord.

The two-way mirror is placed on the front frame (mirror side out) and secured with the mitered oak molding. In order to facilitate removal of the glass (in the event it should break) only the top and side moldings are glued. The bottom molding is held in place with three 3/4" x #6 oval head countersunk wood screws. Make the miter cuts accurately for a good tight fit. A new mirror can be installed by removing the bottom molding and sliding the replacement piece in.

Finish by final sanding all surfaces, then apply several coats of a good polyurethane or Danish oil.

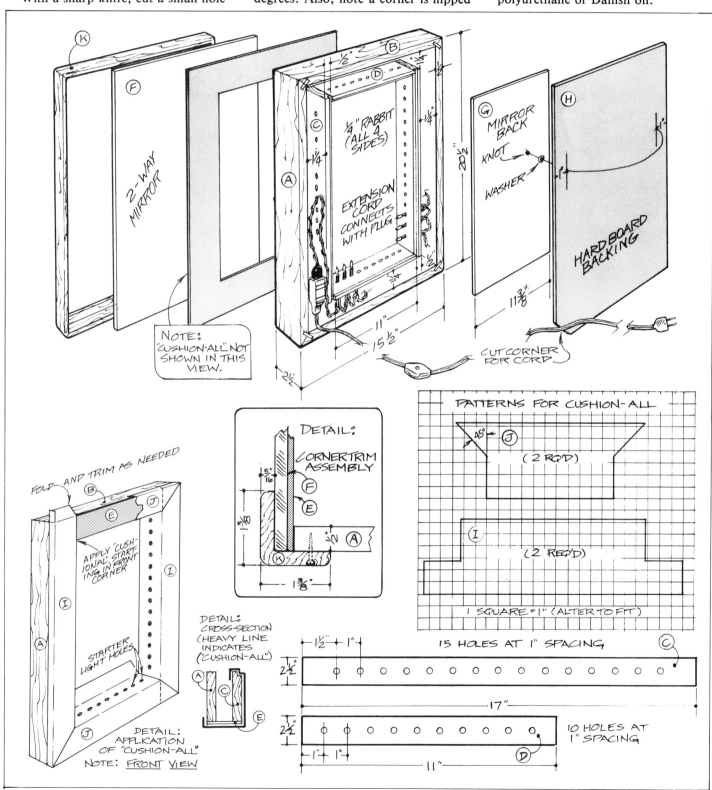

9

Empire Footstool

This maple footstool, dating from the turn of the century, was striped and painted with black paint to simulate rosewood. No doubt it would also have looked good made from cherry, mahogany, or walnut, and a modern craftsman certainly could not be criticized for choosing one of these woods. Whatever wood you use though, make sure it's a hardwood in order to provide adequate strength.

I used 1-inch (actual) wide lumber for the two legs (A). They were cut from solid boards on the original, but readers may find it necessary to glue-up two or more narrower boards if wide stock is not available. Cut the stock to an 11¼″ width and 11¼″ length. Transfer the profile from the grid pattern (note the direction of grain), then cut to shape using the band or saber saw. Sand all edges smooth, then drill a 1-inch diameter by ½-inch deep mortise for the stretcher tenon.

The stretcher (part B) is made from stock measuring at least 1½-inches square. Turn to the dimensions shown, then sand smooth. Note that each end has a 1-inch diameter by ½-inch long tenon.

Assemble the two legs (A) and the stretcher (B) using glue and bar clamps. Make sure the legs are square to the centerline of the stretcher before setting aside to dry overnight.

With the stretcher and legs assembled, the lower frame (parts C & D) can now be made. For maximum strength, the frame is made using dovetail joints, although miter joints with blind splines will make a simplified yet satisfactory alternate. To cut dovetails, use a back saw and a sharp chisel. Refer to the drawing for dovetail dimensions. Make the cuts accurately so that a snug fit and strong joint will result. Note that ⅝″ thick stock is used for parts C and D. Assemble with glue and clamps, once again checking for squareness. Allow to dry overnight. When dry, use a chisel to remove any excess glue squeeze-out.

The upper frame consists of a plywood base (F) and four beveled and mitered sections (E). As shown in the detail, part E is made from 1½ in. square stock cut to a length of 4 feet. If necessary, ¾ in. stock can be glued-up to get the 1½ in. thickness. Pine, or any other wood, can be used here. Make the cut as shown. Use a push stick and keep hands well away from the blade. The beveled stock can now be mitered and glued to part F to form the upper frame.

The dovetailed lower frame (parts C & D) is joined to the legs (A) with four countersunk 1¼ x #10 flat headed wood screws as shown on the drawing.

Cut a piece of 1-inch thick foam rubber to 11¼-inch square to fit the upper frame. Over this, lay about a 16-inch square piece of fabric, then stretch and tuck the fabric around all four sides and staple or tack to the underside of the plywood. Next, use four counter-sunk 1-inch x #10 flat headed wood screws to join the upper and lower frame.

Lightly sand any rough edges or surfaces. The choice of finishes is a matter of personal taste, but if a nice grained wood is used a clear finish is recommended. Two or three coats of satin polyurethane varnish will produce a smooth, hand finish that wears well and is easy to maintain.

Bill of Materials (All Dimensions Actual)			
Part	Description	Size	No. Req'd
A	Leg	1 x 11¼ x 11¼	2
B	Stretcher	1½ x 1½ x 10¼	1
C	Lower Frame	⅝ x 1¾ x 11¼	2
D	Lower Frame	⅝ x 1¾ x 11¼	2
E	Upper Frame	(See Detail)	4
F	Frame Base	¼ x 11¼ x 11¼	1
	Foam Rubber	1 x 11¼ x 11¼	1

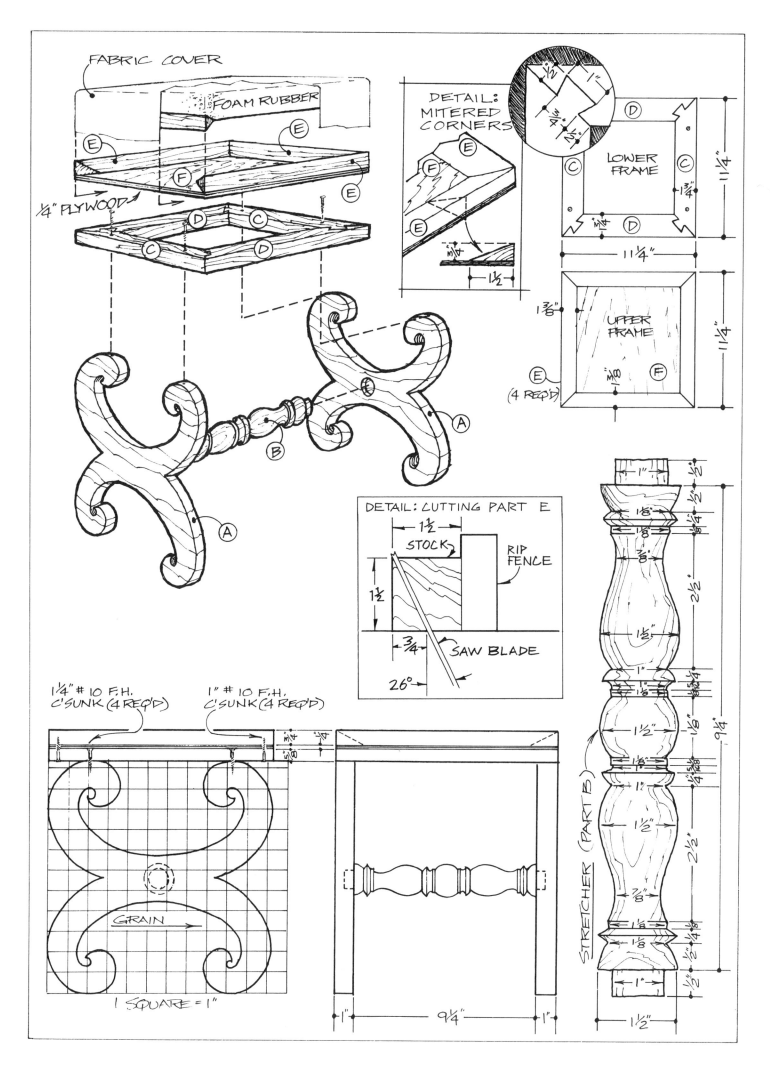

FABRIC COVER

FOAM RUBBER

E

E

F

E

¼" PLYWOOD

C D C D

DETAIL: MITERED CORNERS

F

E

E

¾"

1½

½ 1"
¾ ½

D

C LOWER FRAME C

1¾"

¾" D

11¼"

11¼"

1⅜" UPPER FRAME

E (4 REQ'D)

³⁄₁₆" F

11¼"

A

B

E

A

DETAIL: CUTTING PART E

1½

STOCK

RIP FENCE

1½

¾

SAW BLADE

26°

1"
½ ½
⅛
⅛
8¼"
⅜
2½"
1½"
1"
⅛
8⅜ ⅛
9¾"
1½"
⅛
8⅜
1"
1½"
1½"
2½"
⅞"
⅛
1⅛
½ ¼ ⅛

STRETCHER (PART B)

1"

1½"

1¼" #10 F.H. C'SUNK (4 REQ'D)

1" #10 F.H. C'SUNK (4 REQ'D)

¾"
¼"
⅝"

GRAIN

1 SQUARE = 1"

1" 9¼" 1"

Frog Pull Toy

This delightful toy will "hop" along as it is pulled across the floor...and we think kids will find it lots of fun. We thank the people at Cherry Tree Toys for providing us with plans for the project. If you'd like a catalog of all their plans, write to them at P.O. Box 369, Belmont, OH 43718. Their catalog also lists hardwood toy wheels and parts.

As with most toys, it's a good idea to use a durable hardwood such as maple or birch. Begin with part J, which is made from 1¾″ (actual) thick stock. Transfer the profile to the stock, then lay out the location of the 7/16″ diameter axle holes and the ¼″ diameter eyehole. Use a band saw to cut to shape, then use a drill press to cut the axle and eye holes.

The remaining parts can be cut to the dimensions shown. The ½″ diameter ball (C) can be lathe turned or purchased from Cherry Tree Toys. If desired, they also can furnish the cord holder (A), eyes (B), cam (D), wheels (E), and cord (F).

Give all parts a complete sanding. Round all sharp edges and corners. Assemble as shown in the exploded diagram, taking care to make sure all parts are securely glued. When making toys, it's a good idea to use a non-toxic glue such as Elmer's Glue-All. A final finish is not required.

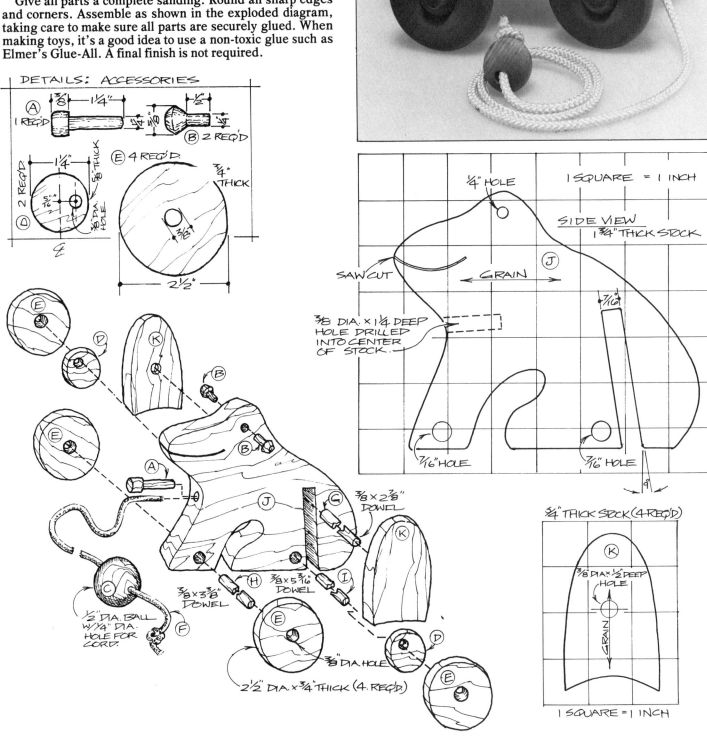

Desk Caddy

This useful desk organizer will hold a large assortment of pens and pencils along with room for lots of letter envelopes. We made ours from mahogany and think the result is very attractive.

Parts A, B, C, D, E, and F can be made from ¼ inch mahogany plywood or powerplaned from thicker solid stock. A sharp hand plane will also do the job. Parts H & I can be made by ripping ⅛ inch strips from a piece of stock measuring ⅜ inch thick by 1½ inch wide by 16 inch long. Before ripping though, crosscut 3/16 inch deep by ⅛ inch wide notches, spaced ½ inch apart as shown. Rip parts H and I for a snug fit in these notches. By the way, you can mail-order ⅛ inch and ¼ inch mahogany solid stock from the company Constantine, 2050 Eastchester Rd., Bronx, NY 10461. Their catalog is available for $1.00.

Make the base (A) from flat stock, cutting it to 3¾ inches wide by 14½ inches long. To make parts B, C, and D, again choose flat stock, then cut to 3¼ inch width by 16½ inch length. This length allows enough stock to cut all four pieces. Set the table or radial arm saw to 45 degrees, then cut all four pieces to length. Before cutting, check the sawblade to make sure it's exactly 45 degrees - don't rely on the saw's tilt scale. We find a 45-degree plastic drafting triangle is a good tool to use for this check. After the four pieces are cut, rip parts B to 2¾ inches.

Parts E and F are also cut from ¼ inch stock. One end of F is mitered to mate with part C. Note that the grain of part E runs vertically, while parts B, C, and D run horizontally.

The entire piece is assembled as shown. All parts are glued and clamped - finishing nails are not necessary if all parts fit up as they should. The thin foam is a nice detail (it cushions the pens and pencils) but not essential.

Sand lightly after assembly. An application of Deftco Danish Oil Finish will provide an attractive satin finish.

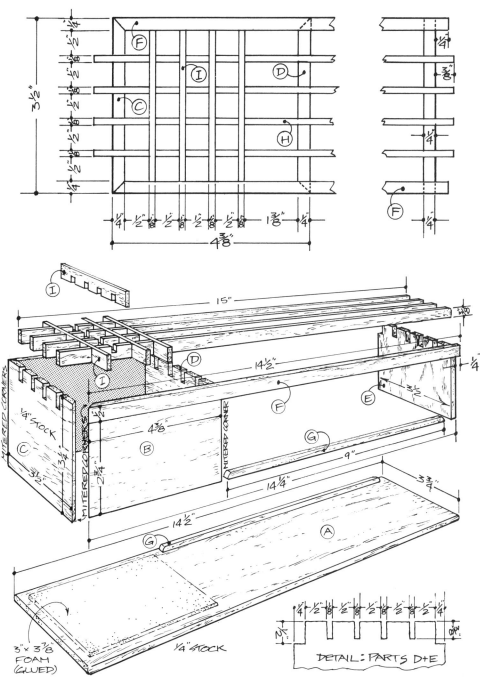

Bill of Materials
(All Dimensions Actual)

Part	Description	Size	No. Req'd
A	Base	¼ x 3¾ x 14½	1
B	Front & Back	¼ x 2¾ x 4⅜	2
C	Left End	¼ x 3¼ x 3½	1
D	Center	¼ x 3¼ x 3½	1
E	Right End	¼ x 3½ x 3¼	1
F	Stretcher	¼ x ½ x 14½	2
G	Retainer	¼ x ¼ x 9	2
H	Long Grid	⅛ x ⅜ x 15	4
I	Short Grid	⅛ x ⅜ x 3	4

Buckboard Seat

This antique buckboard seat was discovered in an antique shop and for those who enjoy a bit of nostalgia it would be perfect in a child's room, a hallway, or as a window seat.

Begin the project with the seat (part A). Whether you use glued-up boards or a single piece of 1 inch (¾ inch actual) thick lumber, you'll have to miter cut the sides and the back edge at a 10-degree angle. Note that on the side edges, there is a stop cut to be made to allow for a molding on the edge of the seat. Also note that this stop cut is beveled at 10 degrees to accept the front edge of part C.

For the sides (parts C), you'll have to make a compound miter for the back edges. Note that there's a left and right side which are mirror images of each other, so the cuts will be different. These can be done on a radial-arm saw with the blade set at a 44-degree angle and the arm at 10 degrees. On the table saw, set the blade at 44 degrees and the miter gauge at 10 degrees. The top and bottom edges will also have to be ripped at 10 degrees. Round the front corner with a saber or band saw, or use a wood rasp.

The back of the seat (part B) can now be cut to size, using the same compound miter procedure. Make the cuts accurately for a good fit with the sides (C) and seat (A). Parts D, the corner blocks, will also have to be compound mitered. These hold the sides and back together with the aid of 1¼ x #10 flat head screws that are plugged with dowels. These screws are driven into D through the sides (C) and back (B).

The legs (part E) with their shoe-foot backs come next.

On the original, these were made from solid pine boards, but I would recommend gluing-up narrower stock. Note the direction of grain. The cloverleaf design can be done with a 1¼ inch spade bit as shown in the detail. The legs are attached to the underside of the seat with ⅜ inch diameter x 2 inch long dowels. The steel straps that are attached to the inside of the legs are very important and should not be excluded. They stiffen them and will keep them from splitting along the grain. The brackets on the underside prevent lateral movement of the seat. To make them, clamp ⅛ inch thick x ¾ inch wide steel flat stock (available in most hardware stores) in a vise and bend to 45 degrees at two points as shown.

Lengths of ⅜ inch thick by ¾ inch wide pine molding act as a trim around the inside and outside edges of the seat. Compound miters at the corners are again required.

Almost any finish would seem to do, even paint. The original has a patina that could be closely duplicated by using Minwax's Puritan Pine stain with a satin varnish finish.

Bill of Materials (All Dimensions Actual)			
Part	Description	Size	No. Req'd
A	Seat	¾ x 13 x 37½	1
B	Back	¾ x 6½ x 39¾	1
C	Side	¾ x 6½ x 13¾	2
D	Corner Blocks	1 x 1 x 6	2
E	Leg	¾ x 13¾ x 14¾	2
F	Outside Molding	⅜ x ¾	As Req'd
G	Inside Molding	⅜ x ¾	As Req'd

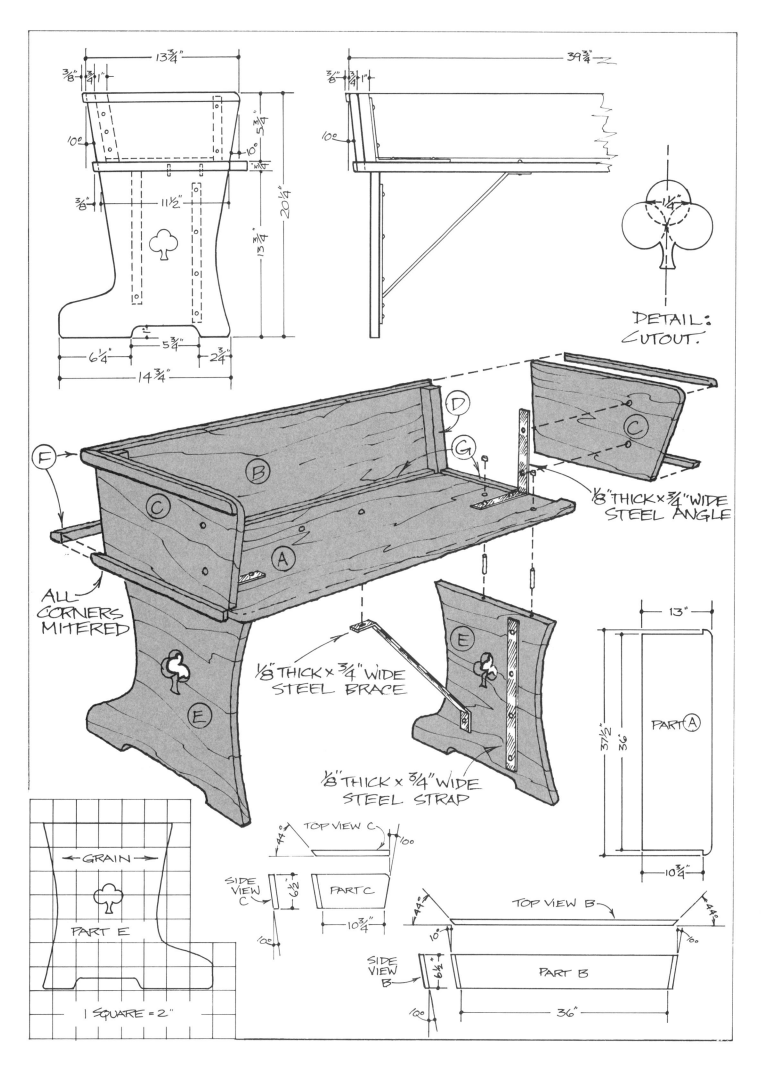

13¾"

³⁄₈" ¾" 1"

10°

5¾"

10°

¾"

20¼"

13¾"

³⁄₈"

11½"

♣

³⁄₈"

6¼"

5¾"

2¾"

14¾"

39¾"

³⁄₈" ¾" 1"

10°

10°

1¼"

DETAIL:
CUTOUT.

F

D

B

G

C

A

⅛"THICK x ¾"WIDE
STEEL ANGLE

ALL
CORNERS
MITERED

⅛"THICK x ¾"WIDE
STEEL BRACE

E

♣

E

♣

⅛"THICK x ¾"WIDE
STEEL STRAP

13"

37½"

36"

PART A

10¾"

← GRAIN →

♣

PART E

1 SQUARE = 2"

44°

TOP VIEW C

10°

SIDE
VIEW
C

6½"

PART C

10°

10¾"

44°

TOP VIEW B

44°

10°

6½"

10°

SIDE
VIEW
B

PART B

10°

36°

Oak File Cabinet

If you're turned off by commercial steel file cabinets in your home office, here's one that's a handsome piece of furniture.

The unit shown was built mainly of ¾″ oak plywood but other hardwood plywoods can be substituted. The cabinet sides, top, bottom and front and back toe rails can be cut from one half of a 4′ x 8′ sheet. The large drawer fronts can be glued up from solid oak or cut from ¾″ plywood. To insure a good permanent fit of the drawer fronts, plywood, which is dimensionally stable, is preferred. The cabinet back is ¼″ oak plywood as are the drawer bottoms. The drawer boxes are of ⅝″ solid oak though ½″ thick stock can be substituted. Note that the overall dimensions of the cabinet include edging strips which are added after assembly.

Start by carefully laying out the cabinet sides, bottom and top on the sheet of plywood. Be sure to arrange the parts so that the grain flows around the cabinet — up the sides and across the top. It's best when rough cutting the plywood parts to cut slightly oversize allowing a slight margin for trimming. If a portable circular saw or saber saw is used to rough cut, keep the face or good side down. Final trimming on the table saw is done with the good side up. To avoid splintering or tearing out when cutting across the grain, use a fine-tooth plywood blade.

After the parts are trimmed to finish size, dado and groove the sides to receive the top, bottom and back panel. Also cut the stopped grooves ¾″ wide x ¼″ deep to house the toe rails. When working with unwieldy workpieces it's easier to use a router for cutting the various grooves and rabbets. The top and bottom are rabbeted as shown to fit in the side dadoes and are also grooved to hold the ¼″ plywood back.

After cutting the back panel and the toe rails, dry assemble the cabinet and check the joints for a good fit. After making any necessary adjustments, the cabinet is glued up and clamped. Check the cabinet for squareness and adjust any clamps to insure that the box is square. This is vital because the drawers will never fit properly if the sides are out of square.

After the glue has cured, the exposed plywood edges are then covered with 3/16″ thick edging strips ripped from solid stock. The strips are glued and clamped in place using pine strips as clamp pads over the full length of the edging. Do the upright strips first, then the horizontals. The top and bottom strips are added last. Note that the top strips stand proud of the cabinet top. The bottom strips are notched to fit around the toe rails which rest on the floor.

Stock for the drawer boxes is resawn to ½″ from a 13/16″ (nominal 1″) board. The drawer sides are dadoed ¼″ deep x ⅛″ wide or the thickness of your tablesaw blade. The front and back are rabbeted so that the tongue fits snugly in the side dadoes. Groove all parts to take a ¼″ plywood bottom. The grooves are cut ⅜″ above the bottom edges.

Again, it's important to check for squareness when gluing and clamping the drawers. Also, make sure the boxes are flat as well. The large drawer fronts are cut from ¾″ plywood to the dimensions given, to be edged or they can be glued up from solid stock and cut to full size. The grain direction should be horizontal. The fronts are screwed to the drawer boxes after the drawer slides are installed.

Two pairs of 22″ heavy duty full extension drawer slides are used. These should require ½″ of space on each side of the drawer. Follow the manufacturer's instructions for mounting the slides and remember to allow ¾″ for the outer drawer front to be inset. Installation of the slides and drawer guides may vary according to the particular hardware you use. On our cabinet, the drawer guides were installed ⅞″ down from the top edges of the drawer sides. The outer drawer fronts, when fastened to the box, should extend ½″ beyond the box at each side and about ⅛″ lower than the bottom edges of the box.

The upper edges of the drawer boxes look best if they are rounded over after assembly using a router and a ¼″ rounding bit. Plane and sand all edging strips flush and finish with a penetrating oil type finish such as Deftco Danish Oil. Drawer pulls are the 3″ wire type that come in brushed aluminum or black.

The installation of wire frame type file racks and hangers for manila folders solves the problem of keeping your files neat and in an upright position. The drawers are sized for these file systems which are available at any office supplies store.

Bill of Materials
(All Dimensions Actual)

Part	Size	No. Req'd
— Case		
Side	¾ x 23⅞ x 28	2
Top	¾ x 14⅞ x 23⅞	1
Bottom	¾ x 14⅞ x 23⅞	1
Back	¼ x 14⅝ x 24	1
Rail	¾ x 3 x 14⅝	2
— Drawers		
Side	½ x 4¾ x 21⅞	4
Front (inner)	½ x 4¾ x 12⅝	2
Back	½ x 4¾ x 12⅝	2
Front (outer)	¾ x 11⅜ x 13¾	2
Edging	3/16 x ¾ x 28½ ft.	
Drawer Pulls	5/16 dia. x 3 wire type	2
Drawer Slide	22″ heavy duty full extension type	2 pr.

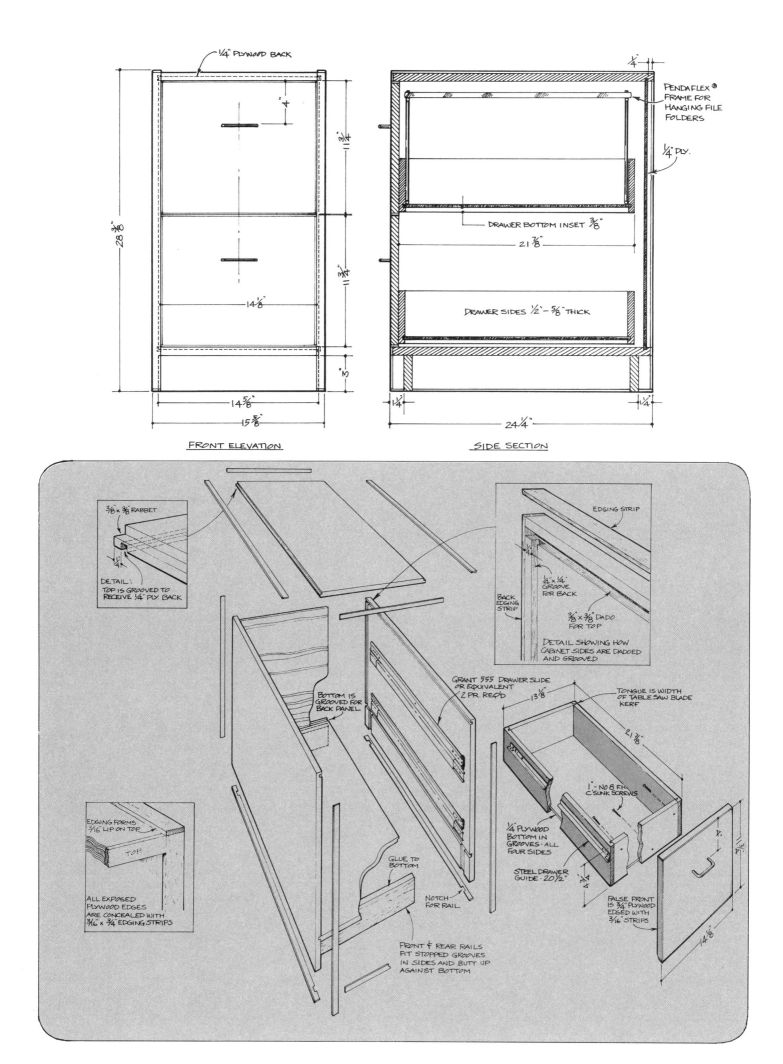

1/4" PLYWOOD BACK

28 7/8"

3 1/4"

11 1/4"

3 1/4"

11 1/4"

14 1/8"

14 5/8"

15 5/8"

3"

FRONT ELEVATION

1/4"

PENDAFLEX ® FRAME FOR HANGING FILE FOLDERS

1/4" PLY.

DRAWER BOTTOM INSET 3/8"

21 3/8"

DRAWER SIDES 1/2" - 5/8" THICK

1/4"

24 1/4"

1/4"

SIDE SECTION

3/8 x 3/8 RABBET

DETAIL: TOP IS GROOVED TO RECEIVE 1/4" PLY BACK

EDGING STRIP

1/4"

1/4" x 1/4" GROOVE FOR BACK

BACK EDGING STRIP

3/8 x 3/8 DADO FOR TOP

DETAIL SHOWING HOW CABINET SIDES ARE DADOED AND GROOVED

EDGING FORMS 3/16" LIP ON TOP

TOP

ALL EXPOSED PLYWOOD EDGES ARE CONCEALED WITH 3/16" x 3/4" EDGING STRIPS

BOTTOM IS GROOVED FOR BACK PANEL

GRANT 555 DRAWER SLIDE OR EQUIVALENT 2 PR. REQ'D

13 1/8"

TONGUE IS WIDTH OF TABLE SAW BLADE KERF

21 3/8"

1" · NO 8 F.H. C'SUNK SCREWS

GLUE TO BOTTOM

NOTCH FOR RAIL

FRONT & REAR RAILS FIT STOPPED GROOVES IN SIDES AND BUTT UP AGAINST BOTTOM

1/4" PLYWOOD BOTTOM IN GROOVES · ALL FOUR SIDES

STEEL DRAWER GUIDE · 20 1/2"

4 3/4"

FALSE FRONT IS 3/4" PLYWOOD EDGED WITH 3/16" STRIPS

4 11/16"

14 1/8"

Early American Chest

This Early American styled chest will require considerable time to build but the final result will be an attractive and useful addition for the traditionally furnished home. Maple was used for most of the construction, though other hardwoods that finish well can be substituted.

Construction is started with the top section. Begin by making the two side panels (A) of the upper section. The rails and stiles of the panel frames are cut to length and dowel holes are located and drilled. Use a router to run stopped grooves along the inner edges of the rails and stiles to take 1/4" thick panels. These panels and the front panels are of 1/4" birch plywood.

The inner edges of stiles and rails are molded as shown using a router and beading cutter. The stiles can be molded along their full length; then the molding is cut away and mitered to meet the rails. An easier alternative is to cut the rails and stiles narrower and apply separate moldings after the panels are assembled. Sand all parts and assemble with dowels and glue, taking care to keep the frames square and flat. When dry, run a 3/8" x 1/2" rabbet along the rear edges to house the 1/2" plywood back.

Next, make up the rails and stiles for the front panel assembly (B). Lay out and drill dowel holes and stopped panel grooves. The molding is cut separately and added after assembly.

The two decorative turnings are made next. When turning on the lathe, leave a square section on each end to serve as a guide against the tablesaw

fence when ripping the turnings lengthwise to form two halves. The decorative molding can be cut with a molding head on the tablesaw. Use a wide board, then rip the molding free. The wide groove can be cut with a standard combination blade, then switch to the molding head and cut the bead portion. Finish with a 3/8" radius cove cutter.

Cut the molding to rough lengths and miter the ends after the panel frame is assembled. The half turnings are then glued to the stiles. Join side panels and front with glue. Clamp up the three parts and square them with scrap strips tacked across the rear edges, then drill for 3/8" x 1 1/2" dowels and drive them in. While this assembly is clamped up and square you can measure and cut the 1/2" plywood back panel for a good fit.

The center frame (C) is made next. Use a router to groove the rails, as shown in the frame joint detail, to accept tongues cut on the stile ends. Glue and clamp up the frame and when dry, sand all joints flush. The front edge is rounded over using a router and rounding cutter and the back edge is notched as shown to receive the plywood back.

Turn the box upside down and place the center frame in position to locate the 3/4" x 3/4" screw blocks or cleats which are screwed to the frame and into the box sides. With the plywood back tacked temporarily in place you can now measure for and cut a 3/8" plywood bottom for a good snug fit all around. The bottom is not fastened but

rests on the cleats.

The drawer case assembly consists of ends (D), two front stiles (E), and a rail (F) screwed to the front of the center frame. The stiles are joined to the ends with blind dowel pins and triangular glue blocks in the corners. The ends are also rabbeted along their back edges for the plywood back.

The bottom frame (G) is similar to the center frame but has wider end stiles for the drawer to ride on. Instead of a notch, the back rail should be rabbeted to 1/2" x 3/8" for the bottom edge of the plywood back. This frame is fastened to the drawer case assembly with screws and cleats.

The base assembly consists of four feet (H), two end rails (I) and a front rail (J). The three rails are beaded along their lower edges and joined to the feet with glue, blind dowel pins and corner glue blocks. This assembly is fastened to the bottom frame G with screws seated in angled pockets as shown in the detail. Glue blocks are also used between the rails and bottom frame.

The plywood back is now fitted and small pilot holes drilled for fastening with 1" nails. A piece of solid stock 3/8" x 3" (K) is cut to fit flush with the top edge of the back and butted against the side panels. This provides a mounting for the offset chest hinges which are mortised into it.

The drawer parts are next cut and grooved for a 1/4" plywood bottom. If you have a dovetail jig, the half-blind dovetails can be easily cut with a router; otherwise join the front and sides with a rabbet joint. The applied front molding is identical to that used for the front panels. The detail shows this molding inset into a shallow rabbet cut around the drawer front.

After the drawer is assembled, two drawer guides are cut and glued to the bottom as shown in the drawer guide detail. The drawer back is notched between the guides. A center guide rail is cut to fit easily between the guides and located on the center stile of the bottom frame so that the drawer is centered in its opening.

The final item is the chest lid which is glued up from jointed 3/4" stock. The front edge and ends are rounded over. Two cleats are screwed to each end of the lid just outboard of the chest sides and the hinges are fastened.

If the chest is to be stained, leave the inside of the box and drawer interior natural. The plywood panels can be stained or painted. Seal both the exterior and interior surfaces with two coats of shellac thinned 50/50 with alcohol and sanded lightly between coats. Vacuum all surfaces and apply two coats of satin finish varnish. Rub down the final coat with fine 4/0 steel wool, until an even luster is achieved. A coat of paste wax, well buffed, completes the project.

(cont'd on next page)

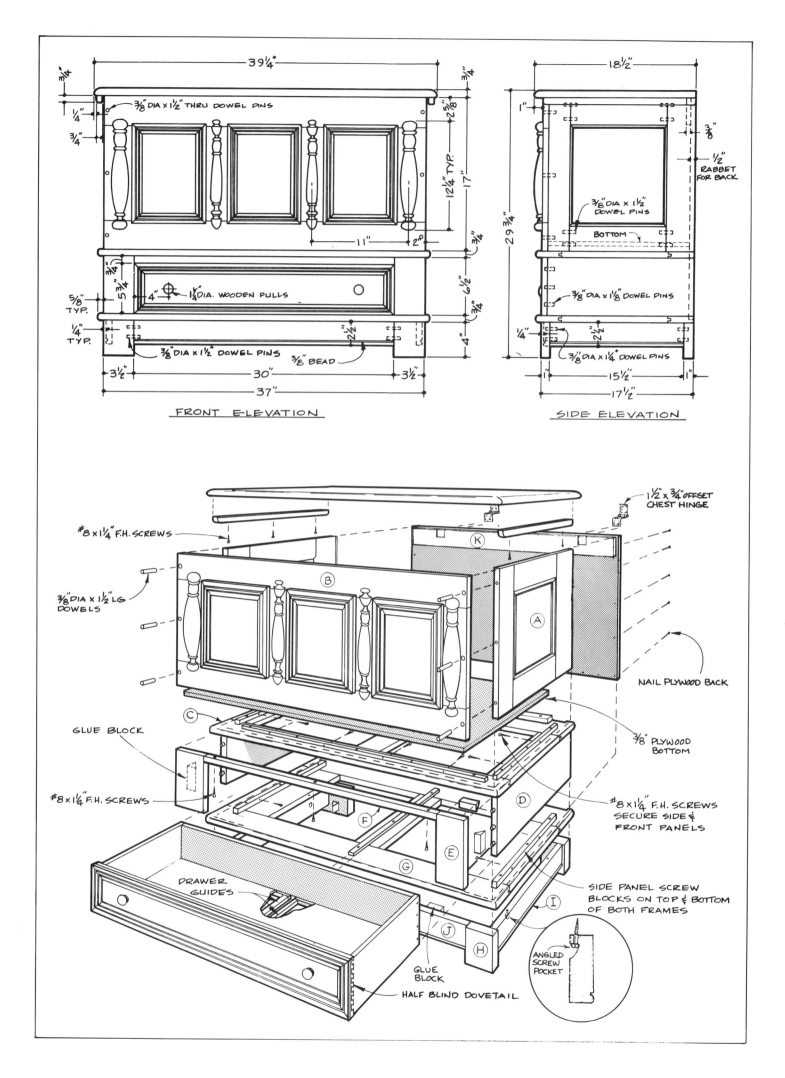

3/8" DIA x 1/2" THRU DOWEL PINS

39 1/4"

3/4"

1/4"

3/4"

2 5/8"

12 1/4" TYP.

17"

11"

2"

3/4"

6 1/2"

3/4"

5 3/4"

5/8" TYP.

4"

1 1/4" DIA. WOODEN PULLS

1/4" TYP.

3/8" DIA x 1/2" DOWEL PINS

3/8" BEAD

2 1/2"

3 1/2"

30"

3 1/2"

37"

FRONT ELEVATION

18 1/2"

1"

3/8"

1/2" RABBET FOR BACK

3/8" DIA x 1/2" DOWEL PINS

BOTTOM

29 3/4"

3/8" DIA x 1 1/8" DOWEL PINS

1/4"

2 1/2"

4"

3/8" DIA x 1 1/4" DOWEL PINS

1"

15 1/2"

1"

17 1/2"

SIDE ELEVATION

1 1/2 x 3/4" OFFSET CHEST HINGE

#8 x 1 1/4" F.H. SCREWS

3/8" DIA x 1 1/2 LG DOWELS

K

B

A

NAIL PLYWOOD BACK

GLUE BLOCK

C

3/8" PLYWOOD BOTTOM

#8 x 1 1/4" F.H. SCREWS

D

#8 x 1 1/4" F.H. SCREWS SECURE SIDE & FRONT PANELS

F

E

G

DRAWER GUIDES

SIDE PANEL SCREW BLOCKS ON TOP & BOTTOM OF BOTH FRAMES

I

J

H

ANGLED SCREW POCKET

GLUE BLOCK

HALF BLIND DOVETAIL

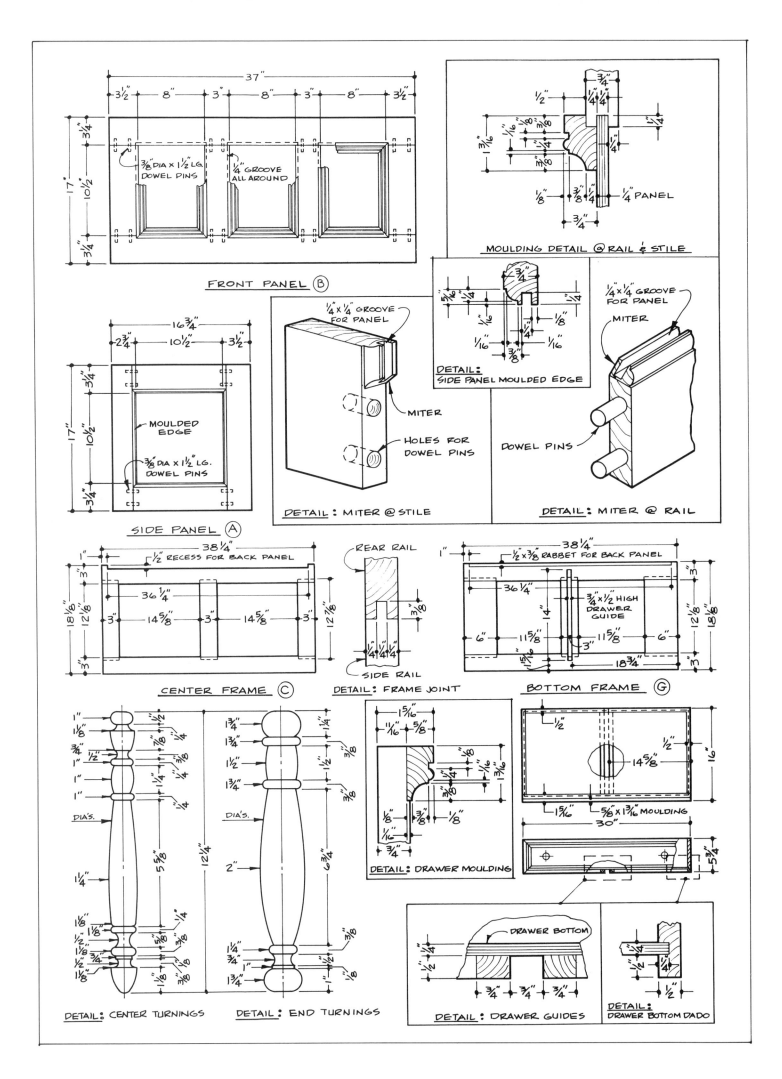

FRONT PANEL Ⓑ

MOULDING DETAIL @ RAIL & STILE

3/8"DIA x 1 1/2" LG. DOWEL PINS

1/4" GROOVE ALL AROUND

1/4" PANEL

DETAIL: SIDE PANEL MOULDED EDGE

1/4" x 1/4" GROOVE FOR PANEL

MITER

DOWEL PINS

SIDE PANEL Ⓐ

MOULDED EDGE

3/8" DIA x 1 1/2" LG. DOWEL PINS

1/4" x 1/4" GROOVE FOR PANEL

MITER

HOLES FOR DOWEL PINS

DETAIL: MITER @ STILE

DETAIL: MITER @ RAIL

CENTER FRAME Ⓒ

1/2" RECESS FOR BACK PANEL

36 1/4"

38 1/4"

REAR RAIL

SIDE RAIL

DETAIL: FRAME JOINT

BOTTOM FRAME Ⓖ

1/2" x 3/8" RABBET FOR BACK PANEL

3/4" x 1/2" HIGH DRAWER GUIDE

DETAIL: CENTER TURNINGS

DIA'S.

DETAIL: END TURNINGS

DIA'S.

DETAIL: DRAWER MOULDING

5/8" x 1 3/16" MOULDING

DRAWER BOTTOM

DETAIL: DRAWER GUIDES

DETAIL: DRAWER BOTTOM DADO

Hutch Clock

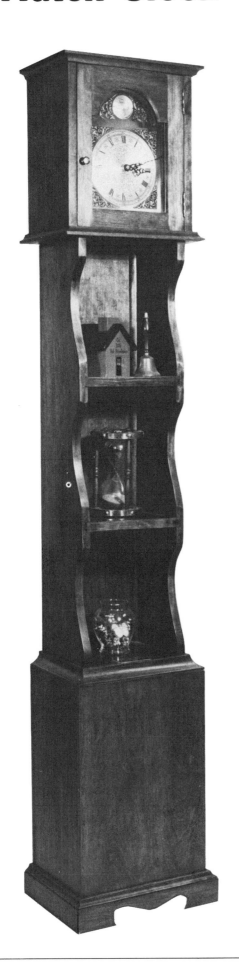

This handsome hutch clock can make an attractive addition to a hallway, den or just about any small area in your home. With three good-sized shelves, there's plenty of room for knickknacks and curios. The clock shown is made of cherry, though almost any hardwood, or even pine, will give beautiful results.

The project should be started by cutting to size the two hutch sides (A) and the three shelves (B). The scalloped edges for parts A are transferred from the grid pattern to the stock, then cut out with a jig or band saw. Full dadoes for the shelves are cut into part A with a table or radial arm saw. A router with a ½ inch rabbet bit can cut the ½ inch by ½ inch rabbets on the back edges. Note that two inches of the rabbeted edge will have to be cut flush to allow for the back panel that widens for the lower section of the clock. A backsaw or dovetail saw can be used for this job.

After sanding, parts A&B can be assembled by gluing and clamping. Make sure the shelves are square to the sides. Next, parts C&D can be cut to size. Part D will require a ¾ inch wide by ½ inch deep rabbet on its outer edges. Also, a ½ inch x ½ inch rabbet is cut on the inside back edge of part C. The two parts F, which are 1 inch square and made of hardwood such as maple, hold C and D together with screws as shown.

Parts E are made next. These are spacers that separate the middle and lower sections. They too should be made of a hardwood. Because of the confined space between the sides A, it might be best to attach parts E to A before the shelves are glued into place and the drill holes made on the insides of A. When the middle and lower sections are joined, a push drill can start the holes in part C.

For the back, part G, I used a ½ inch piece of wide stock instead of a ¼ inch panel, giving the clock a solid look and feel to it. Where it widens for the lower section, 1¼ inch pieces were added on. The back is then attached with 1 inch wood screws countersunk ¼ inch. These are covered with wood plugs that are sanded flush.

(continued on next page)

Bill of Materials (All Dimensions Actual)			
Part	Description	Size	No. Req'd
A	Hutch Side	¾ x 8¼ x 37⅝	2
B	Shelf	¾ x 7¾ x 9	3
C	End	¾ x 9¼ x 20	2
D	Front	¾ x 12½ x 20	1
E	Spacer	½ x 2 x 7¾	2
F	Cleat	1 x 1 x 18	2
G	Back	½ x 12 x 55⅝	1
H	Top & Bottom	¾ x 8¼ x 11½	2
I	Clock Side	¾ x 8¼ x 13	2
J	Lower Dial Frame	¾ x 1½ x 7	1
K	Upper Dial Frame	¾ x 4¼ x 7	1
L	Side Dial Frame	¾ x 1⅞ x 13	2
M	Lower Door Frame	1 x 1½ x 7	1
N	Upper Door Frame	1 x 4¼ x 7	1
O	Side Door Frame	1 x 1½ x 13	2
P	Clock Back	¼ x 10¾ x 13	1
Q	Molding	See Detail	
R	Molding	¾ x 2 x 10¼	2
S	Molding	¾ x 2 x 14	1
T	Molding	See Detail	
U	Movement		

Work can begin on the top and bottom by cutting to size parts H. The lower part H is attached to parts A with wood screws that are located behind where the groove (in part I) for the dial frame will be. Next, make parts I. These will require a ⅜ inch by ⅜ inch groove for the dial frame 1 inch in from the front edges. The back edges will require a ¼ inch deep by ⅜ inch wide rabbet for the back panel, part P, which is made from ¼ inch plywood.

Construct the dial frame by cutting to size parts J, K, and L, doweling, gluing and clamping them together. Once the glue has set, a router with a ½ inch rabbet bit will cut out a groove ⅜ inch deep for the dial.

Now glue and clamp together parts I and the dial frame and attach the back panel with ½ inch brass screws. Turn the assembly over and drill ⅜ inch diameter holes 1 inch deep for the dowel pins, located where they will not be over the screws that hold H to A, but behind the dial frame. Insert dowel centers into the holes and center the assembly on H. Then, ½″ deep holes are drilled into H and dowels are inserted with glue to hold together parts I and H. The same procedure can be used for the upper part H.

The door frame (parts M, N, & O) can now be assembled using dowels and glue. This will also have a rabbet, ⅜ inch deep by ⅜ inch wide, to hold the glass. The door is held with 2 inch brass hinges that are mortised into the door side and screwed flat on the case side. A button magnet catch recessed into the dial frame holds the door closed.

The moldings, parts Q and T, can be bought at most lumber companies as standard cove molding. If you make them as I did, a ½ inch cove bit run along the edge of a ¾ inch board that is ripped ¾ inches wide will make molding T. You'll need about 10 feet. Molding Q can be made on a table saw by running a wide board at an angle over the blade and ripping to shape. All molding, including R, is attached with countersunk nails that are covered with wood filler.

The bow dial and battery movement are both available from the mail-order company Armor Products, Box 445, East Northport, NY 11731. I used their solid brass dial (part no. 30008), however a brass-plated alternate dial (part no. 30007) can be obtained for about one-half the price of the solid brass version. Both dials look exactly alike. I used Armor's part no. 22201 movement, with their part no. 00804 black hands, which are provided with the movement at no extra charge.

The button magnet catch, brass door knob and flexible molding to hold the glass in the door can also be purchased from Armor Products.

I finished the clock with Minwax Jacobean stain followed by several coats of tung oil.

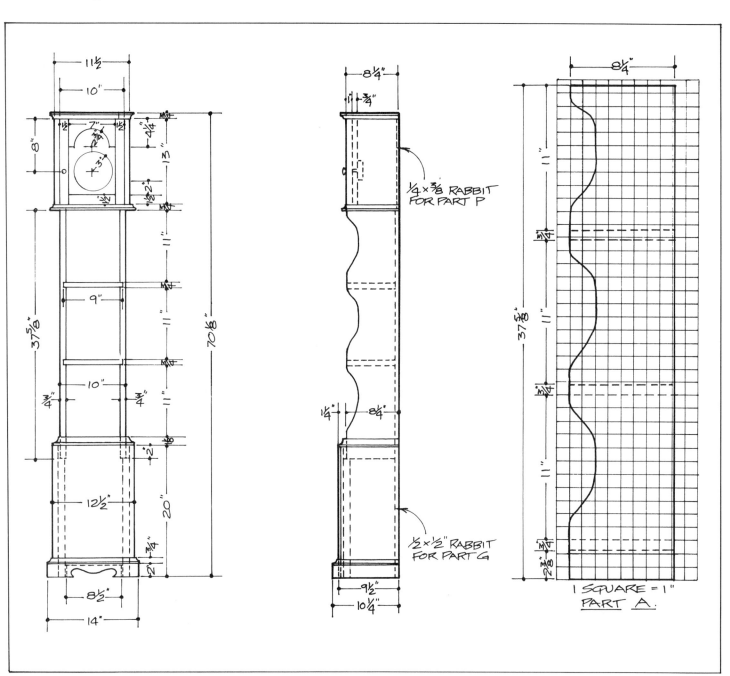

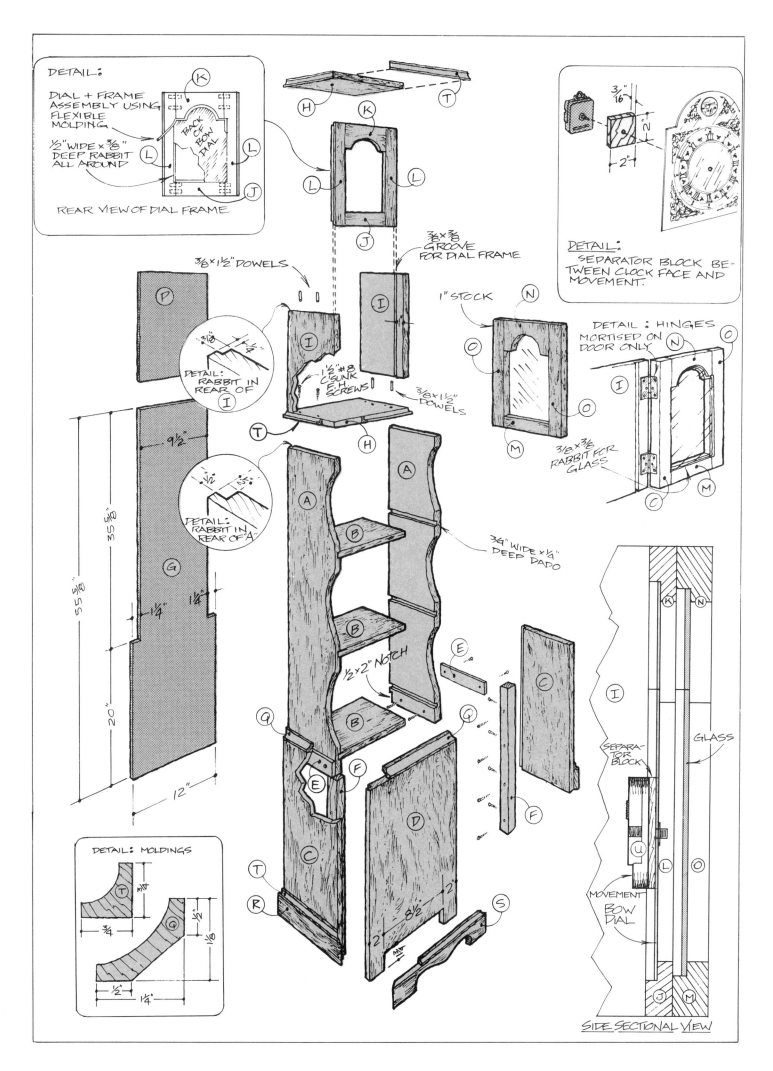

DETAIL:
DIAL + FRAME ASSEMBLY USING FLEXIBLE MOLDING

1/2" WIDE x 3/8" DEEP RABBIT ALL AROUND

BACK OF BOW DIAL

REAR VIEW OF DIAL FRAME

3/8 x 3/8 GROOVE FOR DIAL FRAME

3/8 x 1 1/2" DOWELS

DETAIL: RABBIT IN REAR OF I

1 1/2" #8 C'SUNK F.H. SCREWS

3/8 x 1 1/2" DOWELS

DETAIL: RABBIT IN REAR OF "A"

1" STOCK

DETAIL: SEPARATOR BLOCK BETWEEN CLOCK FACE AND MOVEMENT.

3/16"

2"

2"

DETAIL: HINGES MORTISED ON DOOR ONLY

3/8 x 3/8 RABBIT FOR GLASS

3/8" WIDE x 1/4" DEEP DADO

9 1/2"

35 5/8"

55 5/8"

20"

1/4"

1 1/4"

12"

1/2 x 2" NOTCH

2"

8 1/2"

2"

DETAIL: MOLDINGS

3/4"

1/2"

1/4"

3/4"

1/2"

1/4"

1/8"

SIDE SECTIONAL VIEW

SEPARATOR BLOCK

GLASS

MOVEMENT

BOW DIAL

23

18th Century Corner Shelf

The bowed front of this small corner shelf provides a nice detail, and no doubt, many woodworkers will find this an interesting challenge. There's nothing overwhelming about any of the procedure though, so if time and care is taken, even a novice will be able to build this piece and be pleased with the results.

It seemed appropriate for us to choose mahogany for ours, since early shelves of this style often used that wood. In many ways mahogany is an ideal wood for woodworking. It's hard enough to resist denting and splintering, but not so hard that it becomes burdensome to work with when using hand or power tools. Mahogany is usually straight grained and free of knots, so it planes well.

The two sides can be made first. Use ½ inch thick stock for both parts. Note that one side measures 7¾ inches wide while the other is 7⅜ inches. Cut each side to a 22 inch length, then use a dado head cutter to cut the ⅛ inch deep by ½ inch wide rabbet in the 7¾ inch wide board. Next, transfer the profile to each board, then cut out with a band or saber saw.

In order to make the lower shelf and the bottom you'll need a means to mark the 13¾ inch radius. There are a variety of ways to do it, but perhaps the easiest is to take a strip of scrap stock that measures about ⅛ inch thick and 15 inches long. Drill a small hole for a brad in one end, then measure 13¾ inches and drill a second hole big enough to fit a pencil point. Using the brad as a pivot point, scribe the radius on a piece of ½ inch stock. The piece will look best if the grain runs as shown in the sketch, so try to keep this in mind when you orient the radius on the stock. After scribing both pieces, use a band or saber saw to cut out. Make sure the two back legs meet at 90 degrees or the two sides won't be square when they're glued-up later on.

To make the bowed front, we used a piece of 5/4 inch (1-1/16 - 1-1/8 inch actual) solid mahogany, but it would also be suitable to use 5/4 inch pine and add a mahogany veneer front later on.

Cut the stock to a width of 4 inches and a length of 10 inches. Using the lower shelf or bottom as a template, scribe the 13¾ inch radius on both the top and bottom edge of the stock. If you don't have a band saw to make this cut, clamp the stock securely and use a sharp smooth plane to cut the curve roughly to shape. A belt sander is then used to remove any roughness and further smooth the radius. Hand sanding will finish the job. This technique may sound tedious, but we did it this

way and found it was surprisingly easy. If you plan to veneer, it can be added now. The veneer can run either vertically or horizontally, although in fine cabinetwork it usually runs vertically.

The table or radial arm saw can be used to cut the 45 degree corners as shown. Also, at this time, the front is cut into three separate pieces. Use care here to get a square cut.

The lower shelf, bottom, and bowed front halves can now be assembled (see sketch). A 1⅛ inch square corner block is cut to a length of 4 inches, then the two halves are inset so that their outside ends are flush with the edges of shelf and bottom. Use glue and clipped brads as shown, then clamp securely.

When dry, this sub-assembly is attached to the two sides with glue and finishing nails driven from the back. The upper shelf is cut to size and joined in the same manner. The drawer is made to the dimensions shown using resawn stock. If pine is used for the drawer parts you may want to stain them to match the mahogany. Two drawer guides are also added.

Sand all surfaces thoroughly, especially the edges of the curved sides. Remove all scratched and sharp edges. For a final finish we used Deft's Danish Oil (Natural #1114). This is a penetrating oil that's easy to apply and results in a lovely satin finish. A ⅝ inch diameter brass cabinet knob completes the project.

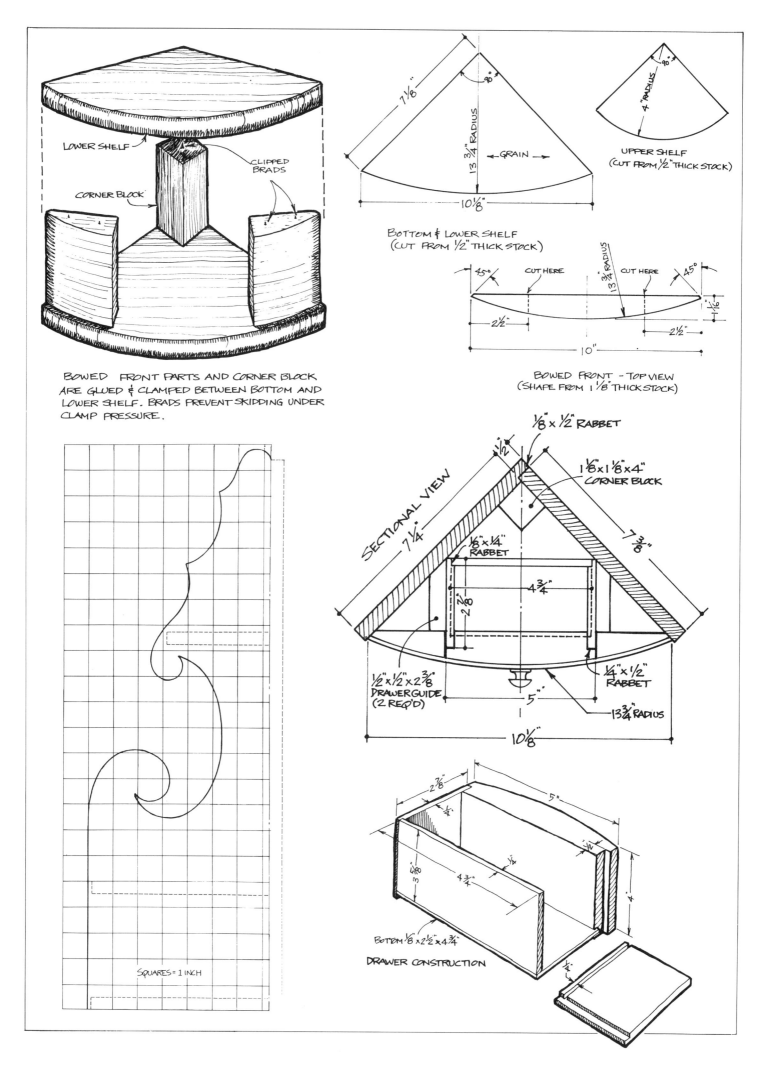

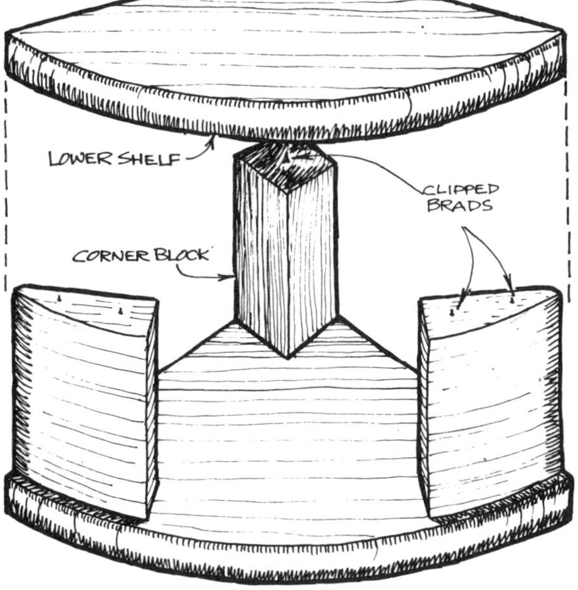
LOWER SHELF
CLIPPED BRADS
CORNER BLOCK

BOWED FRONT PARTS AND CORNER BLOCK ARE GLUED & CLAMPED BETWEEN BOTTOM AND LOWER SHELF. BRADS PREVENT SKIDDING UNDER CLAMP PRESSURE.

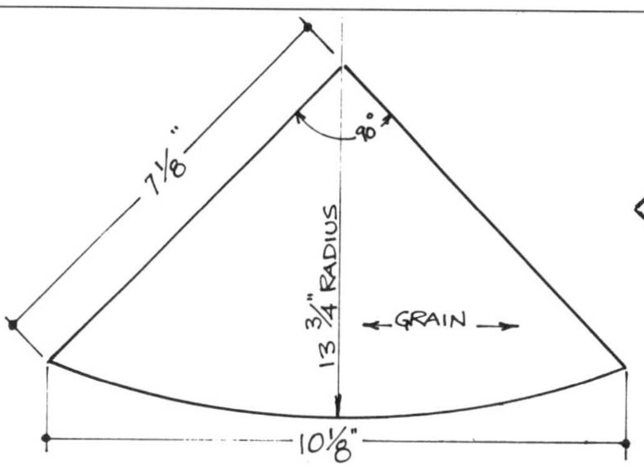
7 1/8"
90°
13 3/4" RADIUS
GRAIN
10 1/8"

BOTTOM & LOWER SHELF (CUT FROM 1/2" THICK STOCK)

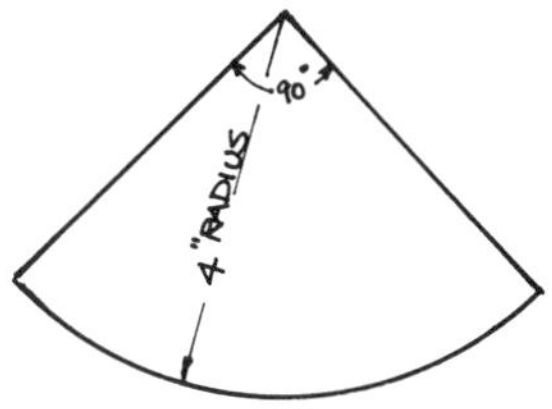
90°
4" RADIUS

UPPER SHELF (CUT FROM 1/2" THICK STOCK)

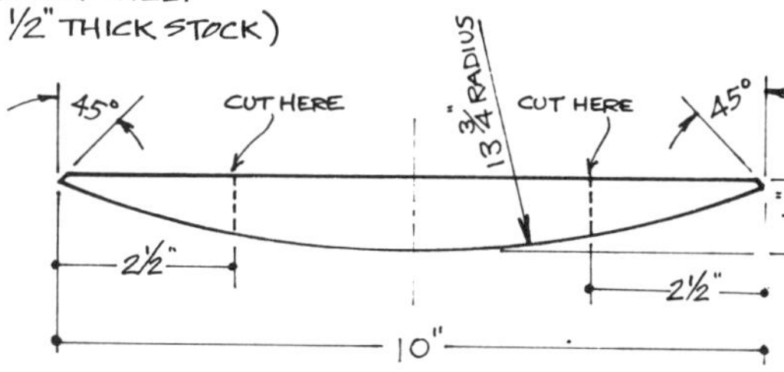
45°
CUT HERE
13 3/4" RADIUS
CUT HERE
45°
1 1/16"
2 1/2"
2 1/2"
10"

BOWED FRONT - TOP VIEW (SHAPE FROM 1 1/8" THICK STOCK)

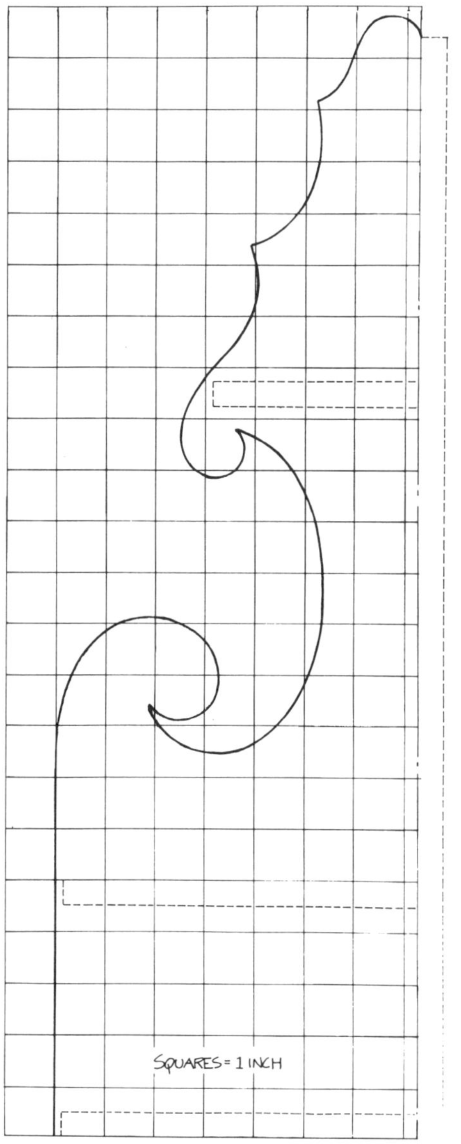
SQUARES = 1 INCH

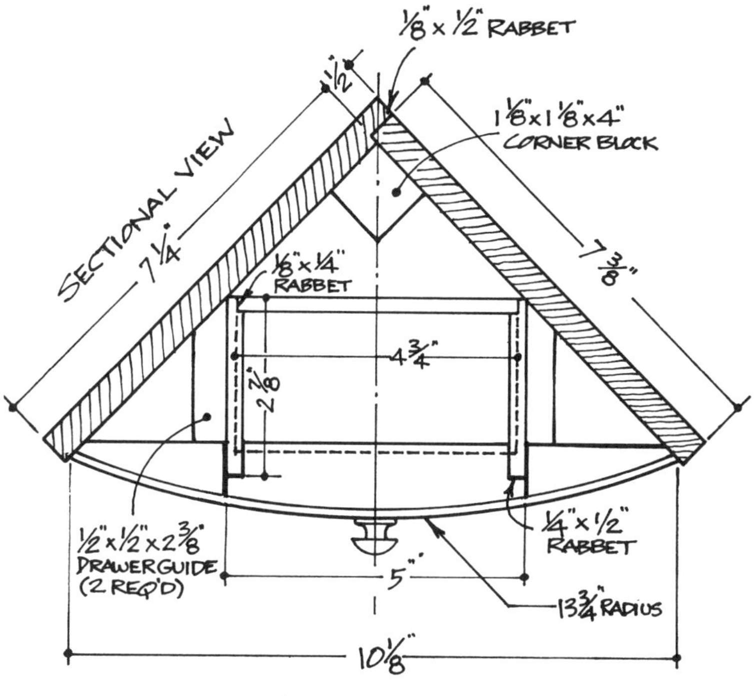
1/8" x 1/2" RABBET
1/2"
1 1/8" x 1 1/8" x 4" CORNER BLOCK
SECTIONAL VIEW
7 1/4"
7 3/8"
1/8" x 1/4" RABBET
4 3/4"
2 7/8"
1/2" x 1/2" x 2 3/8" DRAWER GUIDE (2 REQ'D)
1/4" x 1/2" RABBET
5"
13 3/4" RADIUS
10 1/8"

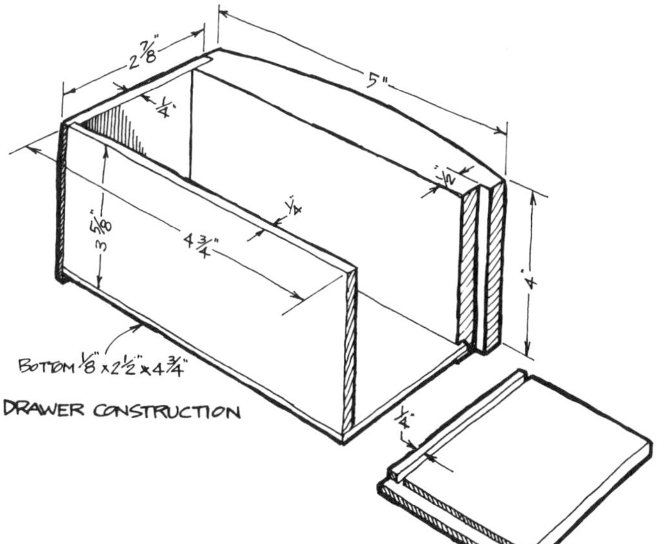
2 3/8"
5"
1/4"
1/2"
3 5/8"
4 3/4"
1/4"
4"
BOTTOM 1/8" x 2 1/2" x 4 3/4"
1/4"

DRAWER CONSTRUCTION

Here is a simple footstool that can be made in a couple of afternoons.

The piece is made entirely of 1″ x 4″ pine stock (which mills out at ¾″ x 3½″). Cut eight sections of board each 18″ in length. Rip four of them down the center with a circular saw so that you end up with four full-width sections and eight of half-width. Arrange them on their edges to form the top of the stool, then coat their faces with glue and clamp. Before gluing, drive a couple of short brads in each board, then clip off the heads so that about ⅛″ is exposed. This will keep the boards from sliding when clamped. When the glue is dry, round over the ends using a hand plane to get it to rough shape, then finish with a belt sander and hand sanding.

Each leg is made up of two 9″ sections of ¾ inch thick stock laminated together. The best course is to draw a full scale template of the leg profile on paper or cardboard, then transfer the shape to the boards.

Coat the wide ends of the finished legs with white glue and drive them into position in their slots on the underside of the top section. When the glue is dry, bore two ¾″ holes in each leg from the side so that they extend completely through the leg and both supporting boards, then drive in glue-covered dowels and sand flush.

Set the stool on a flat surface and level the legs by sanding until the stool no longer rocks. Fine sand the piece overall. Final finish is a matter of personal choice. Ours was finished using red enamel spray paint. No doubt many readers will prefer to stain the piece, then add a polyurethane finish.

Pine Footstool

PATTERN FOR LEGS —

1 SQUARE = 1″

11°

12°

¾ DIA. x 3″ DOWELS (8 REQ'D)

1¾″

1½″

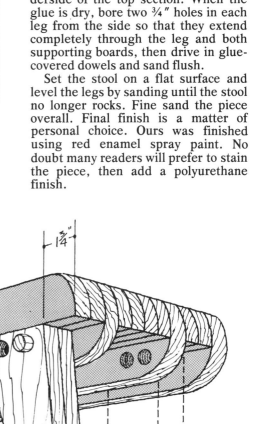

Cheese Cutting Board

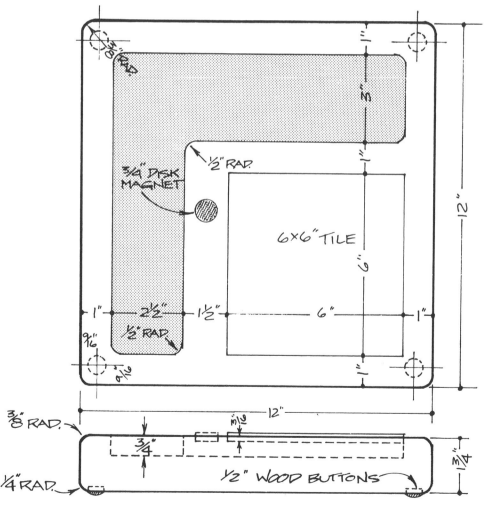

Cutting boards for cheese are always a popular item. This one, 12 inches square, is made of oak, but maple will do just as well.

Using 13/16 inch thick lumber, you'll need to face glue 15 pieces, each one at least 12 inches long and 1¾ inches wide. To provide maximum water resistance, a resorcinol-resin or epoxy glue should be used. Trim to shape after the glue has dried, then sand or plane the board smooth and round the corners.

Next, rout out the recesses for the tile and food stuffs. A router and template or straight guides will make a 3/16 inch deep recess for the tile and a ¾ inch recess for the food. A ⅜ inch rounding-over bit will put the edge on the top of the board and a ¼ inch rounding-over bit will put the edge on the bottom. If desired, a flat ¾ inch diameter magnet can be epoxied into the board to hold a cutting knife.

Drill ½ inch diameter holes for the ½ inch wood buttons, and glue them to the bottom of the board. Before gluing the 6 inch by 6 inch tile in place, finish the board with a non-toxic finish. We used a product called Behlen's Salad Bowl Finish, available from Woodcraft Supply, 41 Atlantic Ave., Box 4000, Woburn, MA 01888.

Mahogany Tripod Table

Mahogany tripod tables came into vogue during the 18th century and are again coming into popularity today. This one, made of solid mahogany, is relatively easy to build and will make an ideal lamp table.

Begin by making the center post. If 3 inch solid mahogany is not available locally you can glue-up two pieces of 8/4 (1¾ inch actual) lumber or you can purchase a 3″ x 3″ x 24″ mahogany turning square via mail-order from Craftwoods, 109 21 York Road, Hunt Valley, MD 21030.

Using the lathe, turn the post to dimensions shown in the detail. After turning, mark the location of the three leg mortises (120 degrees apart), then use a sharp chisel to cut each one to a width of ⅜ inches and a depth of 1¼ inches. If you have one, a ⅜ inch mortising chisel will be helpful here. A mortising chisel has a thick blade without any bevel along the sides. The non-beveled sides act to minimize any tendency for the chisel to twist, making it easier to cut a straight mortise. For a ⅜ inch wide mortise, use a ⅜ inch chisel.

Securely clamp the post in a vise and with the chisel held vertically start chopping near the center of the mortise. Hold the flat face of the chisel toward the center and use a sharp mallet blow to drive it into the workpiece. Work toward one end, levering out chips after each cut. When you reach a point about ⅛″ from the end of the mortise, reverse the chisel and cut from the middle to the other end. Repeat this technique until the 1¼″ depth is reached, then cut slightly deeper to allow a little clearance for the tenon. Finally, trim the remaining ⅛″ of stock on the ends by paring straight down with the chisel held vertically.

After finishing the post, work can begin on the three legs. Made from 4/4 (¾ inch actual) stock, the legs can be cut from boards at least 4¾ inches wide and 15 inches long. Transfer the grid pattern to the stock including the tenon location. With the table saw miter gauge set at 45 degrees, make a cut to establish the end of the tenon. Next, with the miter gauge still set at 45 degrees, use a dado head cutter to cut both sides (cheeks) of the tenon. The dado cuts will establish the ⅜ inch thickness and the 1¼ inch tenon length. Work accurately so that the tenon thickness results in a good fit in the post mortise. The leg profile can now be cut out with a band or saber saw.

Fix the leg in a vise and make a 1½ inch diameter radius as shown in the detail, then use a gouge or chisel to carve a profile that will exactly match the 3 inch diameter post. For the feet, glue ½ inch lumber that measures at least 2 inches high by 3 inches long to either side of the leg bottoms, matching the grain direction if you can. A V parting tool will delineate the toes and their nails, while a small #2 or #3 gouge will help round them out.

The tops of the legs are also rounded, and this can be done with a router and ⅜ inch rounding-over bit. The legs can now be glued to the post.

The top of this table was made of two pieces of grain-matched ½ inch mahogany. If you're afraid of your lumber warping, you may want to glue-up more pieces or use veneer. If veneer is used, the bottom of the table top should also be veneered so the effects of dampness and dryness will be equalized top and bottom.

The cleat or table top support, the ends of which are bevel cut, is a piece of 4/4 lumber that is held with four 1″ x #10 flat head wood screws to the underside of the top. A 1″ diameter hole is drilled through the cleat for the tenon at the top of the post. Glue the tenon and cleat together.

The table was finished with a red mahogany paste filler that can be purchased from Albert Constantine and Son, Inc., 2050 Eastchester Road, Bronx, NY 10461. The filler fills the wood pores resulting in a very smooth surface. It will also add some color. Follow the manufacturer's directions for mixing and application. When dry, several coats of a satin polyurethane will produce a durable final finish.

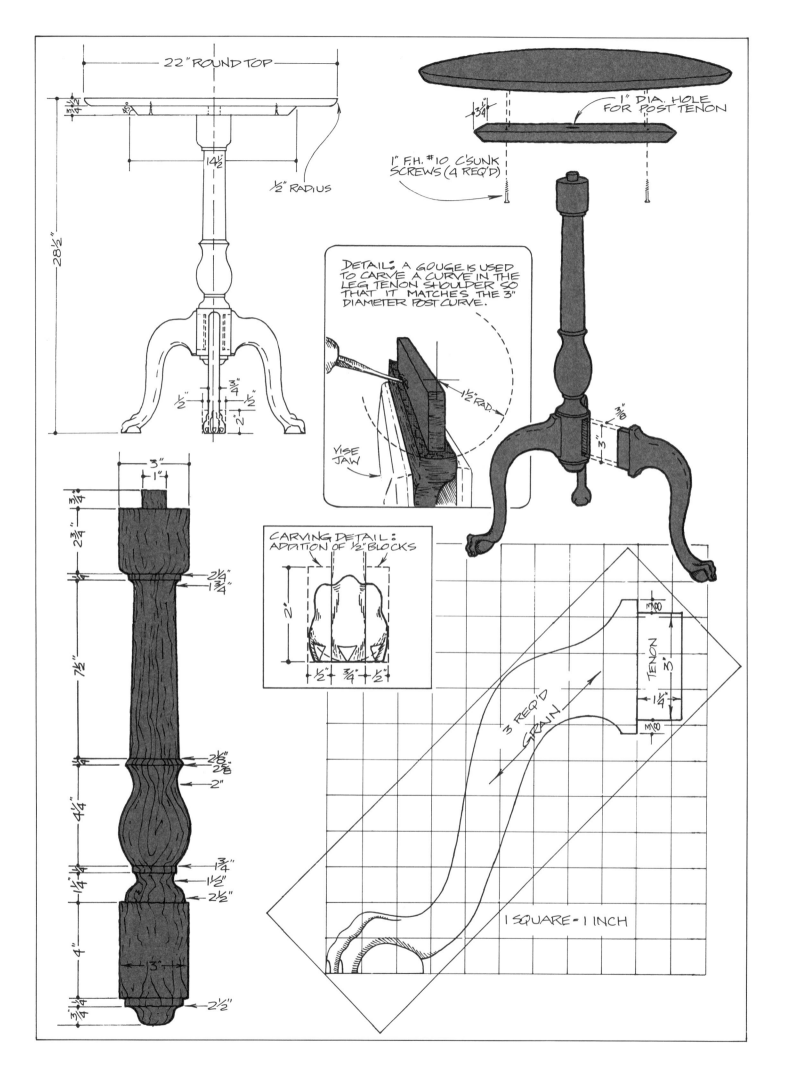

22" ROUND TOP

½" RADIUS

28½"

14½"

¾"
½"   ½"

2"

1" DIA. HOLE
FOR POST TENON

1¾"

1" F.H. #10 C'SUNK
SCREWS (4 REQ'D)

DETAIL: A GOUGE IS USED
TO CARVE A CURVE IN THE
LEG TENON SHOULDER SO
THAT IT MATCHES THE 3"
DIAMETER POST CURVE.

1½" RAD.

VISE
JAW

³⁄₁₆"

3"

3"
½"
3¾"
2¾"

2¼"
1¾"

7½"

2⅛"
2⅝"
2"

4¼"

¼"

3¾"
1½"
2½"

4"

3"

¾"
3¼"
2½"

CARVING DETAIL:
ADDITION OF ½" BLOCKS

2'

½" ¾" ½"

³⁄₁₆"

TENON

3"
1¼"

³⁄₁₆"

3 REQ'D
GRAIN

1 SQUARE = 1 INCH

Pierced Tin Cabinet

Based on an authentic 18th century design, this sturdy wall cabinet will make a lovely addition to any home that enjoys the style of Early American.

The two sides (A) can be made first. Cut to length and width, then with the dado head cutter set to a depth of ⅜ inch, cut a ¾ inch wide rabbet along the top end as shown. The back edge of part A has a ⅜ inch by ¼ inch rabbet to accept part G.

The ¼ inch deep by ⅜ inch wide dado for part D can best be cut with a router equipped with a ⅜ inch straight bit. With part A secured to the workbench, clamp a guidestrip to part A to act as a fence for the router. Stop the router ½ inch short of the front edge, then use a chisel to square the corners. To complete work on part A, drill ¼ inch diameter by ½ inch deep holes for the shelf adjusting pegs.

The base, part B, is made to the dimensions shown, then a router equipped with a ½ inch beading bit is used to apply a molding to the front and sides. After cutting part C to size, a ¼ inch x ⅜ inch rabbet is cut along the back edge to receive the back, part G. Part D has a ¼ inch x ⅜ inch rabbet on each end in order to fit into the dadoes on the sides, part A. Also, note that the two front corners of part D have a ¼ inch x ½ inch notch. The door divider, part I, is tenoned into part D and part F, so both of these parts will require a ⅜ inch wide x 1 inch long through tenon.

Temporarily join the bottom (B) to the two sides (A) using 1½" x #8 counterbored wood screws as shown. Add part D, holding it in place with bar or pipe clamps. After cutting part H to fit the opening between B and D, locate it in it's proper position, then drill through from the top and bottom for ⅜ inch diameter x 1½ inch long dowel pins.

After all parts have been sanded the case can be assembled (parts A through I, except E and G). Use glue on all joints. The wood screws will secure parts A and B, all other parts are held with clamps. Be sure the case is square or else you'll have lots of problems fitting the door frames and drawers. The crown and cove molding (part J) is available at most lumberyards. It's attached with glue and countersunk finishing nails.

Select good flat stock for the door stiles and rails (parts K and L). The through mortise for part K and the tenons for part L are best cut using a table saw tenon jig. Glue and clamp the frame, then check for squareness. When dry use a router with a ⅜ inch by ⅜ inch piloted rabbet bit to cut a recess for part M. Use a chisel to

square the corners.

Tin panels, measuring 11″ x 14″, can be purchased via mail-order from Country Accents, P.O. Box 437, Montoursville, PA 17754. To give the tin an "antique" look use very fine (220 grit) garnet or aluminum oxide paper and give the sheet a thorough sanding.

Bill of Materials (All Dimensions Actual)

Part	Description	Size	No. Req'd
A	Side	¾ x 6½ x 22½	2
B	Bottom	¾ x 7½ x 31	1
C	Top	¾ x 6½ x 28¼	1
D	Lower Shelf	¾ x 6¼ x 28	1
E	Upper Shelf	¾ x 5½ x 27⅜	1
F	Rail	¾ x 2 x 27½	1
G	Back	¼ x 28¼ x 22⅛	1
H	Drawer Divider	¾ x 6¼ x 4	1
I	Door Divider	¾ x 1 x 17¾	1
J	Molding	See Detail	As Req'd
K	Door Stiles	¾ x 1½ x 16¼	4
L	Door Rails	¾ x 1½ x 13¼	4
M	Tin Panel	See Detail	2
N	Molding	¼″ quarter round	As Req'd
O	Drawer Front	¾ x 4 x 13⅜	1/Dwr.
P	Drawer Side	½ x 4 x 5⅞	2/Dwr.
Q	Drawer Back	½ x 3½ x 12⅝	1/Dwr.
R	Drawer Bottom	¼ x 5½ x 12⅞	1/Dwr.

Work in one direction only while maintaining even pressure. Wash the tin and dry completely, then place in a shallow non-metallic container - a glass baking dish or plastic dish pan will do just fine. Add vinegar to the container until the panel is covered with about ¼″ of vinegar. Do only one piece at a time. Soak for 6 - 8 hours, then remove, wash and dry.

Transfer the pattern to the tin, then place the panel on a scrap board for piercing. Nailsets, awls, screwdrivers, square flooring nails, etc. have all been used for piercing tin, each tool producing its own distinctive mark when struck with a hammer. For this project we used a round punch of about ⅛ inch diameter.

After making the drawers and adding the molding, ours was painted with a coat of Williamsburg Powell Waller Red, one of the colonial colors sold by Williamsburg Paint. The piece will also look good if stained and oiled with Minwax's Antique Oil Finish.

The shelf can now be added and the back secured with small common nails. The tin panels are held in place with ¼ inch quarter round molding tacked in place.

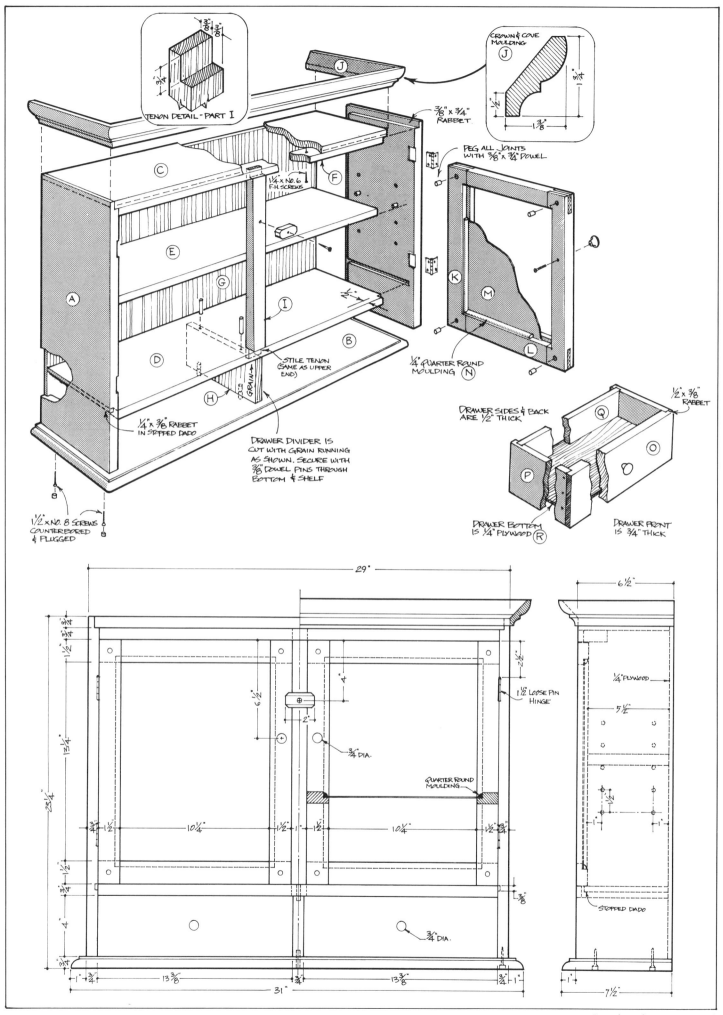

TENON DETAIL - PART I
3/8" 1/8"
3/4"

CROWN & COVE MOULDING J
3/4"
1/2"
1 3/8"

J

3/8" x 3/4" RABBET

PEG ALL JOINTS WITH 3/8" x 3/4" DOWEL

C

1 1/4" x No. 6 F.H. SCREWS

F

A

E

G

I

B

D

H

STILE TENON (SAME AS UPPER END)

1/4" x 3/8" RABBET IN STOPPED DADO

1/2" x No. 8 SCREWS COUNTERBORED & PLUGGED

DRAWER DIVIDER IS CUT WITH GRAIN RUNNING AS SHOWN. SECURE WITH 3/8" DOWEL PINS THROUGH BOTTOM & SHELF

GRAIN

K

M

L

1/4" QUARTER ROUND MOULDING N

DRAWER SIDES & BACK ARE 1/2" THICK

1/2" x 3/8" RABBET

Q

O

P

DRAWER BOTTOM IS 1/4" PLYWOOD R

DRAWER FRONT IS 3/4" THICK

29"

6 1/2"

3/4"
3/4"
3/4"
1 1/2"

6 1/2"

2"

4"

2"

1 1/2" LOOSE PIN HINGE

1/4" PLYWOOD

5 1/2"

13 3/4"

23 1/2"

3/4" DIA.

QUARTER ROUND MOULDING

1/2"

3/4"
1 1/2"

10 1/4"

1 1/2" 1" 1 1/2"

10 1/4"

1/2" 3/4"

1"

1/2"

3/4"

3/8"

4"

STOPPED DADO

3/4"

1"
3/4"

13 3/8"

3/4"

13 3/8"

3/4"
1"

31"

1"

7 1/2"

3/4" DIA.

(continued on next page)

1 SQUARE = 1"

PATTERN FOR TIN PANELS

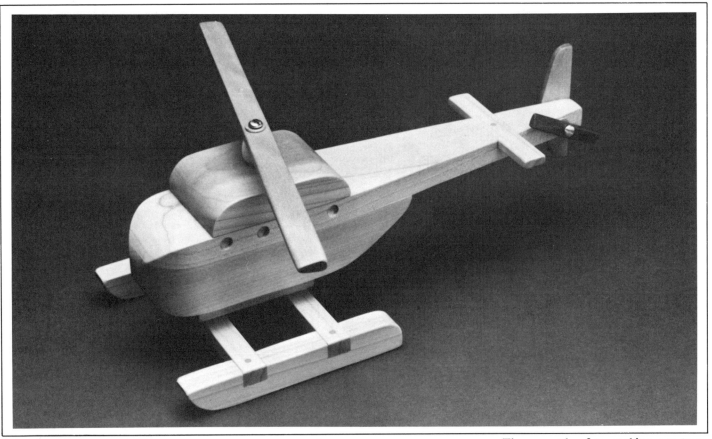

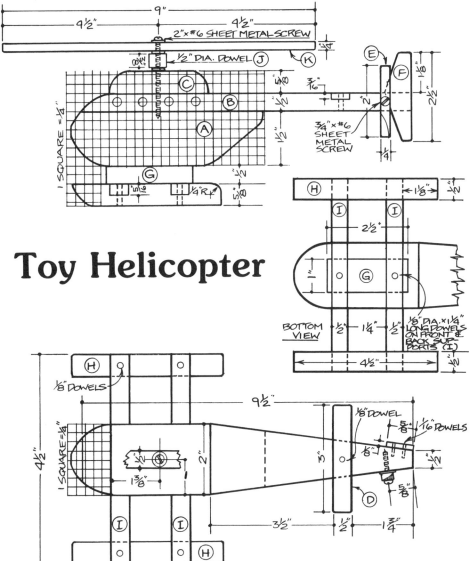

Toy Helicopter

The rewards of toymaking are two-fold; first you enjoy building the toy, then you enjoy watching a delighted child play with it. This one is made from poplar, chosen because it's reasonably priced yet hard enough to stand up to rough service. For maximum durability though, maple is the best choice.

Begin by cutting part A (1½ x 2 x 5¾), part B (½ x 2 x 9½) and part C (⅝ x 2 x 2⅞) to overall thickness, width, and length. Next, cut a 3/16 inch deep by ½ inch wide dado (for part D) across part B as shown. Also, taper the back end of part B down to ½ inch, starting at a point 5¾ inches from the back. Glue parts A, B, and C, locating them in the proper position before clamping. Use a band saw to cut the nose profile as seen from the top, then cut out the side profile. Four ¼ inch diameter by 3/16 inch deep "windows" are drilled into the side of part B.

The remaining parts are cut to the dimensions shown on the drawing. For an authentic look, the rotors (parts K & E) are slightly tapered on each end by cutting off diagonally opposite edges of one surface.

Assemble all parts as shown. Part K is assembled with a 2 inch sheet metal screw, 3 washers and a ½ inch dia. by ⅜ inch long dowel. Part E uses a screw and a washer. (To make sure the screws won't come out it's a good idea to put in a little epoxy in the pilot hole before assembly). Use glue and dowels to join all other parts.

Sand the toy thoroughly, taking care to remove all sharp edges. The best non-toxic finish is no finish at all.

Country Kitchen Cabinet

This handy wall unit serves a variety of uses in our kitchen. Behind the glass door we keep a collection of sugar bowls and creamers. In the drawer is a recipe card file and the pigeon holes provide room for bills, letters, coupons, etc. The towel holder is handy for dishtowels, while on top we keep glass canisters for spaghetti, rice, popcorn and the like.

Make the two sides (A) first. Cut to overall length and width, then lay out and mark the location of the ¼ inch deep by ¾ inch wide dadoes. The left side of part A has three dadoes, the right side has two. Stop the dadoes ½ inch short of the front edge. The dado can be cut with a router or on a table or radial arm saw using the dado head cutter. Transfer the profile from the drawing (note that the top profile is different than the bottom), then cut to shape with a band or jig saw.

Cut the top shelf (part B) to overall length and width, then cut a ¼ inch wide by ¼ inch deep groove for plates. Locate the groove about 1¾ inches from the back edge of part B. Also, cut a ¼ inch by ⅜ inch notch on the two front corners. Part B also has three, ¼ inch deep by ½ inch wide by 7¼ inches long, stopped dadoes cut in the bottom.

The bottom shelf (C) is made next, requiring only that it be cut to length and width. Notches are not needed on the two front corners because part G is inset and will cover the dado end.

Cut the divider (D) to size, then lay out the location of the ¼ inch deep by ¾ inch wide dado. Like the dadoes in the side (A) this one is stopped ½ inch short of the front edge.

Parts F, G, and N can be made next. Transfer the grid pattern to the stock before cutting out with a band or saber saw.

The pigeon hole base (part H) has three, ¼ inch deep by ½ inch wide by 7¼ inch long, stopped dadoes. The drawing shows their locations. Also, the two front corners have a ¼ inch by ⅜ inch notch.

The door rail (P) and stile (Q) are made as shown in the door joint detail. Cut the tenon for a smooth fit in the open mortise. Dry fit the frame for squareness and if all looks okay, add glue and clamp. Double check for squareness before setting aside to dry. When dry, a router equipped with a piloted ¼ inch rabbet bit is used to cut a ¼ x ¼ rabbet on the back. A chisel is used to square the corners. Now the decorative cross-hatch (R) is cut to size, half-lapped at the center, and notched at the ends, then glued to the frame.

The five spindles (I) can be turned to the dimensions shown or a very similar spindle can be purchased from Woodworks, 4013-A Clay Ave., Ft. Worth, TX 76117. Order part no. BS-1010. The rail (O) is simply ¾ inch square stock with a ⅛ inch groove as shown in the detail. The towel holder (part S) is lathe turned to the dimensions shown, or if you don't have a lathe, substitute ⅝ or ¾ inch diameter dowelstock.

The drawer (parts J, K, L, and T) are made to the dimensions shown in the bill of materials. Part K has a ⅜ inch deep by ½ inch wide rabbet cut on each end to accept the side (J), and also a ⅜ inch deep by ¾ inch wide decorative dado down the front. A ⅛ inch wide by 3/16 inch deep groove is cut around the inside of parts J, K, and L to accept the hardboard drawer bottom (T). Locate this groove ¼ inch from the bottom edge of the drawer parts.

Assemble as shown in the drawing. Part D is joined to B & C with glue and three countersunk wood screws. This unit is then joined to the sides in the same manner. Glue is added to the ends of H & M before sliding them in from the back. Add the other parts as shown, then plug the screw holes and sand flush.

Stain to suit, then add two coats of polyurethane satin varnish. When dry, apply a coat of good paste wax.

Pewter knobs were used on the door and drawer, but porcelain will also look good.

Bill of Materials
(All Dimensions Actual)

Part	Description	Size	No. Req'd	Part	Dimension	Size	No. Req'd
A	Side	¾ x 10 x 30	2	L	Drawer Back	½ x 5 x 11	1
B	Top Shelf	¾ x 9⅞ x 23	1	M	Pigeon Hole Dividers	½ x 7¼ x 8¼	3
C	Bottom Shelf	¾ x 9⅛ x 23	1	N	Upper Scroll	¾ x 1½ x 12	1
D	Divider	¾ x 9⅞ x 13½	1	O	Rail	¾ x ¾ x 20	1
E	Adjustable Shelf	¾ x 7½ x 9½	1	P	Door Rail	¾ x 1½ x 9¾	2
F	Back Board	¾ x 6 x 22½	1	Q	Door Stiles	¾ x 1½ x 13½	2
G	Lower Scroll	¾ x 3¼ x 22½	1	R	Cross-Hatch	½ x ¾ x 12½	2
H	Pigeon Hole Base	¾ x 9⅞ x 12½	1	S	Towel Holder	See Detail	1
I	Spindle	See Detail	5	T	Drawer Bottom	⅛ x 11⅜ x 8⅝	1
J	Drawer Side	½ x 5 x 9⅛	2	U	Drawer Stop	¼ x ¼ x 12	1
K	Drawer Front	¾ x 5 x 12	1				

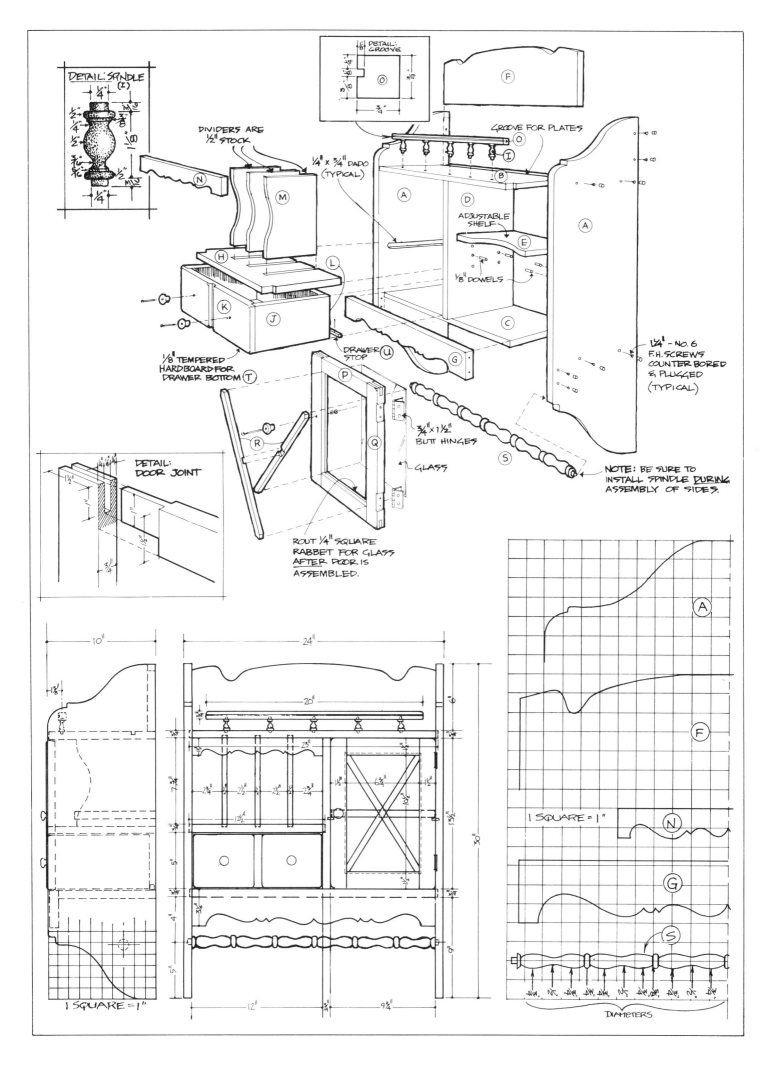

DETAIL: SPINDLE (I)

DIVIDERS ARE ½" STOCK

DETAIL: GROOVE

GROOVE FOR PLATES

¼" × ¾" DADO (TYPICAL)

ADJUSTABLE SHELF

⅛" DOWELS

1¼" - NO. 6 F.H. SCREWS COUNTER BORED & PLUGGED (TYPICAL)

⅛" TEMPERED HARDBOARD FOR DRAWER BOTTOM (T)

DRAWER STOP

¾" × 1½" BUTT HINGES

GLASS

NOTE: BE SURE TO INSTALL SPINDLE DURING ASSEMBLY OF SIDES.

DETAIL: DOOR JOINT

ROUT ¼" SQUARE RABBET FOR GLASS AFTER DOOR IS ASSEMBLED.

1 SQUARE = 1"

10"

24"

20"

1 SQUARE = 1"

DIAMETERS

Rough-Sawn Cedar Clock

Bill of Materials

		(All Dimensions Actual)	
Part	Size	Dimension	No. Req'd
A	Front	¾ x 2¾ x 5-9/16	8
B	Edging	¼ x 1 x 5¾	8
C	Divider	¾ x 3½ x 8⅞	1
D	Door Top	¼ x 2¼ x 8⅞	1
E	Door Sides	¼ x 2¼ x 6¼	2
F	Door Corners	¼ x 2¼ x 3-11/16	2
G	Door Bottom	¼ x 2¼ x 3-11/16	1
H	Door Back	See Detail	1
I	Case Top	¾ x 2½ x 7⅞	1
J	Case Side	See Detail	2
K	Case Corners	¾ x 2¼ x 3-11/16	2
L	Case Bottom	¾ x 2¼ x 3-11/16	1
M	Case Back	¼ x 7⅞ x 21⅛	1
N	Glass		4
O	Dial Board	¼ x 9½ Diameter	1
P	Corner Brace	¾ x 1½ x 1½	2
Q	Movement w/Pendulum		1
R	Brass Hinges		2
S	Brass Hook		1

Rough-sawn cedar is gaining in popularity as interior paneling, wainscoting and trim. Here's the perfect accessory for a room that's been remodeled with rough cedar. It's basically a simplified version of the old standard school clock built out of rough-sawn 1 x 4 nominal (¾ x 3½ actual) cedar fence boards.

Start by cutting the octagonal front (A). Set your tablesaw miter gauge to make a 22½ degree angle and cut the eight pieces needed. Add glue to the miters, then assemble the octagon, securing with a web clamp. When the glue is dry, use a jig saw or coping saw to cut the circular opening for the clock dial. A router is then used to cut a ¼ x ¼ rabbet for the dial board (O) and also to chamfer the front edge of the opening.

Next rip the ¼ x 1 edging (B) that goes around the octagon front (A). When cutting an edge that will be exposed, use the coarsest blade available in order to give it the rough-sawn look. Cut the edging to length with the miter set for a 22½ degree angle. Make sure you make the cuts so that the original rough-sawn face of the edging will be on the outside. Using the web clamp again, glue the edging to the outside of the octagon.

Construction of the case (parts I, J, K, and L) is straightforward enough. The only complication is clamping the 22½ degree miter joints at the bottom. Probably the easiest way to do it is to cut a piece of ¾ inch plywood the exact size and shape of the inside of the case, then clamp the case around the plywood with a web clamp. The door (parts D, E, F, and G) to the pendulum case is made by resawing the cedar to ¼ inch thickness and gluing it to the ¼ inch plywood door back (H). This makes a strong door while using simple miter joints. Part H is cut smaller than the door to form the door lip, and the hole in the center is ½ inch larger to make a ¼ inch rabbet for the glass (see detail). The door is attached with two small brass hinges (R).

If you want to simplify construction, you can make a non-opening door. Cut parts E, F, and G from ¾ " thick cedar and cut a ¾ " x ½ " rabbet on the outside edge. Part D is cut the same except do not cut the ¾ " x ½ " rabbet. Omit the ¼ " x ¼ " stopped rabbet on part J and the front rabbet on parts K and L. (See the alternate cross-sections on plan). Attach this door to the case with glue and small finish nails.

Any nails used on the door and elsewhere on the case can be effectively hidden with natural color plastic wood dough. Apply the wood dough with the tip of a small screwdriver in order to avoid getting it on the surrounding wood. Leave the surface of the dough rough and it will blend right in with the rough-sawn wood.

The paper clock dial (available from the Mason and Sullivan Co., 586 Higgins Crowell Rd., West Yarmouth, MA 02673; order part no. 2820P, specify 8½ inch diameter time ring) is attached to a ¼ inch hardboard dial board (O). The Mason and Sullivan dial will have Roman numerals, not the Arabic style shown. After the paper dial has been attached to part O, glue it into the rabbet in the octagonal front (A).

The octagon front (A) is attached to the case by means of screws through the corner braces (P) and the case divider (C). The clock shown uses a battery operated quartz pendulum movement (Q) also available from the Mason and Sullivan Co. Order part no. 3722X. However, if you prefer, you can substitute a non-pendulum movement, Mason and Sullivan part no. 3723X. If you choose a pendulum movement, install the clear glass (N) in the pendulum door and put the back (M) on the case. If you choose a movement without a pendulum, you can install a mirror in place of the glass and a decorative decal can be placed on the mirror. If you choose the latter method, the alternative door can be used and the back of the case (M) can be omitted. In either case, the glass or mirror is held in place with glazier's points. It's a good idea to cover the back of the mirror with cardboard before installing the glazier's points to protect the silvered back.

No finish is necessary, but a thin coat of clear sealer will help keep that fresh-cut look.

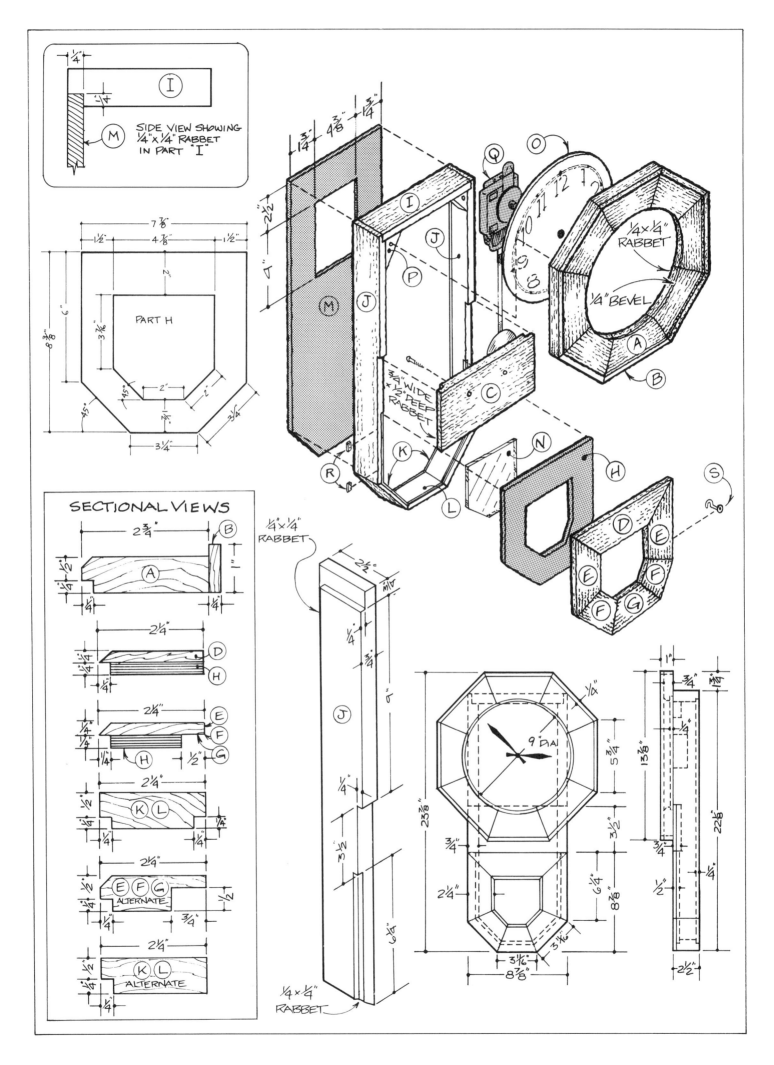

SIDE VIEW SHOWING
¼" x ¼" RABBET
IN PART "I"

PART H

SECTIONAL VIEWS

ALTERNATE

ALTERNATE

¼" x ¼"
RABBET

¼" x ¼"
RABBET

¼ x ¼
RABBET

¼" BEVEL

¾" WIDE
x ½" DEEP
RABBET

9" DIA

Editor's Note: Readers will note that the crib has fewer spindles than shown in our drawing. We added the extra spindles in order to meet the requirements of a Consumer Product Safety Commission ruling which states that, for infant safety, the distance between crib components (such as spindles, slats, crib rods and corner posts) shall not exceed 2⅜ inches.

In designing this cradle I felt that it had to be functional, trim in appearance and stable. Cherry is used for all parts.

Begin by turning the spindles (Part A) to the dimensions shown in the detail. Since thirty-four spindles are required, it's well worth taking the time to make a full-size template of the profile. Draw the profile, full-size, on a piece of ¼ inch hardboard or plywood, then cut to shape on a jig or band saw. As you turn each spindle, the template is used to check the progress and accuracy of the profile.

After the four corner posts (D) are turned from 1½ inch square stock, the two lower side rails (B) and two upper side rails (F) can be cut to length and width. Lay out and mark the location of the spindle holes, then use a drill press or doweling jig to drill ⅜ inch diameter by 7/16 inch deep holes to accept the spindle tenons. Also drill the ⅜ inch dia. by 13/16 inch deep dowel pin holes on each end (see Sketch A).

The two lower end rails (C) are cut to length and width, then a ½ inch wide by ⅜ inch deep groove is cut along the entire length of one side, after adding spindle holes. Each end is cut at a 10 degree angle before drilling the two dowel pin holes.

Cut the two upper end rails (G) to length and width, then add spindle holes before cutting the 10 degree angle on each end. Add the two dowel pin holes, then mark the 15¼ inch radius. Cut to shape.

Cut the support (H) to length and width. Locate in its proper position on part G and scribe the 15¼ inch radius. Use a dado head cutter to cut a ½ inch deep rabbet, stopping the rabbet just short of the scribed radius. Use a sharp chisel to remove the remaining stock while making sure that the radius on part H matches that of part G. Now, transfer the grid pattern from the drawing and cut to shape.

The bottom (E) is made from tongue and groove, random width, V-groove flooring, resawn to slightly less than ½ inch thickness. If flooring is not available, ½ inch hardwood plywood can also be used.

Parts I & J are made as shown. Note that part I has a mortise cut to take the stretcher tenon (K).

Part K is made from two pieces of ¾ inch stock. Cut each end to form a 3/16 x 1⅛ x 3⅞ tenon when the two halves are joined. Dry clamp the two halves

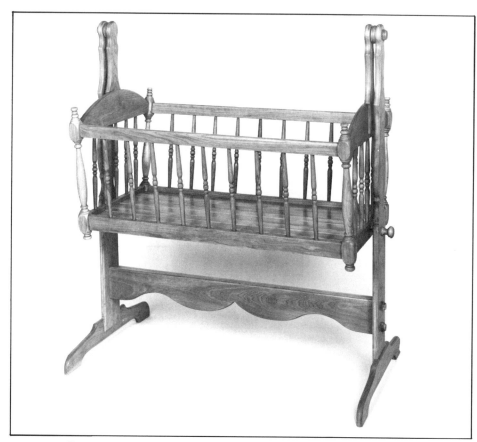

Swinging Cradle

and fit into the leg (I) mortises, then drill two holes through part I and into part K. Remove the clamps, then use a chisel to cut a groove equal to one-half the bolt head width. The groove will keep the bolt from spinning when the nuts are assembled. Put the bolt in place and glue the two halves. The glue joint is then covered with veneer.

Give all parts a thorough sanding. To assemble, eleven spindles are glued to parts B & F, while six spindles are glued to parts C & G. Clamp lightly and make sure spindles are square to the rails.

Cut flooring to fit, notching it around the corner posts (D) and beveling the two side edges to match the slope of parts B. Add dowel pins and dry assemble, checking for fit. If all looks o.k., the corner posts can be assembled to parts B & F. Clamp securely. When dry, put the bottom (E) in place, then join the part A-B-D-F subassembly to the part A-C-G subassembly.

The rest of the cradle is assembled as shown. After turning the knobs (M), drill a hole the width and depth of the hex nut. Mark the outside of the nut on the knob and cut the six corners with a chisel. Use epoxy to hold the nut in the knobs. The washers (N) are turned to match the adjoining parts.

The safest and most functional way to support the cradle is with two bolts and four screw inserts. Constantine, 2050 Eastchester Rd., Bronx, NY 10461, is one source for the inserts.

The last step is to assemble and line up the cradle before drilling a pilot hole for the plug. Before drilling the ½" plug hole in the lower rail, cut out the recess for the brass washer. Using a 1¼" hole saw drill to a depth equal to the thickness of the washer. With a sharp chisel clean out the inside of the circle and inlay the washer. Drill two countersunk holes in the washer for two #4 brass wood screws.

Make the locking pin (L) overlength and trim it after testing. Also, the hole for the tapered locking pin should be spotted in place after assembly.

As for finishing, I have painted one white, stained and varnished another and this one was waxed. It is a personal preference.

Bill of Materials (All Dimensions Actual)			
Part	Description	Size	No. Req'd
A	Spindle	(See Detail)	34
B	Lower Side Rail	¾ x 2 x 34½	2
C	Lower End Rail	¾ x 2 x 15¼	2
D	Corner Post	(See Detail)	4
E	Bottom	½" T & G Flooring	As Req'd
F	Upper Side Rail	¾ x 1⅝ x 34½	2
G	Upper End Rail	¾ x 5¼ x 19 9/16	2
H	Support	¾ x 4 x 13¼	2
I	Leg	¾ x 4½ x 43⅛	2
J	Foot	¾ x 4⅜ x 23½	2
K	Stretcher	1½ x 4⅝ x 39⅛	1
L	Locking Pin	(See Detail)	1
M	Knob	(See Detail)	6
N	Washer	9/16 x 2¼ dia.	2

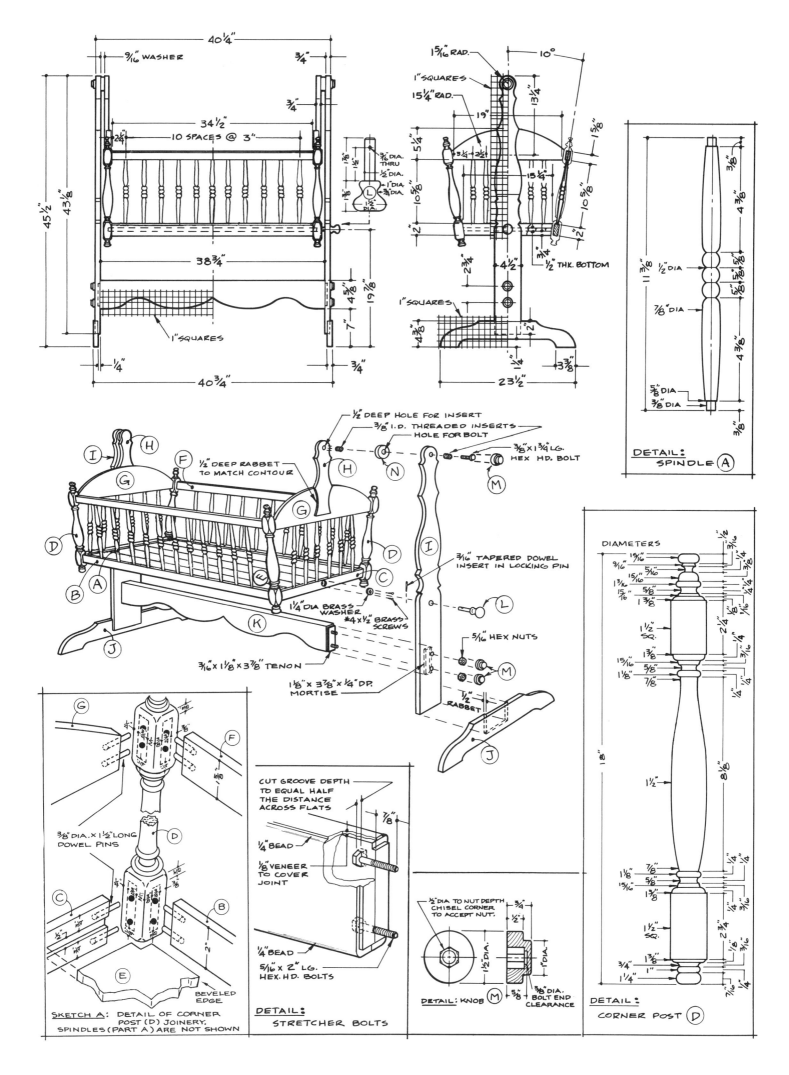

40¼"

9/16" WASHER

¾"

34½"

10 SPACES @ 3"

2¼"

45½"
43⅛"

38¾"

4⅝"
19⅞"

7"

1" SQUARES

¼"

40¾"

¾"

1⅞"
½"
1⅛"

¾" DIA. THRU
½" DIA.
1" DIA.
⅝" DIA.
½" DIA.

L

15/16" RAD.

1" SQUARES

15¼" RAD.

10°

19"

13¼"

5¼"

10⅝"

3¼" 2½"

15¼"

1⅝"

10⅝"

2"
23¾"
4½"

½" THK. BOTTOM

3¼"

1" SQUARES

4⅜"

¼"
2"

3⅜"

23½"

DETAIL: SPINDLE Ⓐ

⅜"
4⅜"

11"

⅜" DIA   ½" DIA

⅝" ⅝" ⅝"
⅝" ⅝"

7/8" DIA

4⅜"

⅝" DIA
⅜" DIA

⅜"

½" DEEP HOLE FOR INSERT
⅜" I.D. THREADED INSERTS
HOLE FOR BOLT

⅜" X 1¾" LG. HEX HD. BOLT

Ⓘ Ⓗ

Ⓕ

Ⓖ

½" DEEP RABBET TO MATCH CONTOUR

Ⓗ

Ⓖ

Ⓝ

Ⓜ

Ⓓ

Ⓒ

Ⓑ Ⓐ

3/16" TAPERED DOWEL INSERT IN LOCKING PIN

Ⓘ

Ⓛ

Ⓓ

1¼" DIA BRASS WASHER
#4 X ½" BRASS SCREWS

Ⓚ

Ⓙ

3/16" X 1⅛" X 3⅞" TENON

1⅛" X 3⅜" X ¼" DP. MORTISE

5/16" HEX NUTS

Ⓜ

½" RABBET

Ⓙ

DIAMETERS

½"
3/16"
¼"

15/16"
9/16"
5/16"
15/16"
13/16"
15/16" 5/8"
16"   1⅜"

½"
2¼"
3/16"
¼"

1½" SQ.

15/16" 1⅜"
5/8"
1⅛" 7/8"

3/16"
¼"

8⅝"

18"

1½"

1⅛" 7/8"
5/8"
15/16" 1⅜"
1⅛"

¼"
3/16"
¼"

1½" SQ.

¾" 1⅜"
1¼" 1"

2¾"

7/16" ¼"

DETAIL: CORNER POST Ⓓ

Ⓖ

3/8" DIA. X 1½" LONG DOWEL PINS

Ⓓ

Ⓒ

Ⓔ

Ⓕ

Ⓑ

BEVELED EDGE

SKETCH A: DETAIL OF CORNER POST (D) JOINERY. SPINDLES (PART A) ARE NOT SHOWN

CUT GROOVE DEPTH TO EQUAL HALF THE DISTANCE ACROSS FLATS

7/8"

¼" BEAD

⅛" VENEER TO COVER JOINT

¼" BEAD

5/16" X 2" LG. HEX. HD. BOLTS

DETAIL: STRETCHER BOLTS

½" DIA TO NUT DEPTH CHISEL CORNER TO ACCEPT NUT.

¾"
½"

1½" DIA.

1" DIA.

⅝"

⅜" DIA. BOLT END CLEARANCE

DETAIL: KNOB Ⓜ

This easy-to-make project provides an attractive way to transport a hot casserole dish from the kitchen to the dinner table. It can be put right on the table since it also serves to protect the table from the hot dish. Ours is made from red oak along with birch dowel stock, but just about any wood species can be used. Very little stock is required, so check your scrap bin before starting. Also, those looking for a marketable item might want to consider this one.

The dimensions we've provided are based on using a Pyrex 33 x 23 x 5 cm. dish. If a different size dish is used, the dimensions will need to be altered as necessary.

Cut the two ¾ x 2⅝ x 11 end pieces and the two ¾ x 1 x 11 handles to size. Locate and drill the ½ inch diameter dowel holes as shown, then cut the dowel stock to length. Sand smooth before gluing and clamping. When dry apply a slight chamfer to all edges of the ends and handles. Use a sharp chisel to clean up any excess glue squeeze-out. An application of Watco Clear Danish Oil will complete the project.

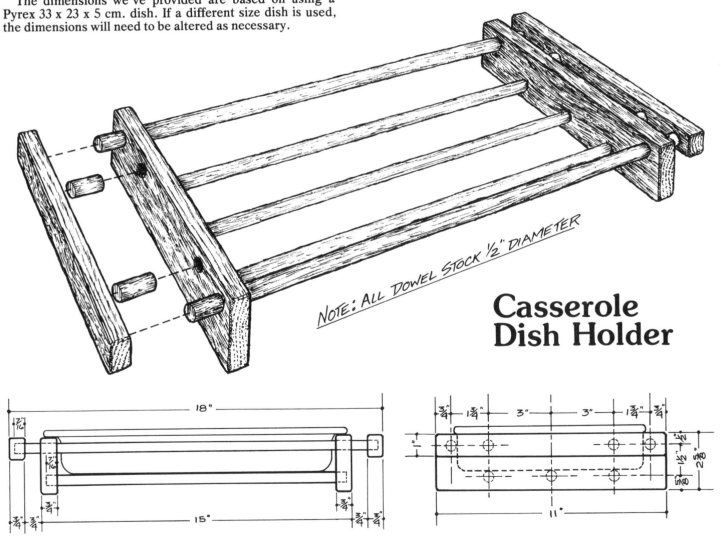

NOTE: ALL DOWEL STOCK ½" DIAMETER

Casserole Dish Holder

Ship's Wheel Weather Station

A fairly easy lathe project that will make use of your scrap wood, this weather station is made from pine and maple, but most any other wood will do.

The 1⅛-inch thick wheel (A) is mounted to a piece of scrap wood with glue and newspaper between, then attached to a lathe turning plate. Turned to a 5¾-inch diameter with the point of a skew chisel held 90 degrees to the wood, the hub has a slight (⅛-inch) radius on the front edge. The groove that holds the ⅜-inch diameter manilla rope is ¼-inch deep and ⅜-inches wide, and the hole that holds the mechanism housing of the weather instrument is 3 inch diameter by ⁷⁄₁₆ inch deep. The hole diameter should be exact since the housing is force fitted into the hole. The eight spokes (B) are turned from a 1-inch diameter maple dowel.

The 3⅞-inch diameter brass bezel weather station instrument (D) is available as either a barometer, humidity, or temperature unit from the Craft Products Company, 2200 Dean St., St. Charles, IL 60174, (the dial face will differ somewhat from the one shown). Order their part no. 3613G85 for the thermometer, part no. 3623G85 for the barometer, and part no. 3632G85 for the hygrometer.

The spokes (B) are glued to the wheel and all parts are finished with Minwax Special Walnut Stain and a satin finish polyurethane. The manilla rope is force fitted into the groove and its edges are cut with a razor blade and butted closely together at the top. A piece of felt is applied to the back with Elmer's glue, then cut to size with a sheetrock knife.

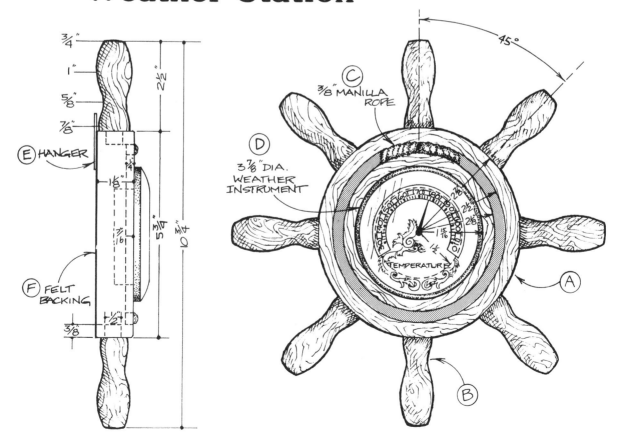

Handsome and massive are words that can best be used to describe this contemporary desk. Perhaps the most difficult part of building it will be securing the 2″ thick oak for the base, although it is possible to laminate thinner stock to achieve the 1¾″ thickness of the base.

Building the base unit is a simple mortise and tenon job. After milling parts A, B & C to 1¾″, cut the legs to length, secure them side by side and lay out mortises. End rails B and back stretcher C are tenoned as shown in the detail.

Assemble two end units (A & B) first with glue and pipe clamps, then join them with stretcher C and back rail D which is screwed to the legs. The top is of ¾″ oak plywood edged with solid strips. Turn the top upside down and locate cleats (E) butting against end and front strips. Bore two ¼″ holes through each cleat and ½″ deep into the top. Enlarge the top holes to ⅜″ and screw in ¼″ threaded inserts. Hex head ¼″ machine bolts and washers are then temporarily inserted to join cleats and top. Spread glue on leg tops and set top in place. When dry, remove the bolts and top and fasten cleats to legs with screws; then re-attach the top.

Mill oak stock to ¾″ thickness for the tambour units. After sides A are shaped, make a ¼″ plywood template for routing the ¼″ x ¼″ tambour grooves. A single template is used and flopped to rout the opposing groove, thus slight template irregularities will be transferred on opposite sides.

Make register marks on the centerline of template and each side (A) so the template can be positioned exactly the same on each side. Temporarily secure template to the side to be grooved with screws. These holes are later filled. The groove is cut with a ¼″ straight bit and 7/16 O.D. template bushing fitted to the router. Sand and wax the grooves after cutting.

Drawer box parts B are cut and tenoned as shown to fit mortises in the sides. When assembling parts A and B make sure they are square and the sides are parallel; otherwise the tambours will not track properly. Cut parts D to fit snugly between parts B and glue them to the sides. Add guides E before gluing back C in place.

Tambour strips are ripped from a board resawn and planed to 5/16″. You will probably have to rip about 50 strips to get 32 for one unit as some will warp in a day or two. Cut strips to an oversize length of 17¼″ and sand them, rounding off the face corners slightly.

Insert strips into a jig as shown, forcing them together and leveling them. The fabric backing of denim or light artist's canvas is cut to 15″ width

Tambour Desk

and long enough to cover the tambours with a ½″ overhang front and back. Apply a thin coat of Titebond glue to strips and lay fabric in place along penciled guide lines. Use a roller lightly, to smooth the fabric.

When dry, curl the tambour to separate strips that are glued together. The tambour can now be trimmed to finish width of 17″ or as determined by carefully measuring the distance between groove bottoms. Strips are shouldered using a router and guide strips clamped square to the tambour. Trim fabric and cover the front edge behind a thin slat glued to the first strip as shown.

Insert tambours in their grooves and join the units with the top (J).

Back G is added, screwing and gluing to the top. The entire assembly is fastened to the desk with screws driven through the desk top (F) and into sides A.

Drawers are built of ½″ stock as shown. Small strips will need to be glued to the part B bottoms to stop the drawer fronts flush. The pigeonhole box is made of ¼″ oak, sized for a snug fit between desk top and J. Dividers are ⅛″ thick, cut to 4″ deep and fitted into ⅛″ by ⅛″ dadoes, top and bottom.

We finished our desk with Watco Danish Oil and when dry fastened the leather tambour pulls with small brass R.H. screws and washers to notches cut in the first tambour.

Bill of Materials (All Dimensions Actual)					
Base			Tambour Unit		
Part	Size	Qty	Part	Size	Qty
			A	¾ x 6 x 24	4
A	1¾ x 3½ x 27	4	B	¾ x 6¼ x 17¼	4
B	1¾ x 2½ x 23¼	4	C	¾ x 5 x 16½	2
C	1¾ x 3½ x 61	1	D	¾ x ¾ x 3½	4
D	¾ x 7 x 61½	1	E	½ x ¾ x 5½	4
E	¾ x 1¾ x 27¼	2	F	Drawer Assembly	2
F	¾ x 27¼ x 61½	1	G	¾ x 6 x 25½	1
G	¾ x 1¾ x 120″		H	Tambour Assembly	2
			I	Pigeon Hole Unit	1
			J	¾ x 12 x 61½	1

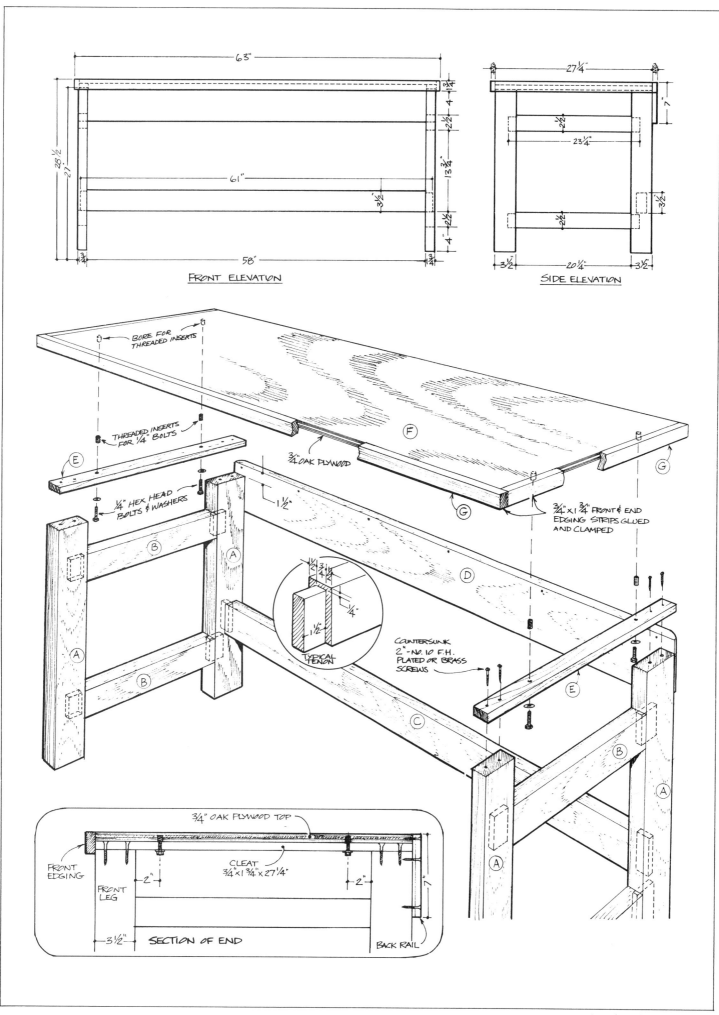

FRONT ELEVATION

SIDE ELEVATION

BORE FOR
THREADED INSERTS

THREADED INSERTS
FOR 1/4 BOLTS

1/4" HEX HEAD
BOLTS & WASHERS

3/4" OAK PLYWOOD

3/4" x 1 3/4" FRONT & END
EDGING STRIPS GLUED
AND CLAMPED

TYPICAL
TENON

COUNTERSUNK
2"- No. 10 F.H.
PLATED OR BRASS
SCREWS

3/4" OAK PLYWOOD TOP

FRONT
EDGING

FRONT
LEG

CLEAT
3/4" x 1 3/4" x 27 1/4"

SECTION OF END

BACK RAIL

(continued on next page)

43

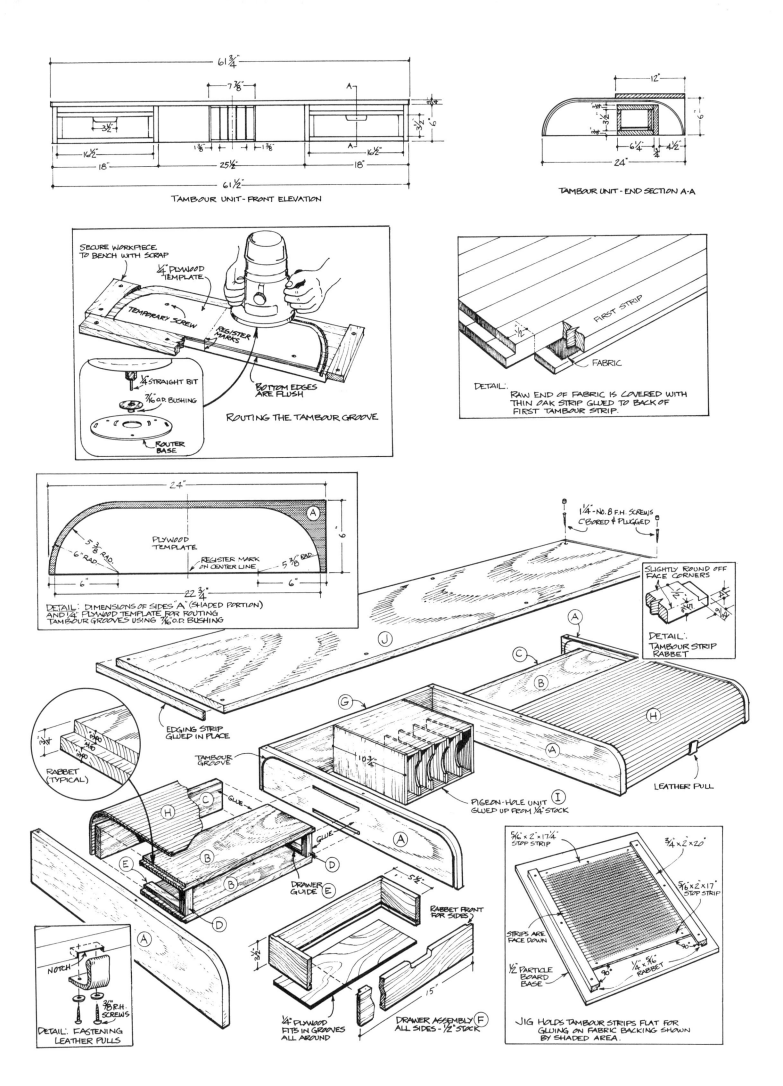

TAMBOUR UNIT - FRONT ELEVATION

TAMBOUR UNIT - END SECTION A-A

SECURE WORKPIECE TO BENCH WITH SCRAP

¼" PLYWOOD TEMPLATE

TEMPORARY SCREW

REGISTER MARKS

¼" STRAIGHT BIT

7/16" O.D. BUSHING

ROUTER BASE

BOTTOM EDGES ARE FLUSH

ROUTING THE TAMBOUR GROOVE

FIRST STRIP

FABRIC

DETAIL: RAW END OF FABRIC IS COVERED WITH THIN OAK STRIP GLUED TO BACK OF FIRST TAMBOUR STRIP.

24"

PLYWOOD TEMPLATE

5 3/8" RAD.

6" RAD.

REGISTER MARK ON CENTER LINE

5 3/8" RAD.

6"

6"

22 3/4"

DETAIL: DIMENSIONS OF SIDES "A" (SHADED PORTION) AND ¼" PLYWOOD TEMPLATE FOR ROUTING TAMBOUR GROOVES USING 7/16" O.D. BUSHING

1¼" - No. 8 F.H. SCREWS C'BORED & PLUGGED

EDGING STRIP GLUED IN PLACE

SLIGHTLY ROUND OFF FACE CORNERS

DETAIL: TAMBOUR STRIP RABBET

RABBET (TYPICAL)

TAMBOUR GROOVE

GLUE

GLUE

DRAWER GUIDE

PIGEON-HOLE UNIT GLUED UP FROM ¼" STOCK

LEATHER PULL

NOTCH

3/8" R.H. SCREWS

DETAIL: FASTENING LEATHER PULLS

¼" PLYWOOD FITS IN GROOVES ALL AROUND

RABBET FRONT FOR SIDES

DRAWER ASSEMBLY ALL SIDES - ½" STOCK

5/16" x 2" x 17¼" STOP STRIP

¾" x 2" x 20"

5/16" x 2" x 17" STOP STRIP

STRIPS ARE FACE DOWN

½" PARTICLE BOARD BASE

¼" x 5/16" RABBET

JIG HOLDS TAMBOUR STRIPS FLAT FOR GLUING ON FABRIC BACKING SHOWN BY SHADED AREA.

44

Band Saw Boxes

A well seasoned log and a band saw are all that's needed to make one of these beautiful little wooden boxes. They are great fun to build, with the size and shape of an individual box limited only by the woodworker's imagination and the capacity of the band saw. Of the boxes shown, the shortest measures about 2 inches high while the tallest has a height of about 4½ inches. Their unique appearance, plus the fact that they are relatively easy to build, makes them ideal as gift items or for sale at craft fairs.

It is most important that the log be well seasoned or else there will be cracking problems after the box is cut. Since these boxes have somewhat of a rustic look, a few slight cracks can be considered acceptable, but if the moisture content is too high, the cracking will be severe and the box rendered useless.

The sliding jig shown is not essential, although it will prove helpful, especially if you plan to make a bunch of boxes. It's made from ½ inch plywood cut to a length and width that's suitable for your band saw table. The 1 x 1½ fence and ¾ x 3 cleat are glued to the plywood, then further secured from the bottom with a few screws. The hardwood track is sized to ride smoothly in the saw table's miter gauge slot.

To make a box, follow steps 1 through 9 which correspond to the sketches. Before starting, keep in mind that when cutting across the stock, it will tend to want to spin out of your hands, especially without a jig, so hold firmly and keep hands a safe distance from the blade.

Step 1: Cut the log to length. Try to select a log that's reasonably straight.

Step 2: With the log standing on end, cut into the log, then all around to remove the bark.

Step 3: Use a pencil to mark an alignment line along the length, then slice off the lid, bottom inset, and top inset. If you want to make curved or angled lids (as are some of the boxes shown) it is done freehand, without the aid of a jig.

The thickness of the lid is a matter or personal taste,

influenced by the diameter and length of the log. They can be as narrow as ½ inch or as wide as 1 inch or more. To keep all the parts properly orientated, use a pencil to label the top and bottom of each piece.

Step 4: With the log on end, remove the core, forming a wall ¼ to ⅜ inches thick. If desired, this core can serve as the basis for another box, one that will fit inside the larger box.

Step 5: Apply glue to the seam and clamp with heavy rubber bands. Use enough rubber bands to insure a good clamping force. A web clamp will also do the job. When dry, remove the rubber bands, then give the inside a thorough sanding.

Step 6: Use a sharp pencil to follow the inside contour, scribing a line on both the top and bottom inset.

Step 7: Cut out on the scribe lines. Sand lightly and check for a good fit.

Step 8: Locate the box on the lid with the top inset in place. Use the alignment line to match up the grain. Carefully remove the box without disturbing the location of the inset, then hold the inset in place while scribing a pencil line around it. Apply glue to the underside of the top inset and secure to the lid with 2 or 3 brads. Replace the box to make sure everything fits up all right. If it does, remove the box and clamp the top inset to the lid with a few spring clamps. Remove the brads when dry.

Step 9: Sand the top of the bottom inset, then add glue to its edge and glue in place. Allow to dry. Sand the lid and top inset. Also sand the bottom and the exterior of the box. These boxes look best when sanded very smooth, so finish up with 220 grit aluminum oxide paper. Break the edges with light sanding. Watco Danish Oil is easy to apply and results in a finish that's very attractive. When dry, a piece of felt is glued to the bottom, adding a nice finishing touch. If desired, a pair of ⅛ or 3/16 inch diameter pins can be inserted in the lid. A matching pair of holes in the box then serve to make it easy to properly align the lid to the box.

(continued on next page)

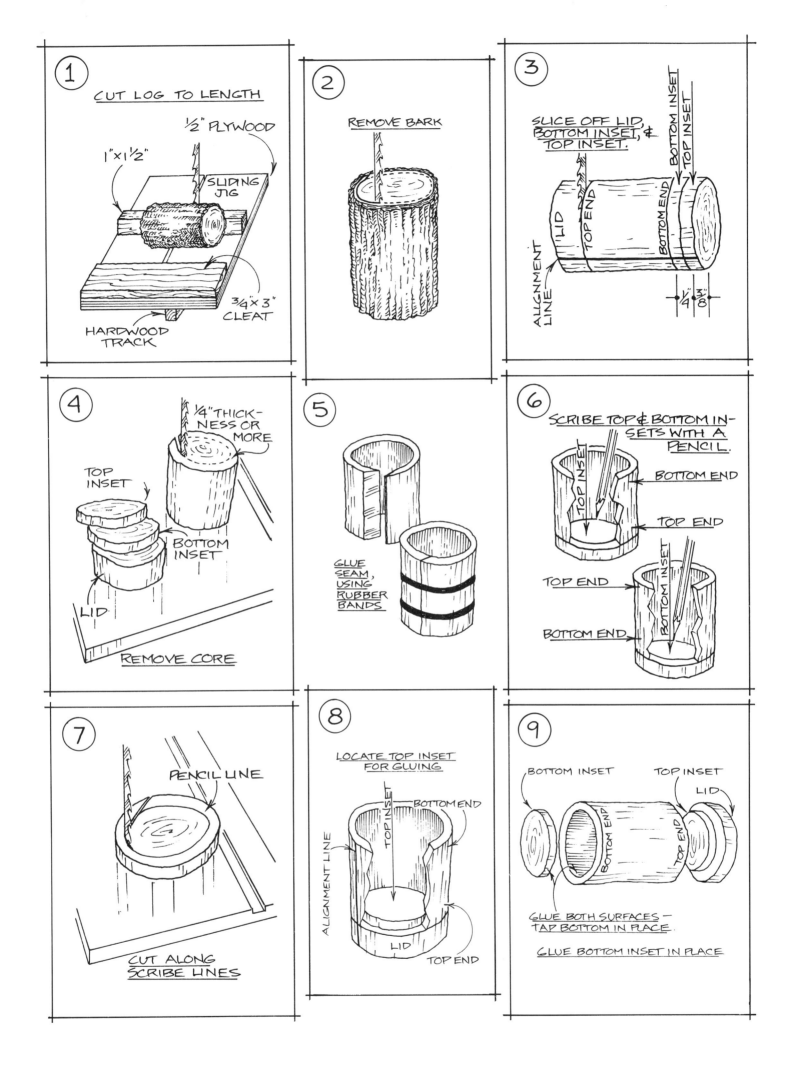

1 CUT LOG TO LENGTH

½" PLYWOOD
1" × 1½"
SLIDING JIG
¾" × 3" CLEAT
HARDWOOD TRACK

2 REMOVE BARK

3 SLICE OFF LID, BOTTOM INSET, & TOP INSET.

BOTTOM INSET
TOP INSET
LID
TOP END
BOTTOM END
ALIGNMENT LINE
¼" ⅜"

4 ¼" THICKNESS OR MORE

TOP INSET
BOTTOM INSET
LID
REMOVE CORE

5 GLUE SEAM, USING RUBBER BANDS

6 SCRIBE TOP & BOTTOM INSETS WITH A PENCIL.

TOP INSET
BOTTOM END
TOP END
TOP END
BOTTOM INSET
BOTTOM END

7 PENCIL LINE

CUT ALONG SCRIBE LINES

8 LOCATE TOP INSET FOR GLUING

TOP INSET
BOTTOM END
ALIGNMENT LINE
LID
TOP END

9 BOTTOM INSET
TOP INSET
LID
BOTTOM END
TOP END

GLUE BOTH SURFACES — TAP BOTTOM IN PLACE.

GLUE BOTTOM INSET IN PLACE

46

Here's an attractive way to display that favorite plant. Rough-sawn cedar adds a natural look, while its inherent resistance to decay makes it suitable for outdoor as well as indoor use. If you do plan to use it outdoors though, be sure to use a glue that's highly water resistant such as plastic resin.

Our planter was sized for a pot that measures 5 inches high by 8 inches in diameter. A seven foot length of 1 x 12 nominal (¾ x 11¼ actual) cedar provided enough stock for the entire project. Keep in mind that if you use a pot that's larger or smaller, the planter dimensions (and the amount of stock that's needed) will need to be altered to suit.

Cut the four legs to size (¾ x 4¾ x 26), then add a 22½ degree bevel along each edge. Do the same for the four (¾ x 4¾ x 10) side pieces. You will need to first rip the stock to a slightly greater width, and then use the bevel rips to establish the final widths as indicated. The saw blade must be set at exactly 22½ degrees because even a small error will add up to a large gap when you have eight joints. To check the accuracy of your saw angle, it's a good idea to first make a test octagon from scrap stock.

As shown in the exploded view, we used ¼ inch diameter by ¾ inch long dowel pins to keep the legs and side pieces aligned for glue-up. To insure accuracy of the dowel pin holes, it's a good idea to build a jig (see detail) to support the stock in the drill press. Lay out and mark the hole locations, then use a ¼ inch diameter bit to bore each hole to a ⅜ inch depth. Since the pins serve only to align the parts, you'll just need two pins at each joint.

After boring the holes, apply glue to the mating edges of the legs and side pieces. The dowel pins don't need any glue. Assemble the parts making sure the top edges are flush, then clamp with two or three web clamps.

When dry, screw the ¾ inch square by 3⅛ inch long cleats in place using 1¼ inch long by no. 8 flathead wood screws as shown. The bottom, which is made from ¾ inch thick stock, can now be cut to fit inside the planter. The addition of your favorite potted plant completes the project.

Octagonal Planter

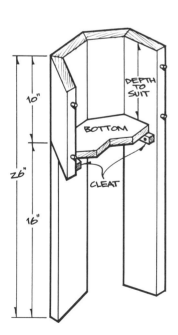

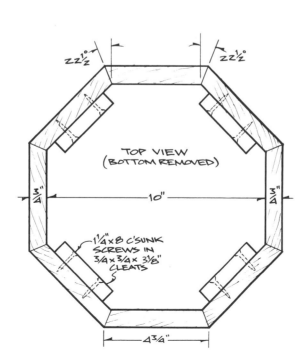

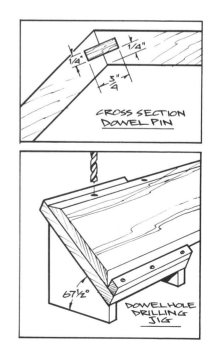

Here's a project that we think will prove to be a useful item to have around the house, especially in the kitchen near those high cabinets. And when it's not being used as a step stool, it functions very nicely as a chair.

The one shown was made in Denmark sometime around 1890, probably by a country cabinetmaker. Although this one was made from hard pine, we recommend oak in order to insure adequate strength.

Before starting, all 1 inch nominal stock (13/16 inch actual) should be surface planed to ¾ inch actual thickness. Make the step unit (parts A, B, C, D, and E) first. Cut part A to overall width and length, then lay out and cut the tenons and the notch for part E. Refer to the drawing for dimensions to make the remaining cuts.

Cut parts B and C to size, then lay out the location of the dovetails (see dovetail layout on drawing). Make all cuts with care so that a strong, neat fitting joint will result.

Part D is made to the dimensions shown, then the ¾ inch wide by 2 inch long by ¾ inch deep mortises are cut. Sand all parts thoroughly before assembling the step unit as shown. Use glue and clamp securely. Check for squareness before setting aside to dry.

The chair unit is made next. Part F and the two upper steps (parts G & H) are made and assembled in the same manner as parts A, B, and C.

The leg (K) is made from 5/4 stock (1-1/16 inch thick actual). Be sure to select stock that's free of knots or any other defects. Transfer the profile to the stock, then cut out with a band or saber saw. Lay out the location of the ³⁄₈ inch wide by ⅞ inch deep mortises for parts L & M, then cut out with a sharp chisel.

A framing square is used to determine the location of the leg in relation to the seat (I). Cut the seat to length and width, then clamp in your workbench so that the seat end is flush with the workbench top. Lay the framing square on the workbench so that one edge butts against the seat bottom (see Detail A). Locate the square so that its other edge extends 1½ inches past the back edge of the seat. Now, place the leg on the framing square as shown (15¾ inches from the bottom of the seat and 2¼ inches from the corner of the frame). With the leg held in place, use a pencil to scribe the curve of the leg on the seat end. Repeat this procedure on the other end. Now cut the ½ inch deep by ¾ inch wide rabbet on each end of the seat, then with the remaining scribe mark as a guide, use a sharp chisel to cut a notch equal to the leg thickness. Repeat on the other side.

Again clamp the seat in the workbench, only this time have the leg notch flush with the bench top. Locate

19th Century Step-Chair

the framing square as before, then insert the leg into the notch in its proper position in relation to the seat. Use this set-up to mark the length of the half-lap joint on the leg. Note the half-lap is ¾ inches deep.

After giving all parts a thorough sanding, the seat (I) can now be assembled to the leg (K). Parts L & M are added at the same time. Use glue and clamp securely. Check for squareness before setting aside to dry.

The sub-assembly consisting of parts F, G, and H is now fitted into the rabbet on part I and secured with glue and two screws driven through the half-lap of each leg. Note that the two front corners of part F are rounded to allow clearance as the unit is pivoted.

Part J is cut to size and its ends rounded over. The part of J that extends beyond part F should have its thickness reduced about 1/16 inch.

This will allow some slight clearance as the units are pivoted.

Lay out the pivot pin location on J (see Detail), then drill a ¼ inch diameter by ¾ inch deep hole. Also, at this time locate the pivot pin location on the step-unit. Make this hole ¼ inch diameter by 9/16 inch deep. Cut ¼ inch diameter steel rod to a length of 1¼ inches, then epoxy it into the step unit pivot hole. Fit part J on the pivot pin, then secure it to the chair unit with four countersunk wood screws as shown. Check for a smooth pivoting action. The countersunk holes can be filled with wood plugs.

Give the project a final sanding, taking care to round-off sharp edges. Finish up with 220 grit paper. Generally, we feel that a project like this looks best with just a clear finish, so we would suggest a penetrating oil such as Watco or Deftco Danish oil.

Bill of Materials	(All Dimensions Actual)		
Part	Description	Size	No. Req'd
A	Step Unit End	¾ x 8⅝ x 17	2
B	First Step	¾ x 4⁷⁄₁₆ x 13½	1
C	Second Step	¾ x 4-5/16 x 14	1
D	Foot	1 x 1¾ x 15½	2
E	Step Unit Stretcher	½ x 1⅛ x 14	1
F	Chair Unit End	¾ x 8⅝ x 16¼	2
G	Third Step	¾ x 4-5/16 x 13½	1
H	Fourth Step	¾ x 4-5/16 x 13½	1
I	Seat	¾ x 9 x 14	1
J	Cleat	1 x 1¾ x 12¾	2
K	Leg	See Detail	2
L	Inside Stretcher	⅝ x 1 x 13⅝	1
M	Outside Stretcher	⅝ x 1½ x 13⅝	1

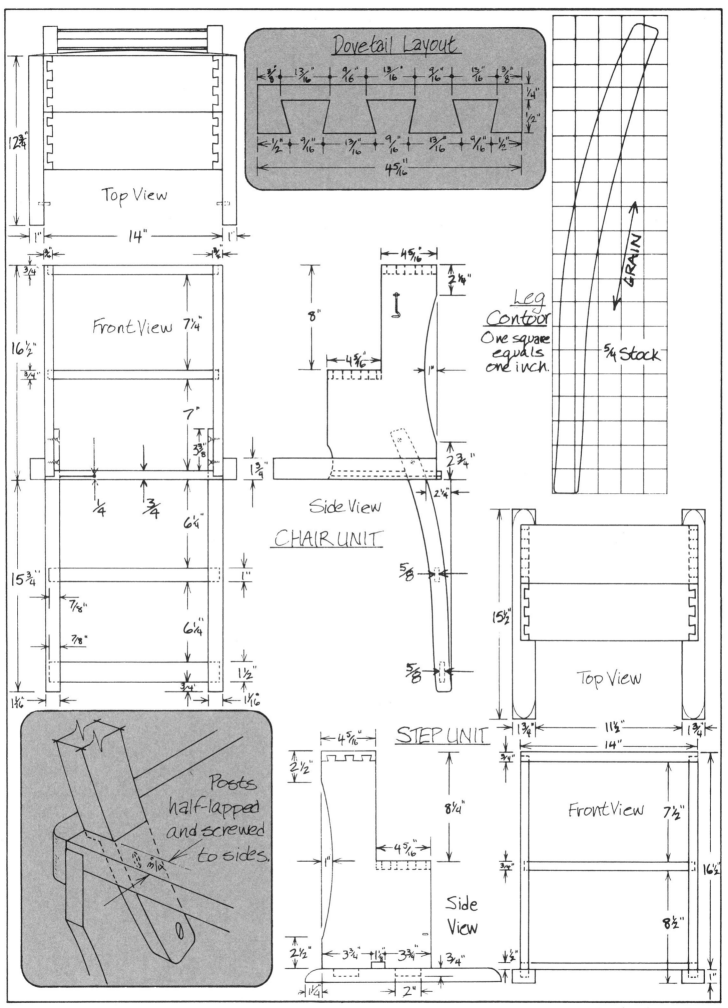

Top View

Dovetail Layout

$\frac{3}{8}$" $\frac{13}{16}$" $\frac{9}{16}$" $\frac{13}{16}$" $\frac{9}{16}$" $\frac{13}{16}$" $\frac{3}{8}$"

$\frac{1}{4}$"

$\frac{1}{2}$"

$\frac{1}{2}$" $\frac{9}{16}$" $\frac{13}{16}$" $\frac{9}{16}$" $\frac{13}{16}$" $\frac{9}{16}$" $\frac{1}{2}$"

$45\frac{1}{16}$"

12$\frac{3}{4}$"

1"   14"   1"

$\frac{3}{4}$"

$\frac{3}{4}$"

Front View   7$\frac{1}{4}$"

16$\frac{1}{2}$"

$\frac{3}{4}$"

7"

$3\frac{3}{8}$"

$1\frac{3}{4}$"

$\frac{1}{4}$ $\frac{3}{4}$

6$\frac{1}{4}$"

15$\frac{3}{4}$"

1"

$\frac{7}{8}$"

$\frac{7}{8}$"

6$\frac{1}{4}$"

1$\frac{1}{2}$"

$\frac{3}{4}$"

$1\frac{1}{16}$ $1\frac{1}{16}$"

Posts half-lapped and screwed to sides.

$\frac{3}{4}$

CHAIR UNIT

$45\frac{1}{16}$"

8"

$4\frac{5}{16}$"

$2\frac{1}{4}$"

1"

2$\frac{3}{4}$"

2$\frac{1}{4}$"

$\frac{5}{8}$

$\frac{5}{8}$

Side View

Leg Contour

One square equals one inch.

GRAIN

$\frac{5}{4}$ Stock

15$\frac{1}{2}$"

Top View

1$\frac{3}{4}$"   11$\frac{1}{2}$"   1$\frac{3}{4}$"

14"

STEP UNIT

$4\frac{5}{16}$"

2$\frac{1}{2}$"

8$\frac{1}{4}$"

$4\frac{5}{16}$"

1"

$\frac{3}{4}$

$\frac{3}{4}$

Front View   7$\frac{1}{2}$

16$\frac{1}{2}$

8$\frac{1}{2}$

Side View

2$\frac{1}{2}$"   3$\frac{3}{4}$" 1$\frac{1}{4}$" 3$\frac{3}{4}$" $\frac{3}{4}$"

1$\frac{1}{4}$"   2"

$\frac{1}{2}$"

1"

(continued on next page)

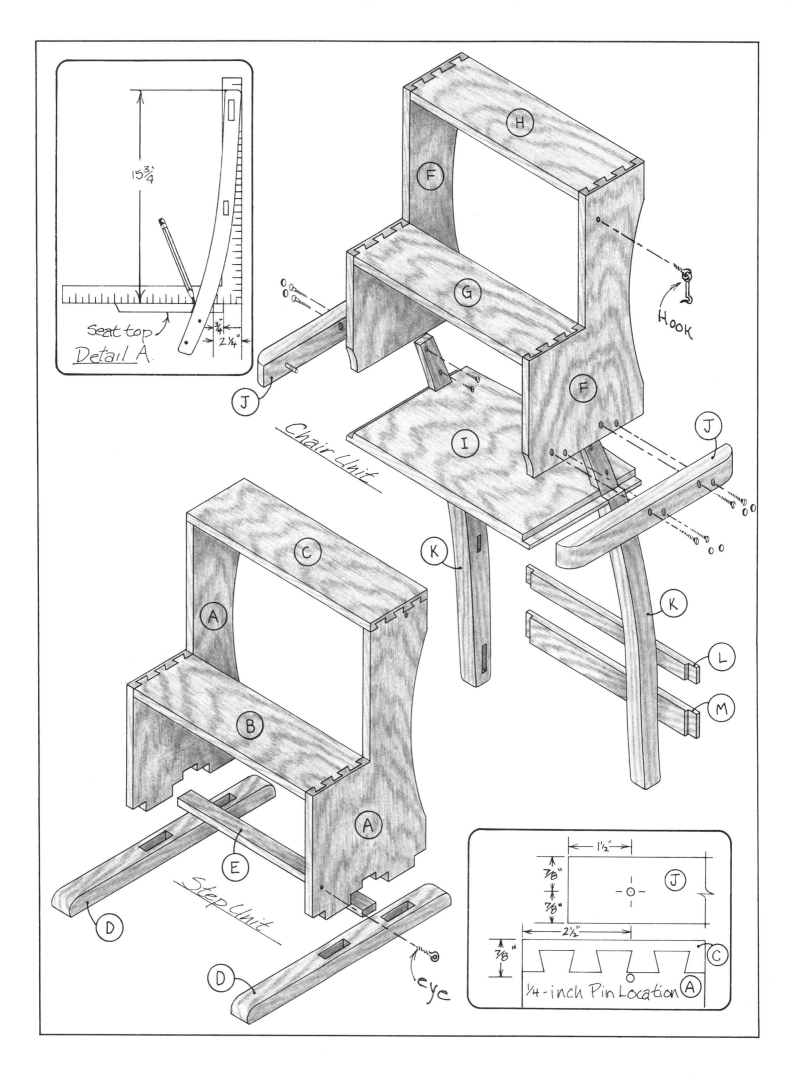

15 3/4"

seat top

Detail A.

3/4"
2 1/4"

Hook

Chair Unit

H

F

G

F

J

J

I

K

K

L

M

C

A

B

A

E

Step Unit

D

D

eye

1 1/2"

7/8"
7/8"

J

2 1/2"

7/8"

C

1/4-inch Pin Location

A

Sailing Ship Weather Vane

We think you'll agree that this is an uncommonly handsome weather vane. With her mainsail set, this replica of an early 19th century U.S. revenue cutter will keep her bows facing into the wind and safely ride out the summer squalls and winter gales of many years. Construction is simple and all materials should be readily available at building supply and hardware stores.

Start by enlarging the grid pattern for the hull (not including the keel) and transfer the pattern to a piece of 5/4″ clear pine (1-1/16″ actual thickness) as shown in Fig. 1. Tack two pieces of 5/4″ stock together and bandsaw the shape as shown in Figs. 1 and 2. If no bandsaw is available cut the sides separately, then clamp them together and sand them so they are identical. Bow and stern cuts can be planed and filed.

Fig. 3 shows how the two thick hull sides are glued to a central ½″ x 6″ x 24″ pine board so that the top edges are flush. Be sure to use a water resistant glue such as Weldwood plastic resin or resorcinal.

Before cutting the keel and rudder to shape, lay out the mast locations. The ⅜″ dia. holes are best drilled with a drill press while either the assembly or the table is tilted at 5 degrees. Lacking a drill press, use a simple bored block as a doweling jig. Take care that the holes are drilled in the same planes. The masts must rake at the same angle and line up when viewed from fore and aft.

The sheerline can now be bandsawn or shaped by hand. A compass or steel washer can be used as shown to mark a cutting line around the bow stem and along the keel (Fig. 4).

The hull is now carved using the photo and Figs. 5 and 6 as a guide. The stern section is hollowed with a gouge or round rasp until the stern presents a "wineglass" shape. About 4 inches forward of the stern, this hollow section is faired into the slightly rounded section amidships. The bow should be tapered smoothly to the stern and down to the keel. Don't fret over the hull shape too much because after it is painted and mounted high on your roof it will look fine.

The various spars are cut from dowel as indicated on the drawing. Mast tops and the ends of the yards are tapered only for a short distance using a block plane and sandpaper. File flat sections on masts and their tops and join them with quick setting epoxy, then wrap the joints with windings of 20 gauge copper wire. Tuck the free ends into small holes drilled through the masts. The bowsprit and jib boom are joined in a similar manner.

Before gluing masts and bowsprit into place, drill them and the other spars with small holes to take the 20 gauge copper rigging wire. Where the shrouds pass through the masts drill ⅛″ diameter holes.

Pad the hull and lock it in the bench vise. Glue masts and bowsprit in place with quick setting epoxy. Four small copper or galvanized nails are driven into the hull on each side just behind each mast. These anchor the shrouds which are led up one side, through the ⅛″ holes in the masts and down to the opposite side. Pull the shrouds as taut as possible without bending the masts.

The double back stays supporting the foremast are paired like the shrouds and terminate at a nail on each side of the deck. The stays from the foremast to the bowsprit are next added along with the bowsprit rigging and bobstay which is anchored to the stem with a nail.

Join gaff and main boom to the mizzenmast with copper strips as shown in the detail. The yards are then added and rigged with a continuous length of wire running from a nail on deck, up through the yard tip to the mast and down to the opposite side of the deck.

After the mizzenmast has been rigged and the gaff and boom are firmly in place, cut a sheet copper sail to fill the area between these spars. We used ordinary copper chimney flashing though thin galvanized steel can also be used. Holes are punched in the edges of the sail as shown and it is laced to the spars with rigging wire.

The ship is finished by applying two coats of spar varnish to the deck and all spars. The hull is given two coats of flat black and white enamel using masking tape to assure a neat job of edging at the waterline and gunwales. The copper sail can be polished and

(continued on page 53)

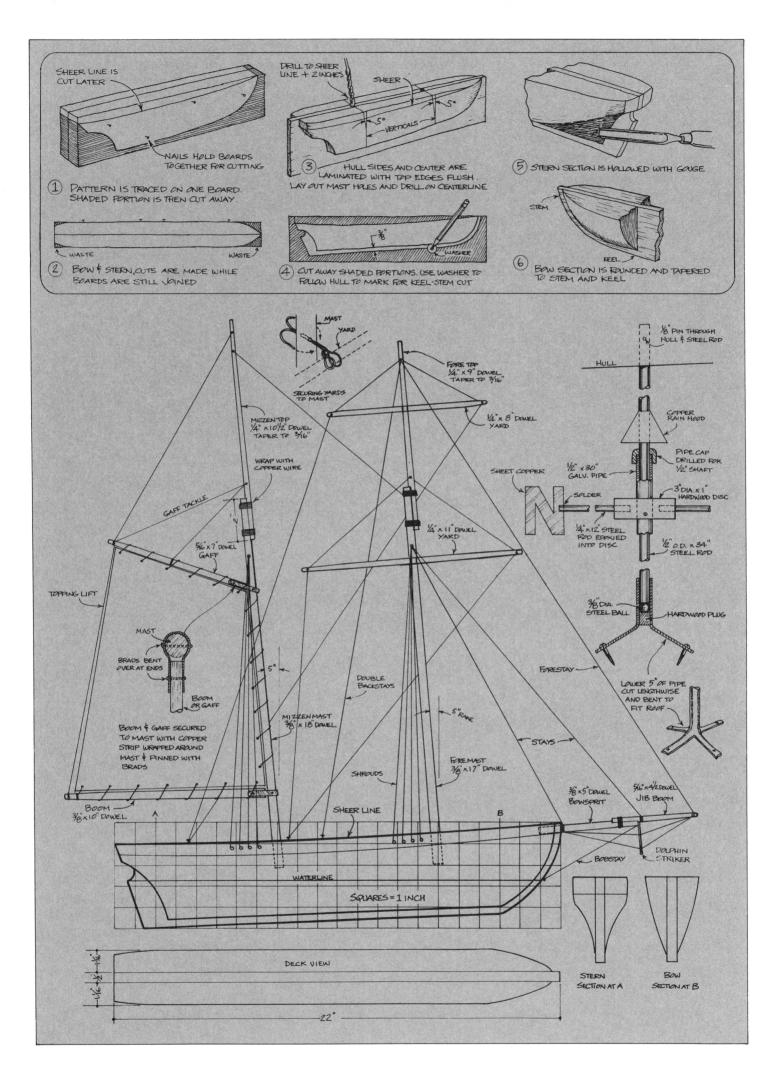

SHEER LINE IS CUT LATER

NAILS HOLD BOARDS TOGETHER FOR CUTTING

① PATTERN IS TRACED ON ONE BOARD. SHADED PORTION IS THEN CUT AWAY.

WASTE   WASTE

② BOW & STERN CUTS ARE MADE WHILE BOARDS ARE STILL JOINED

DRILL TO SHEER LINE + 2 INCHES

SHEER

5°

5°

VERTICALS

③ HULL SIDES AND CENTER ARE LAMINATED WITH TOP EDGES FLUSH. LAY OUT MAST HOLES AND DRILL ON CENTERLINE

3/8"

WASHER

④ CUT AWAY SHADED PORTIONS. USE WASHER TO FOLLOW HULL TO MARK FOR KEEL-STEM CUT

⑤ STERN SECTION IS HOLLOWED WITH GOUGE

STEM

KEEL

⑥ BOW SECTION IS ROUNDED AND TAPERED TO STEM AND KEEL

MAST

YARD

SECURING YARDS TO MAST

FORE TOP 1/4" x 9" DOWEL TAPER TO 3/16"

MIZZEN TOP 1/4" x 10 1/2" DOWEL TAPER TO 3/16"

1/4" x 8" DOWEL YARD

WRAP WITH COPPER WIRE

GAFF TACKLE

SHEET COPPER

1/4" x 11" DOWEL YARD

5/16" x 7" DOWEL GAFF

TOPPING LIFT

MAST

BRADS BENT OVER AT ENDS

BOOM OR GAFF

BOOM & GAFF SECURED TO MAST WITH COPPER STRIP WRAPPED AROUND MAST & PINNED WITH BRADS

5°

DOUBLE BACKSTAYS

MIZZEN MAST 3/8" x 18" DOWEL

5° RAKE

FOREMAST 3/8" x 17" DOWEL

SHROUDS

BOOM 3/8" x 10" DOWEL

A

SHEER LINE

B

1/8" PIN THROUGH HULL & STEEL ROD

HULL

COPPER RAIN HOOD

PIPE CAP DRILLED FOR 1/2" SHAFT

1/2" x 30" GALV. PIPE

SOLDER

3" DIA. x 1" HARDWOOD DISC

1/4" x 12" STEEL ROD EPOXIED INTO DISC

1/2" O.D. x 34" STEEL ROD

3/8" DIA. STEEL BALL

HARDWOOD PLUG

FORESTAY

LOWER 5" OF PIPE CUT LENGTHWISE AND BENT TO FIT ROOF

STAYS

3/8" x 5" DOWEL BOWSPRIT

5/16" x 4 1/2" DOWEL JIB BOOM

BOBSTAY

DOLPHIN STRIKER

WATERLINE

SQUARES = 1 INCH

1/16" 1/2" 1/16"

DECK VIEW

STERN SECTION AT A

BOW SECTION AT B

22"

Weather Vane (Cont'd)

varnished or left to weather naturally.

Lay the completed ship on the workbench with the masts hanging over the edge and find the balance point with a short length of dowel. This should be somewhere near the mizzenmast. Drill up into the keel with a ½" bit to a depth of 2 inches and perpendicular to the waterline. A solid ½" dia. x 34" steel rod is inserted in the hole and locked in place by drilling through the hull and rod a hole sufficiently large enough to drive in a steel pin cut from a nail.

The staff that supports the steel rod consists of a 30" length of standard ½" galvanized pipe threaded on one end to take a pipe cap. Cut a 1" thick x 3¼" square piece of hardwood and scribe intersecting lines from the center of each side to mark locations of the holes which will hold the letters representing the four points of the compass. Drill ¼" holes in each side to a depth of about 1 inch, then scribe a 3" dia. circle and cut the disc or mount it on a face plate and lathe-turn it.

A central hole is bored through the disc for a snug fit over the galvanized pipe. A ¾" spade bit is used after which the hole should be carefully reamed until the disc just slips over the pipe. Later it will be locked in place on the pipe, after you've determined the proper orientation of the north, south, east and west arms.

The ¼" steel rods which fit the disc are cut to 12" lengths and a slot is hacksawed in one end for the letters which are cut with aviation snips and soldered or epoxied to the rods. Spread some epoxy in the disc holes and drive in the rods.

By carefully hacksawing four lengthwise slits in the unthreaded end of the galvanized pipe, as shown, you can bend the four resulting strips out to conform to your roof. Two strips ride the ridge while the other two fit the slope on either side. Drill through these feet to take long galvanized screws which are driven into ridge and rafters.

After bending the mounting feet cut a hardwood plug to fit tightly in the pipe bottom. Epoxy this plug in place and also seal its bottom face with epoxy. Center-drill the pipe cap with a ½" bit and screw the cap on the galvanized pipe.

Lock the galvanized pipe in the vise and drop a steel ball of about ⅜" dia. down into the pipe. Now place the steel rod with the ship attached into the hole in the pipe cap and let it rest on the ball bearing. A small copper rain hood is then cut and soldered to the solid rod just far enough above the pipe cap to prevent water from entering and without interfering with the movement of the weather vane. For better visibility against the sky, the entire assembly can be given a couple of coats of black enamel.

To mount the weather vane it will be necessary to use a hand compass to determine the direction of magnetic north. If you're a sailor you'll know that this isn't likely to be true north but it's close enough for our purposes. The galvanized staff should be fastened to the roof, applying caulking under the feet where the screws are driven into the roof. The disc with the four direction arms is located about 5" below the pipe cap and rotated to the proper orientation. Hold it in place while you drill a pilot hole for a screw through the disc and into the pipe without touching the inner rotating rod. A bit of motor oil poured down through the pipe cap will keep the ball bearing well lubricated and operating smoothly for years. Be prepared to take orders for this weather vane when your friends see it.

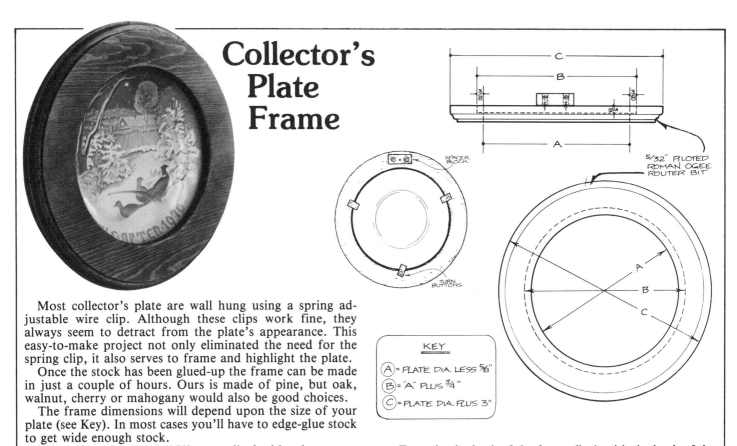

Collector's Plate Frame

KEY

Ⓐ = PLATE DIA. LESS ⅝"
Ⓑ = "A" PLUS ¾"
Ⓒ = PLATE DIA. PLUS 3"

Most collector's plate are wall hung using a spring adjustable wire clip. Although these clips work fine, they always seem to detract from the plate's appearance. This easy-to-make project not only eliminated the need for the spring clip, it also serves to frame and highlight the plate.

Once the stock has been glued-up the frame can be made in just a couple of hours. Ours is made of pine, but oak, walnut, cherry or mahogany would also be good choices.

The frame dimensions will depend upon the size of your plate (see Key). In most cases you'll have to edge-glue stock to get wide enough stock.

Dimensions "A" and "C" are scribed with a bow compass, then cut out with a saber saw. It's best to cut just on the waste side of the scribed line, then carefully sand down to the line to provide a smooth curve. The rabbet is cut using a router with a ⅜ inch piloted rabbet bit. A 5/32 inch piloted Roman ogee bit cuts the outside molding.

To make the back of the frame flush with the back of the plate, a small spacer block is secured to the frame back. A ⅛ inch diameter hanger hole is drilled in it for a finishing nail. The plate is held to the frame with three small wooden turnbuttons made from ⅛ inch stock.

Sand thoroughly, then stain and final finish to suit.

19th Century Danish Washstand

Nowadays we all wash-up at the bathroom sink, but before the advent of modern plumbing, it was the washstand that served this function. The bowl was filled from a pitcher, and here one would wash away the dirt and sweat of a long hard day's work.

Built in the late 1800's, this well-constructed washstand was obviously the work of a skilled country craftsman. The liberal use of rabbets and dadoes, along with the dovetail and mortise and tenon joints, is evidence that it was built to last — not just for a dozen years, but rather a dozen generations. And last it did, for in spite of the many years of daily use, it remains basically a sound and functional piece of furniture.

Like most pieces of American or European country furniture, it was made from pine. Of course, most any wood can be used for a reproduction, but pine would probably be your best choice. Look for stock with a minimum of warp and reasonably free of knots.

The two sides (part A) can be made first. Since 13½ inch wide boards are a rarity these days, you'll have to edge-glue two or more narrower boards in order to get enough width. There's an assortment of dadoes and grooves cut on part A. Refer to the exploded view and the detail drawing for locations and dimensions of each groove. These cuts can best be made with a router equipped with a straight bit. Use guidestrips and stop blocks to control the router. Next, transfer the curved profile from the grid pattern and cut out with a band or saber saw.

After cutting part B to size, the half-dovetails can be laid out and cut. Make the cuts with care to insure a good fit.

The bottom (C), center shelf (D), and base shelf (E) are identical and can be made next. Refer to the detail for the dimensions of the ¼ inch by ⅜ inch rabbet on each end. This cut can be made by making repeated passes with the table or radial arm saw, or with a router and piloted ⅜ inch rabbet bit. When cutting the rabbets, try to make them slightly thicker than the dadoes. Then, when the rabbeted board is sanded, it will result in a good snug fit.

The plinth (part F) can be cut to overall length and width as shown. Make repeated passes on the table or radial arm saw to form the ⅜ by ⅜ inch tongue on each end. Transfer the curved pattern from the grid before cutting out with the band or saber saw.

Part G, the front, can now be cut to size. Since this piece shows prominently, try to select stock with an attractive figure. Note the detail drawing showing the ⅜ inch by ⅜ inch rabbet on each end. This rabbet can be cut in the same manner as the shelf rabbets were.

The back cleat (part H) is made from 5/4 nominal stock (1⅛ inch actual). As shown in the detail, a ¼ inch wide by ⅜ inch deep groove is cut along its length. A couple of passes over the table saw will cut this groove in short order. The 45 degree bevel serves to make the cleat less noticeable after the project has been assembled.

The two side cleats, part I, are cut to a 10½ inch length. Later, when installed, this length will allow a slight gap between the back cleat(H) and the front (G). It's a good idea to have this gap because as the sides (A) tend to shrink during

(continued on next page)

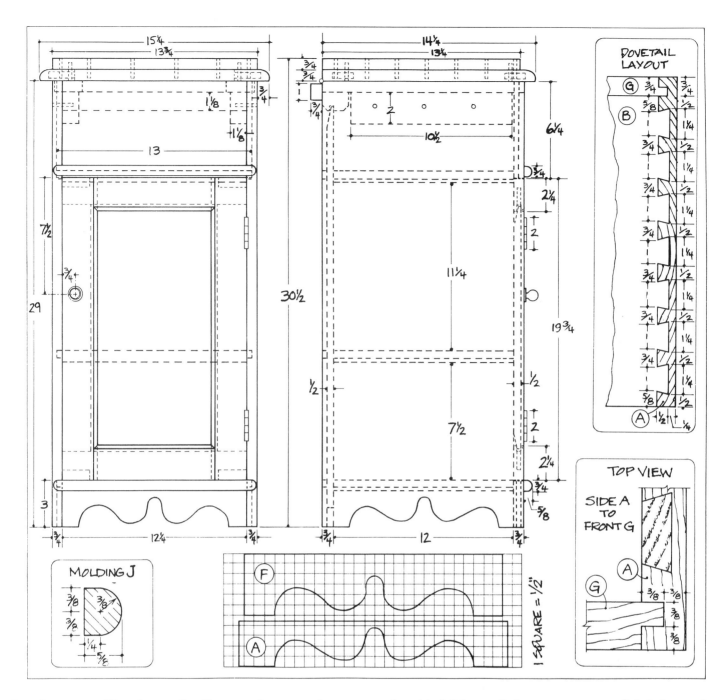

the winter, part H and part G will move closer together. Cutting the cleat (I) a little short allows this movement without putting any stress on part G or part H.

Parts J, the two molding strips, are made from ¾ inch stock. The dimensions are shown in the detail. Probably the easiest way to duplicate the ⅜ inch radius is to cut a piece of wide (around 1½ inches or so) stock to a length of 27½ inches, then clamp it in a vise. Mark the radius on each end, then use a sharp hand plane to round the edges. Finish rounding with coarse, then smooth, sandpaper. Now use the table or radial arm saw to rip the molding to a ⅝ inch width, then cut to 13½ inch lengths and round the ends.

The back (K) is made of edge-glued ½ inch thick stock. The beveled edge (on the sides and top only) can best be cut by setting the table saw blade to an angle of 17 degrees, then running the stock (as it's held against the rip-fence) through the blade on edge. The location of the rip-fence and the height of the blade must be carefully adjusted before making the cut.

The door assembly (parts L, M, and N) can now be made. Referring to the detail, note that the door rails and stiles have a bevel around their inside edges. The procedure for making these parts is shown in the step by step drawing on page 57. As can be seen, the joint can be cut with a table saw. Mortises are drilled out and cleaned up with a mortis-

ing chisel. It's usually best to cut tenons slightly larger than necessary and allow them to protrude to be later trimmed flush with the stiles. When allowing for extra tenon length remember that the critical rail dimension is the distance between tenon shoulders.

The bevels on the rails are coped or cut at an angle to fit against the stile bevels giving the appearance of a mitered corner. After completing step 8, the corner joint should fit together perfectly without further trimming. Tenon haunches can be quickly cut with a dovetail or small backsaw or by using the miter gauge and making repeated passes over the table saw blade.

The top frame (parts O and P) is joined with mortise and tenon joints. All dimensions are shown in the detail. Note that the inside edges of parts O and P have a curved radius. These curves were applied to allow the frame to fit over the lip of the washbowl. Even if you don't plan to use this as a washstand, the curves are a nice detail and worth including.

Before assembly give all parts a complete sanding. Check all joints for proper fit-up, then assemble as shown. Glue and clamp, then add the ¼ inch diameter dowel pins where shown. Do not glue the back (K) and door panel (N). However, part K should be joined to parts C, D, and E, with a single dowel at the center (measuring across the back) of each shelf. Two blocks (R) to support the open top are glued

(continued on page 57)

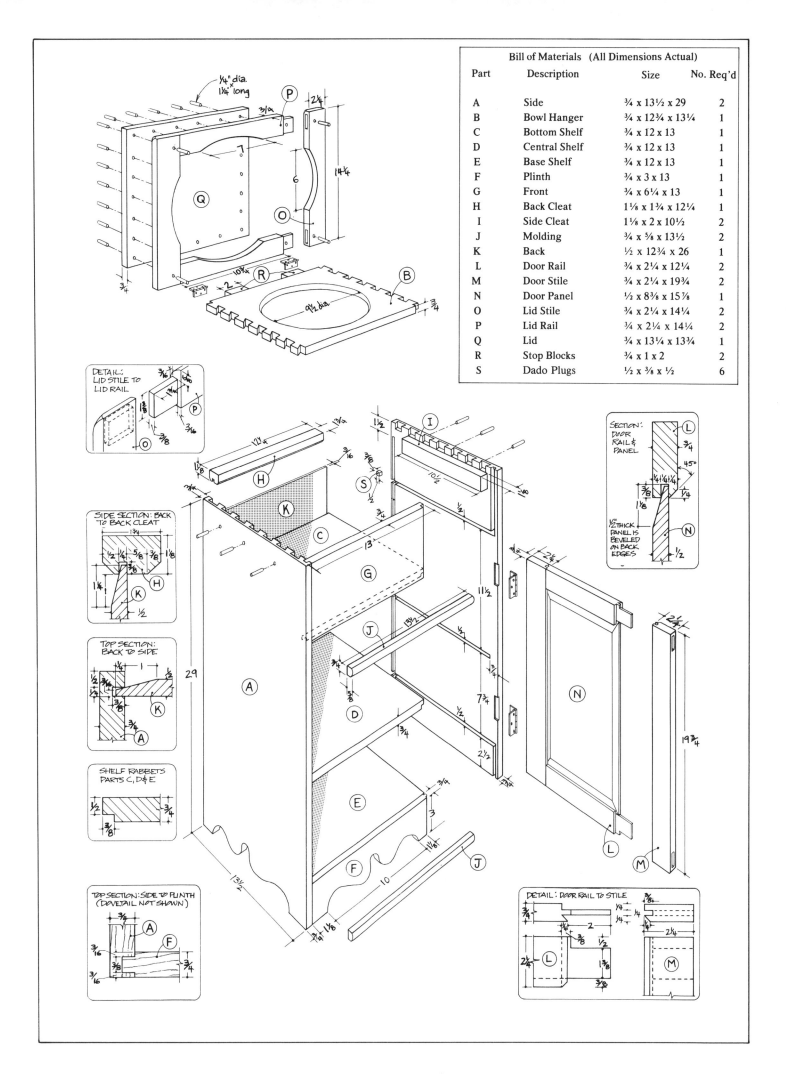

Bill of Materials (All Dimensions Actual)			
Part	Description	Size	No. Req'd
A	Side	¾ x 13½ x 29	2
B	Bowl Hanger	¾ x 12¾ x 13¼	1
C	Bottom Shelf	¾ x 12 x 13	1
D	Central Shelf	¾ x 12 x 13	1
E	Base Shelf	¾ x 12 x 13	1
F	Plinth	¾ x 3 x 13	1
G	Front	¾ x 6¼ x 13	1
H	Back Cleat	1⅛ x 1¾ x 12¼	1
I	Side Cleat	1⅛ x 2 x 10½	2
J	Molding	¾ x ⅝ x 13½	2
K	Back	½ x 12¾ x 26	1
L	Door Rail	¾ x 2¼ x 12¼	2
M	Door Stile	¾ x 2¼ x 19¾	2
N	Door Panel	½ x 8⅜ x 15⅞	1
O	Lid Stile	¾ x 2¼ x 14¼	2
P	Lid Rail	¾ x 2¼ x 14¼	2
Q	Lid	¾ x 13¼ x 13¾	1
R	Stop Blocks	¾ x 1 x 2	2
S	Dado Plugs	½ x ⅜ x ½	6

DETAIL: LID STILE TO LID RAIL

SIDE SECTION: BACK TO BACK CLEAT

TOP SECTION: BACK TO SIDE

SHELF RABBETS PARTS C, D & E

TOP SECTION: SIDE TO PLINTH (DOVETAIL NOT SHOWN)

SECTION: DOOR RAIL & PANEL

½" THICK PANEL IS BEVELED ON BACK EDGES

DETAIL: DOOR RAIL TO STILE

Frame & Panel Joint With Decorative Bevel

1

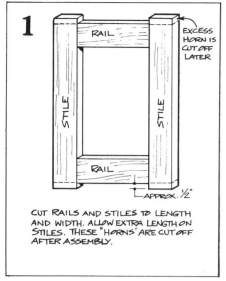

CUT RAILS AND STILES TO LENGTH AND WIDTH. ALLOW EXTRA LENGTH ON STILES. THESE "HORNS" ARE CUT OFF AFTER ASSEMBLY.

2

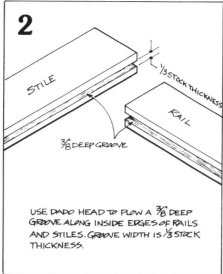

USE DADO HEAD TO PLOW A ⅜" DEEP GROOVE ALONG INSIDE EDGES OF RAILS AND STILES. GROOVE WIDTH IS ⅓ STOCK THICKNESS.

3

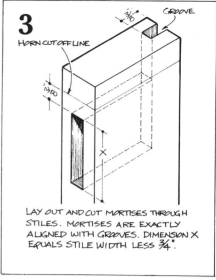

LAY OUT AND CUT MORTISES THROUGH STILES. MORTISES ARE EXACTLY ALIGNED WITH GROOVES. DIMENSION X EQUALS STILE WIDTH LESS ¾".

4

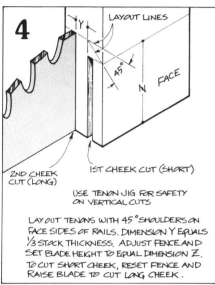

LAY OUT TENONS WITH 45° SHOULDERS ON FACE SIDES OF RAILS. DIMENSION Y EQUALS ⅓ STOCK THICKNESS. ADJUST FENCE AND SET BLADE HEIGHT TO EQUAL DIMENSION Z. TO CUT SHORT CHEEK, RESET FENCE AND RAISE BLADE TO CUT LONG CHEEK.

USE TENON JIG FOR SAFETY ON VERTICAL CUTS

5

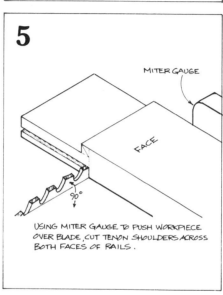

USING MITER GAUGE TO PUSH WORKPIECE OVER BLADE, CUT TENON SHOULDERS ACROSS BOTH FACES OF RAILS.

6

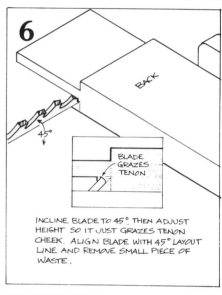

INCLINE BLADE TO 45°, THEN ADJUST HEIGHT SO IT JUST GRAZES TENON CHEEK. ALIGN BLADE WITH 45° LAYOUT LINE AND REMOVE SMALL PIECE OF WASTE.

7

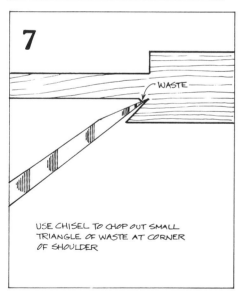

USE CHISEL TO CHOP OUT SMALL TRIANGLE OF WASTE AT CORNER OF SHOULDER

8

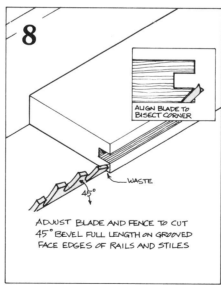

ADJUST BLADE AND FENCE TO CUT 45° BEVEL FULL LENGTH ON GROOVED FACE EDGES OF RAILS AND STILES

9

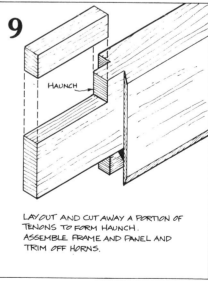

LAYOUT AND CUT AWAY A PORTION OF TENONS TO FORM HAUNCH. ASSEMBLE FRAME AND PANEL AND TRIM OFF HORNS.

and screwed to part B as shown. Also, small filler blocks (S) are used to plug the dado groove cutouts in the back edge of parts C, D, and E.

Final sand all parts, giving all edges a thorough rounding to simulate years of wear. Stain to suit. We would suggest a stain that provides an antique look, and one of our favorites (with pine) is a single coat of Minwax Special Walnut followed by two coats of their Antique Oil Finish.

While we can't provide a source for an exact reproduction of the knob, we can suggest a 1¼ inch diameter wooden knob available from Horton Brasses, Nooks Hill Rd., Cromwell, CT 06416. It's painted black with a brass face. Order part no. WCT-2. A small mortise is cut in the inside of part A to accept the knob's locking lever.

Toy Jeep

During World War II there were over 60,000 jeeps manufactured in this country, and it was a rare G.I. who didn't spend at least a few bone-jarring hours riding in one of them. With four-wheel drive and powered by a 60 h.p. Willis engine, it was a no-nonsense driving machine that kept rolling through almost any terrain.

In proportion to size, the toy jeep shown here is pretty close to the real one. And it's a sturdy design, so kids don't have to worry about being rough with it. Although pine can be used, a hardwood such as maple or birch will minimize the nicks and dents.

Begin by cutting parts C & D to size, then rounding over the top, outside edge of part D. Glue and clamp the three parts together to form the hood, noting that C is positioned ⅛ inch above parts B. The pin (N) can be made as shown or purchased from Craftsman Wood Service Co., 1735 W. Cortland Court, Addison, IL 60101.

Cut the frame (A) to size, then glue the hood (parts C & D) to the frame. When secured it should be flush with the front of the frame. The back end (F) is then cut and glued to the back of the frame.

The fender (B) is made as shown in the detail. After rounding the front end it is glued to the frame, hood, and back end. Add finishing nails to secure.

Make the axle holders (K) as shown in the detail, making sure that the groove allows the axles to turn easily. Glue the axle holders so that they overhang the frame by about 1/16 inch on each end. Also, the center of the axle groove should be 1⅜ inches from the front of part A.

Round-off the two upper corners of the dashboard (E), then glue in place. Drill a ¼ inch dia. by ¾ inch deep hole for the steering column (part O) and steering wheel (part P). Round-off the upper corners of the seat backs (I), then glue parts I and H in place against the ends of the side seats (G). Now fasten the bumper (J) using glue and a few finishing nails.

Next attach the spare wheel to the center of the back end. It can be glued or fastened with a short length of ¼ inch diameter dowel, or use the pin (N).

The wheels (M) can now be mounted along with the axles (L). By the way, if you prefer to purchase wheels rather than make them, they can also be ordered from Craftsman Wood Service.

Sand all parts thoroughly taking care to round all sharp edges. To avoid the dangers of a toxic finish, no final finish was applied.

Bill of Materials (All Dimensions Actual)

Part	Description	Size	No. Req'd
A	Frame	½ x 3½ x 7½	1
B	Fender	⅝ x 1¾ x 8⅛	2
C	Inner Hood	1¾ x 2 x 3	1
D	Outer Hood	¾ x 1⅝ x 3	2
E	Dashboard	5/16 x 2¼ x 3½	1
F	Back End	¾ x 1¾ x 3½	1
G	Side Seats	¾ x ¾ x 2	2
H	Front Seats	¾ x 1½ x 1	2
I	Seat Back	⅜ x 1½ x 1¾	2
J	Front Bumper	⅜ x ¾ x 4¼	1
K	Axle Holders	¾ x 1¾ x 3⅝	2
L	Axles	¼ " dia. x 4¾ " long	2
M	Wheels	2" dia. x ½" thick	5
N	Pin	See Detail	3
O	Steering Post	¼" dia. x 1½" long	1
P	Steering Wheel	1" dia. x ¼" thick	1

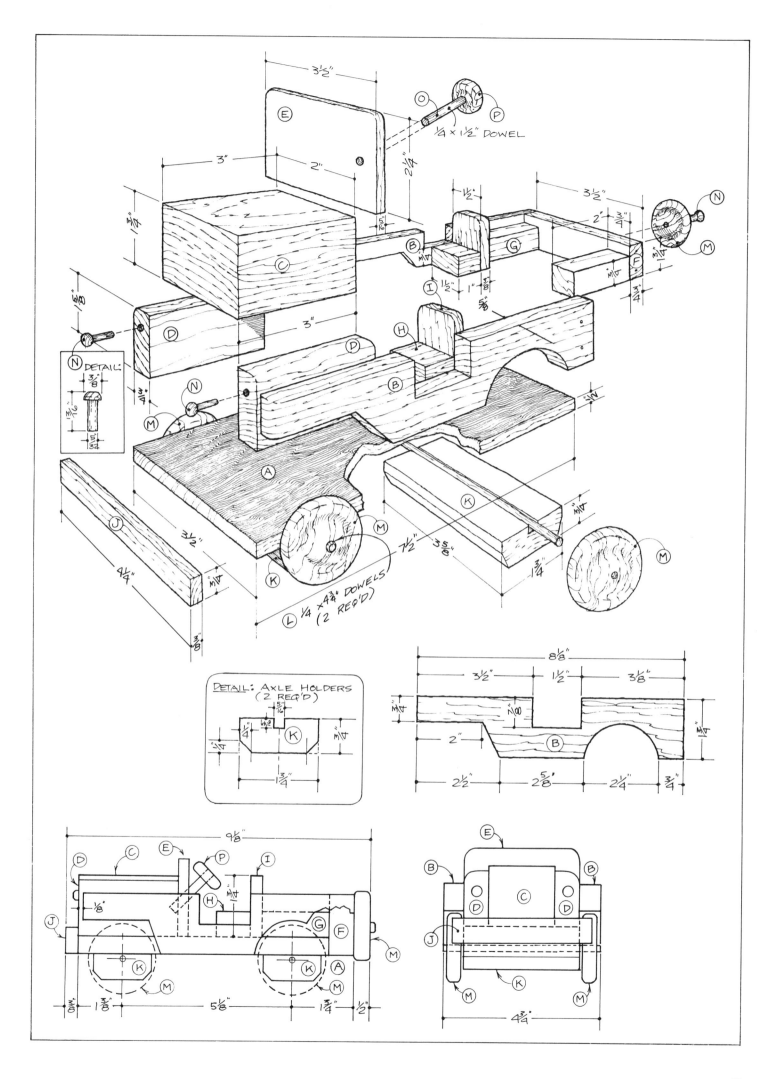

1/4 x 1 1/2" DOWEL

N DETAIL:

DETAIL: AXLE HOLDERS (2 REQ'D)

1/4 x 4 3/4" DOWELS (2 REQ'D)

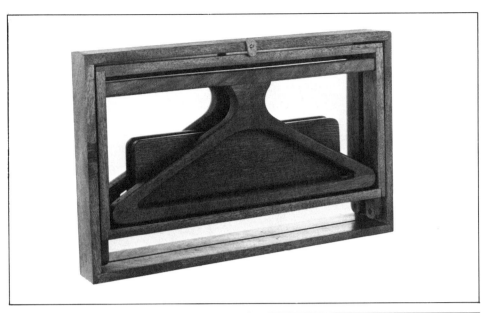

deep dado as shown. If you don't have a dado cutter, you can form the same joint by making repeated passes over the table saw blade. The 1 inch diameter radius can now be scribed as shown, then cut out with a band or saber saw.

The tray (F) is cut to overall length and width, then a router equipped with a ¼ or ⅜ inch diameter straight bit is used to rout the 5/16 inch deep recess as shown. Run the router against guidestrips to establish the perimeter of the recess, then clean up the rest freehand. In order to have the router properly supported you'll need to butt the back of part F against a piece of ½ inch thick scrap stock.

The hanger (H) is made from a glued-up and doweled frame as shown in the detail. Once the frame is made, transfer the grid pattern, then cut out with a band or saber saw. It can then be glued and doweled to part G.

Give all parts a thorough sanding, especially the hanger. Remove all rough surfaces and give edges a good rounding.

Assemble the frame (parts A and B) with glue and clamps. Before setting aside to dry, check for squareness. Make adjustments as necessary. Join part E to F (glue and clamp) and when dry, parts C, D, E, and G can be joined in the same manner. Again check for squareness. Check that part G rotates freely.

Join the two frames by applying glue to the hole in part A, then pushing dowels through part C and into part A. Trim dowels flush with both surfaces.

After sanding, ours was stained with one coat of Minwax Mahogany stain followed by two coats of Minwax Antique Oil Finish.

Attach two small brass hangers to the back edge, then cut ⅛ inch mirror to fit in the back rabbets. Secure with short brads driven into ¼ inch square retaining strips. A small turnbutton made from 3/16 inch stock completes the project.

Mahogany Wall Valet

This unique wall valet offers a number of useful features. When open it has a tray big enough to hold a wallet, pocket change, and watch, along with a hanger for your suit and tie. On the back there's a mirror in case you want to make sure your tie's on straight. It can also be folded flat so it will hang nicely on the back of a closet door when not in use.

Begin by making the frame sides, top and bottom (parts A, B, and C), referring to the detail drawings for all dimensions. Note that part A has a rabbet cut on both ends and the back, while part B has the rabbet cut only on the back. The back rabbets are cut ⅜ inch deep to accept a ⅛ inch thick mirror glass plus the ¼ inch square

retaining strips.

Part C is made next. After cutting to width, cut it to a length of 10⅛ inches. This is ⅝ inch longer than its final length, but this extra amount will make it easier to drill the pivot holes.

The method shown in Sketch A will insure that the pivot holes are drilled accurately. Parts A and C are taped together so that their front and bottom edges are flush with each other. Use some masking tape to clamp the four parts together, then lay out the location of the 5/16 inch diameter hole. Now use the drill press to drill through all four pieces.

Next, the extra ⅝ inch length can be cut from parts C. Use the dado head cutter to cut a ½ inch wide by ¼ inch

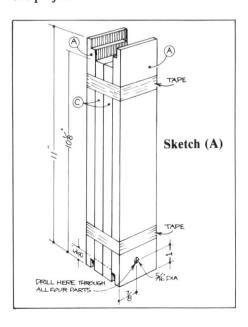

Sketch (A)

DRILL HERE THROUGH ALL FOUR PARTS

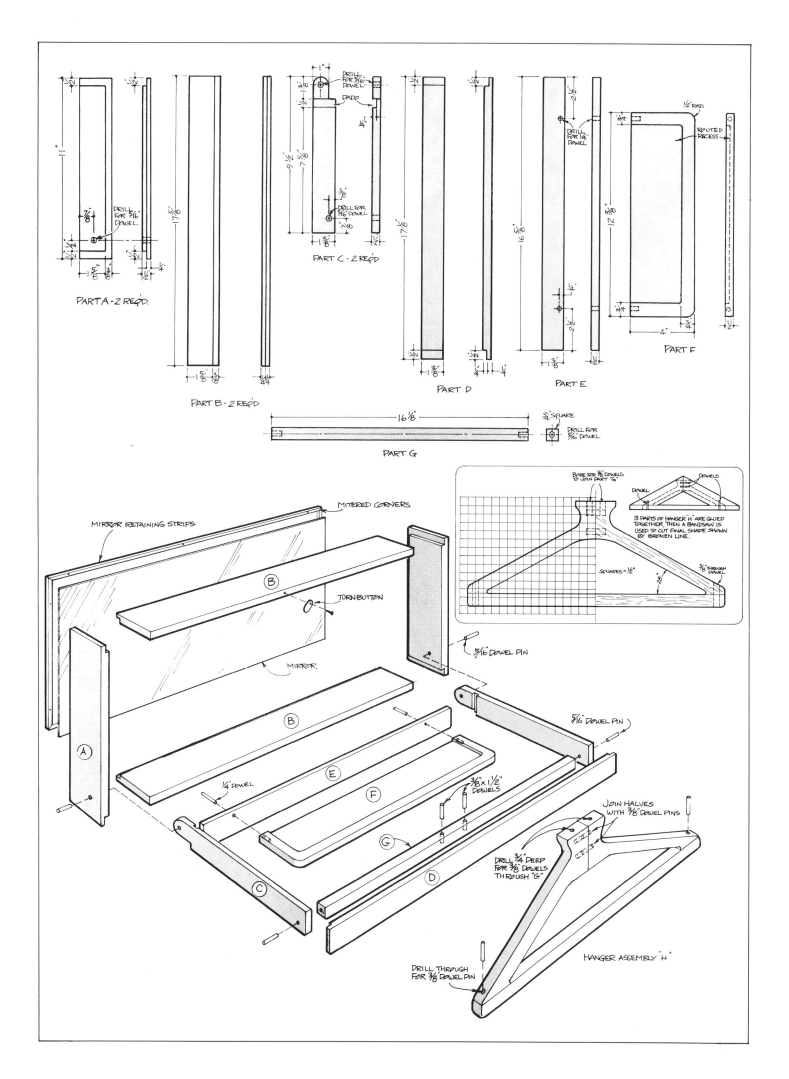

PART A - 2 REQ'D.

PART B - 2 REQ'D

PART C - 2 REQ'D

PART D

PART E

PART F

PART G

DRILL FOR 5/16 DOWEL

DRILL FOR 5/16 DOWEL

DADO

DRILL FOR 1/4 DOWEL

DRILL FOR 1/4 DOWEL

ROUTED RECESS

1/2 RAD.

3/4 SQUARE

MITERED CORNERS

MIRROR RETAINING STRIPS

TORN BUTTON

MIRROR

5/16" DOWEL PIN

5/16" DOWEL PIN

1/4" DOWEL

3/8" x 1/2" DOWELS

BORE FOR 3/8 DOWELS TO JOIN PART "G"

DOWELS

DOWEL

3 PARTS OF HANGER "H" ARE GLUED TOGETHER, THEN A BANDSAW IS USED TO CUT FINAL SHAPE SHOWN BY BROKEN LINE.

SQUARES = 1/2"

3/8" THROUGH DOWEL

JOIN HALVES WITH 3/8" DOWEL PINS

DRILL 3/4" DEEP FOR 3/8" DOWELS THROUGH "G"

HANGER ASSEMBLY "H"

DRILL THROUGH FOR 3/8" DOWEL PIN

Dovetailed Footstool

If you've never done dovetail work, yet would like to give it a try, why not consider this small footstool for your next project. There are few joints that can match its attractive appearance and even fewer that have such inherent strength. This particular type of dovetail joint, called a through dovetail, is not as difficult to make as you might think, and the process goes pretty quickly once you get started.

Before beginning though, give your chisel a good sharpening. Trying to cut dovetails with a dull chisel is just asking for aggravation. Also, it's helpful to have a fine-tooth dovetail or back saw. You just won't get a good clean cut if you try to cut them with a coarse sawblade.

At this point, it's also worth pointing out some basic dovetail terminology. A dovetail joint consists of mating segments cut on the ends of the two boards to be joined. Each segment on one board is cut in the shape of the tail of a dove, and appropriately called the dovetail, or sometimes just the tail. The other board is cut to receive the dovetails and the resulting segments are called pins. Referring to the drawing, the dovetails are cut in the top (part A) and the pins are cut in the sides (part B). Also, a single dovetail is cut on the end of the stretcher (C).

Begin by laying out the dovetails on the ends of part A, referring to the drawing for all dimensions. Ideally, the length of the tail should be equal to the thickness of part B, plus about 1/32 inch. Later, when the joint is assembled, the tails will stick out 1/32 inch, allowing them to be sanded perfectly flush with the side. As you lay out the dovetail locations, work accurately, and use a hard sharp pencil.

Once the tails have been laid out, mark the waste material between dovetails with an "x" to avoid confusion. Scribe the tail location not only on the face surface of the board, but also on the end grain. Secure the top (A) in a vise and use the fine-tooth saw to make the angled cuts. Work carefully, cutting on the waste side of the line, just grazing but not removing it.

Bring the cuts almost, but not quite to the scribed bottom line. A coping saw can now be used to cut across the grain, removing the waste. Remove the workpiece from the vise and clamp it flat on the bench over a scrap board, then use the chisel to dress the sides and bottom of the cutouts.

The pins on the sides (part B) can best be laid out and scribed by using the finished dovetails as a template. To do this, clamp part B in the vise, end up. Lay the dovetailed top (A), in its proper position, on part B and trace

the dovetails with a sharp knife or pencil. Use a square to carry the scribed lines to the face of the board. For reasons mentioned earlier, this distance should be equal to the thickness of A, plus 1/32 inch.

Once again, mark the waste portions with an "x", then cut out in the manner used to cut the dovetails. A well fitted joint should go together with only light tapping from a mallet and scrap block. If needed, trim further with the chisel. When the fit is good, apply glue to all surfaces and clamp securely.

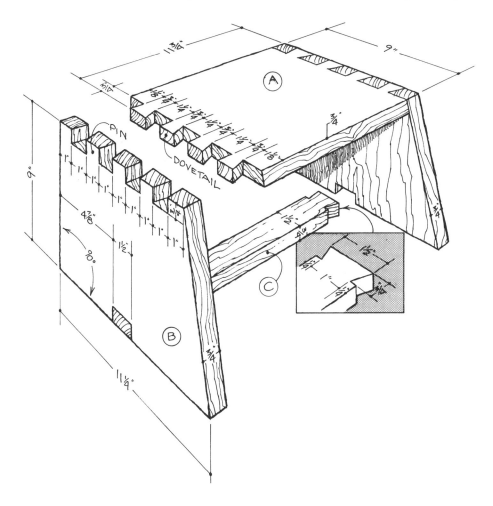

Plant Stand

Plant stands are always popular with our readers, and this one should have a special appeal to those who enjoy the style of Early American. It could also serve as a small night stand for a lamp, perhaps in a bedroom or hallway.

Using 1 inch nominal stock (¾ inch actual), make the two sides first. Since they measure a full 12 inches wide at the bottom it will be necessary to edge glue two narrower boards. Glue and clamp firmly, then allow to dry overnight. When dry, rip to a width of 12 inches, then set the table saw blade for a 3 degree angle. Now, using the miter gauge, crosscut the sides to length.

Next, lay out the location of the shelf dadoes and replace the regular sawblade with a dado head cutter (the angle should still be set at 3 degrees). Set the dado head gauge to cut the dado as shown in the drawing.

The sides taper from 12 inches at the bottom to 9 inches (before cutting the notch) at the top. To cut the taper, clamp the two sides together, then mark the taper with a straightedge and pencil. A sharp plane will cut to the taper line in short order.

To complete work on the sides, lay out the apron notches and the curved bottom profile. A back saw will cut out the notches while a band or saber saw will remove the bottom curve.

Cut the two aprons to size (¾ x 2 x 11), then lay out and cut the curved profile.

The top can be cut from a piece of 1 x 12 (¾ x 11¼ actual) but the shelf, which is 12 inches wide, will require edge-gluing. Cut both parts to length as shown.

Assemble all parts as shown using glue and 1½ x #8 wood screws, countersunk and plugged. Sand all parts thoroughly and round edges to simulate years of wear. Ours was finished with one coat of Minwax Special Walnut followed by two coats of Minwax Antique Oil Finish.

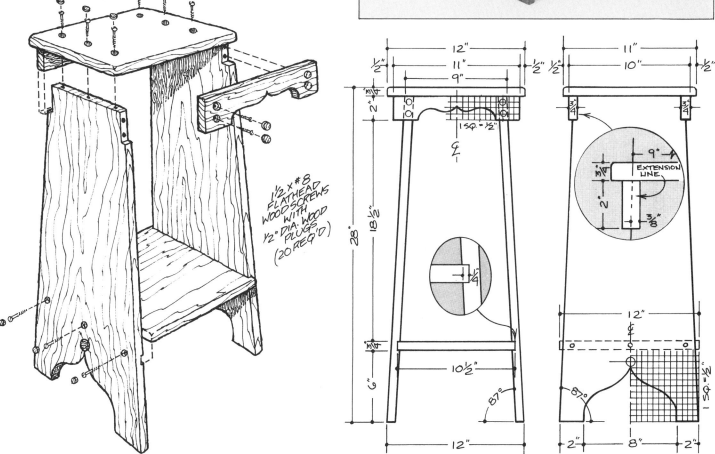

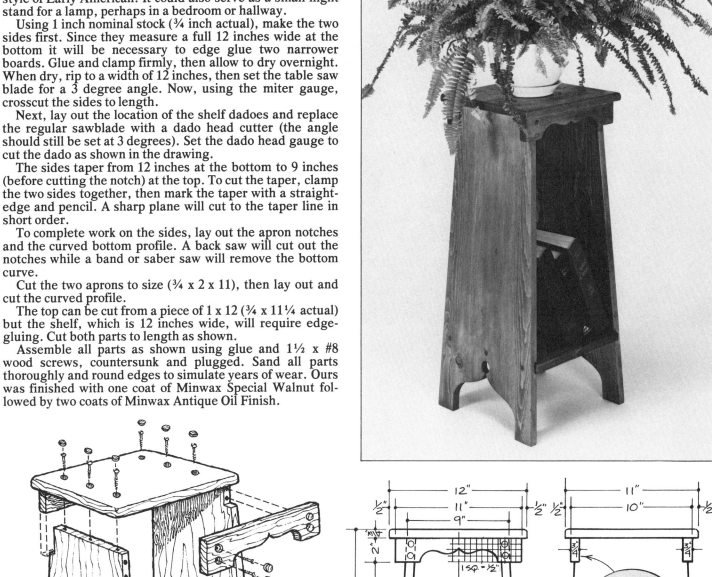

18th Century Lawyer's Case

Originally used by lawyers to store files, abstracts, and titles, this handsome case will find modern use as a place to keep books and magazines handy. This one is made from cherry, but walnut or mahogany would also be good choices.

If wide stock is not available you'll need to edge-join two or more narrower boards. If you are able to select your own hardwood stock, do it with care. Try to choose boards that have a pleasing grain pattern (a better word to describe grain pattern is "figure"). The boards should also be flat and free of any splits, cracks, or other obvious defects.

While dowel pins were once commonly used in edge-joining, from a strength standpoint they actually reduce the glue surface, and thereby the strength in a good long grain-to-long grain joint. However, they do provide a very useful service by keeping the mating boards in line when

clamp pressure is applied. This is especially helpful when working with long boards.

Perhaps most important to the success of an edge-joint is a clean, smooth surface on both mating parts. This allows close contact between both surfaces resulting in maximum glue strength. Ripping to width on the table or radial arm saw will usually leave a fairly rough edge, so it's best to smooth it out with a sharp plane. Take several light cuts, don't try to do it in one pass, and of course, plane with the direction of the grain. When planing, it's important that the edge remain square to the face of the board. Check for this by using a square.

After edge-joining, parts A and B can be cut to overall length and width. Note that part B is ¼ inch narrower than part A. Also, part B has three, ¼ inch deep by ⅜ inch wide stopped dadoes. These are best cut with a router equipped with a ⅜ inch diameter

bit. Lay out the location of the dadoes, then securely clamp a fence (made from a piece of scrap stock) to serve as a guide for the router. Stop the dado at a point 5½ inches from the back edge, then cut the corners square with a chisel.

Part A has a ¼ x ¼ rabbet cut along the entire length of the inside back edge. This can be cut on the table or radial arm saw or with a router equipped with a piloted ¼ inch rabbet bit.

Next, cut part C to overall length and width, then lay out the location of the ¼ inch deep by ⅜ inch wide dadoes. Except for the fact that these are stopped on both ends, the method for cutting them is the same as for part B. After cutting the dadoes, use the router and a piloted ¼ inch radius cove bit to apply a cove to all four edges.

Parts E and F are identical. Cut to length and width, then use a piloted 5/32 inch Roman ogee bit to rout a molding around all four edges.

The dividers, part D, are made from ⅜ inch thick stock. If you have fairly narrow pieces of heavier stock (1½ - 2 inches wide) they can be resawn on the table saw. These resawn boards can then be edge-glued to form the wide divider panels. Of course, if you have a band saw you'll be able to resaw much wider stock. Perhaps the easiest way to get ⅜ inch stock is to hand plane ¾ inch stock. It doesn't take very long, and besides, most woodworkers agree that hand planing a piece of wood is one of the most pleasurable aspects of this hobby.

Once you have stock for the dividers, transfer the profile from the grid pattern shown. Use a saber saw or band saw to cut out, then sand the edges of the curves to remove all rough spots.

For the back (G), ¼ inch hardwood plywood should be used.

Sand all parts, then assemble as shown using glue and wood screws, countersunk and plugged. Allow glue to dry before giving the project a thorough final sanding. Lightly round all corners and sharp edges. Finish to suit. The one shown, made of cherry, was not stained. Instead it was simply finished with two coats of Watco Danish Oil.

Bill of Materials
(All Dimensions Actual)

Part	Description	Size	No. Req'd
A	End	¾ x 8½ x 12	2
B	Top	¾ x 8¼ x 15⅜	1
C	Bottom	¾ x 9½ x 17⅞	1
D	Partition	⅜ x 7¾ x 11¾	3
E	Crown	¾ x 10½ x 18⅞	1
F	Base	¾ x 10½ x 18⅞	1
G	Back	¼ x 15⅞ x 12	1

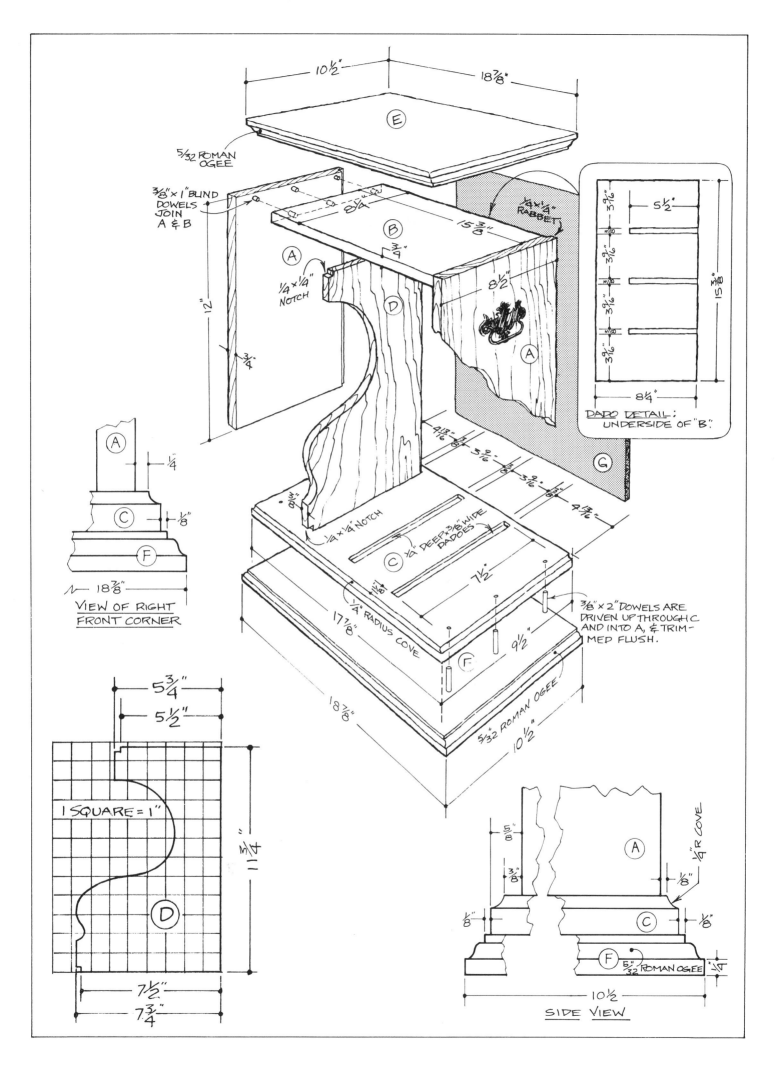

10½"

18⅞"

E

5/32 ROMAN OGEE

3/8" × 1" BLIND DOWELS JOIN A & B

¼"×¼" RABBET

8¼"

15¾"

B

A

¾"

¼ × ¼ NOTCH

12"

¾"

8½"

D

A

DADO DETAIL: UNDERSIDE OF "B"

5½"

3/16"
3/16"

3/8"

3/16"
3/16"

3/8"

3/16"
3/16"

15⅝"

8¼"

G

A

C

¼

F

⅛"

18⅞"

VIEW OF RIGHT FRONT CORNER

4 13/16"

5 9/16"

3 9/16"

4 13/16"

Ø¾"

¼ × ¼ NOTCH

C

¼" DEEP × 3/8" WIDE DADOES

7½"

3/8" × 2" DOWELS ARE DRIVEN UP THROUGH C AND INTO A, & TRIMMED FLUSH.

¼" RADIUS COVE

17⅞"

F

9½"

18⅞"

5/32 ROMAN OGEE

10½"

5¾"

5½"

I SQUARE = 1"

11¾"

D

7½"

7¾"

⅝"

A

¼"R COVE

3/8"

⅛"

⅛"

C

⅛"

F

5/32 ROMAN OGEE

¼"

10½"

SIDE VIEW

65

Blanket Chest

The attractive traditional design and simple construction of this chest make it an ideal project, even for a novice woodworker. A table saw, router, sabersaw, and drill are the only power tools required.

While the chest shown was made from pine, a hardwood such as cherry or walnut, or an aromatic cedar (a softwood), would be excellent alternate selections.

We opted to include a pair of friction lid supports, which will hold the lid open in the desired position, providing easy access to the chest. A lock might also be added, if you prefer. Both the friction lid supports (order part no. 75J87L, and 75J87R) and the chest lock are available from: Constantine's, 2050 Eastchester Rd., Bronx, NY 10461. Note that you will need two lid supports; a left-hand and a right-hand version.

Make the front (A), two sides (B), and back (C) first. Standard 1 x 12 (¾ x 11¼ actual) pine will provide the necessary width, but if 1 x 12 is not available, you'll have to edge-join narrower stock.

Note that part A has a ¾ inch wide by ½ inch deep rabbet on each end, while part B has a ¾ inch wide by ⅜ inch deep rabbet on one end. These rabbets are best cut using a dado head cutter, although they can also be done by making repeated passes over a regular sawblade.

Parts A, B, and C can now be assembled. Use glue and clamp securely with pipe or bar clamps. Some short pieces of scrap stock should be used to protect the worksurface from clamp marks.

It's most important that this box be square. If it isn't, loosen the clamps and make adjustments before setting aside to dry overnight.

The bottom (D) is made next. Cut it slightly wider and longer than the box (parts A, B, & C), then attach it to the box bottom with glue and finishing nails. When dry, use a hand plane to remove the overhanging edges. This results in a flush edge all around.

The two lid supports (G) are cut to fit snugly between parts A and C. Add glue to the ends and the edge that contacts part B, then clamp in place. Make sure it's flush with the top edges of the box.

The spacers (part O) can now be cut to size and glued to the underside of part G. Secure in place with a clamp until dry.

Cut the two lid frame ends (I) and lid frame back (J) to size. Fasten in place with glue and 1¼" x #8 flat head wood screws. Slightly countersink the screw heads.

The two top sides (L) and the top back (M) are cut to overall length and width, then the corners are spline mitered as shown. The spline groove is cut ⅛ inch wide (or the width of your table or radial arm sawblade kerf). In order to have maximum strength the spline should be cut so that its grain runs in the same direction as parts L and M, or another alternative is to use plywood as the spline material. After cutting the spline, transfer the curved profile from the grid pattern to the stock. Use a band saw or saber saw to cut to shape. Parts L and M can now be assembled to the box using blind dowels as shown. The dowel spacing isn't critical, just be sure to avoid the screwholes.

The top (H) will require that two or more boards be edge-joined in order to get adequate width. After the stock has been edge-glued and allowed to dry it can be cut to overall width and length. Since wide boards have a tendency to warp, it's a good idea to add the two cleats (N). Secure with a screw at the center, and one about one inch from each end of the cleat, screwing up and into the top (H). The cleat should not prevent the top from moving due to changes in humidity — if it does the top might crack. Don't use glue here. Also, it helps if the screw hole on each end of the cleat is slotted, thereby allowing unrestrained movement of the top.

Next, make the base front and back (E) and the base ends (F). Cut a little on the long side, then cut the miters to fit the exact dimensions of the box. The ⅛ inch by 1 inch notch can be cut with the dado head or with a regular sawblade. After cutting the 45 degree bevel and the curved profile, add glue to the notch and the mitered end, then secure to the box with pipe or bar clamps. Allow to dry overnight.

Cut and fit glue block (K) for added strength, then give all surfaces a thorough final sanding. Give corners a liberal rounding. Add 2 inch brass butt hinges and friction lid supports as shown.

Ours was finished with a coat of Minwax Special Walnut stain followed by two coats of Minwax Antique Oil Finish. After drying, the friction lid supports were adjusted to support the lid in any position.

Bill of Materials (All Dimensions Actual)			
Part	Description	Size	No. Req'd
A	Front	¾ x 11¼ x 44	1
B	Side	¾ x 11¼ x 16¾	2
C	Back	¾ x 11¼ x 43¼	1
D	Bottom	½ x 17 x 44	1
E	Base Front & Back	¾ x 4 x 45¼	2
F	Base Ends	¾ x 4 x 18¼	2
G	Lid Support	¾ x 3 x 15½	2
H	Lid	¾ x 14¾ x 38	1
I	Lid Frame End	¾ x 3¾ x 14¾	2
J	Lid Frame Back	¾ x 3¾ x 45½	1
K	Glue Block	1 x 1 x 2¾	4
L	Top Sides	¾ x 4¾ x 16¾	2
M	Top Back	¾ x 6½ x 44	1
N	Cleat	¾ x 1½ x 12	2
O	Spacer	¾ x 3 x 4	2

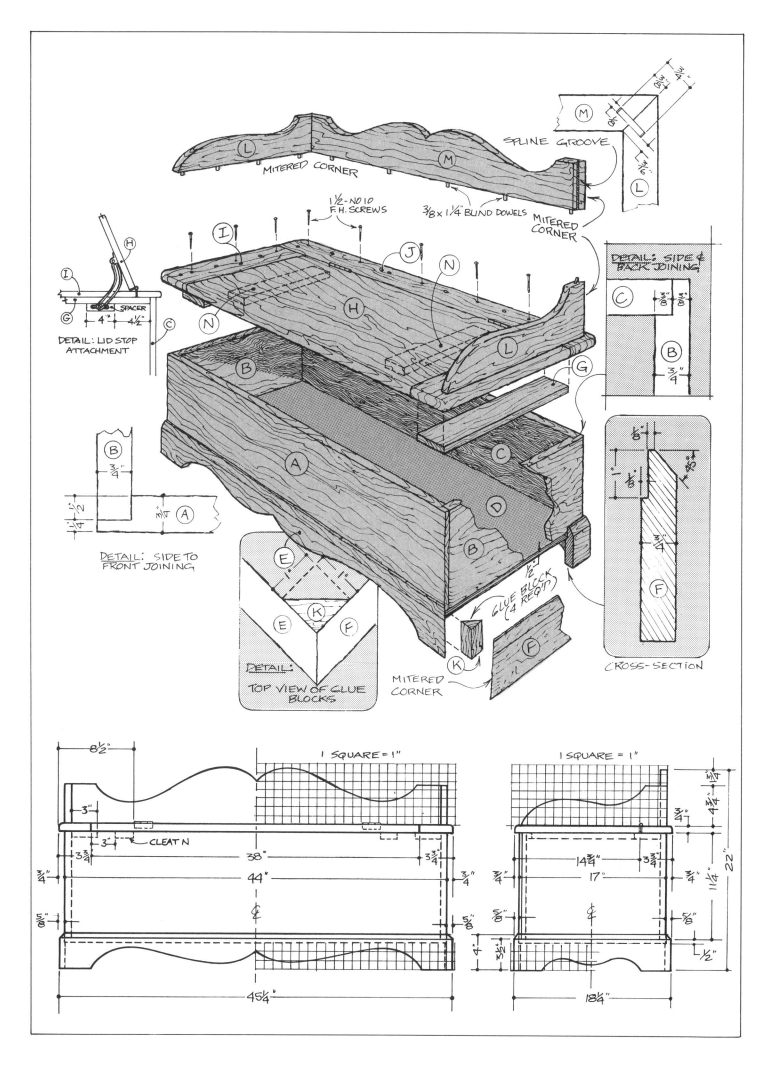

MITERED CORNER

SPLINE GROOVE

1½ - NO 10
F.H. SCREWS

⅜ × 1¼ BLIND DOWELS

MITERED
CORNER

DETAIL: SIDE &
BACK JOINING

DETAIL: LID STOP
ATTACHMENT

SPACER

DETAIL: SIDE TO
FRONT JOINING

DETAIL:
TOP VIEW OF GLUE
BLOCKS

GLUE BLOCK
(4 REQ'D)

MITERED
CORNER

CROSS-SECTION

1 SQUARE = 1"

1 SQUARE = 1"

CLEAT N

Early American Wall Cupboard

With space at a premium in the homes of most early Americans, wall cabinets enjoyed a great deal of popularity because they added some much needed storage area.

While not an original piece, the one shown offers many of the characteristics that make early American designs so appealing to many of us. To simplify construction, dowels are used for most joints, although experienced woodworkers will no doubt choose to incorporate the mortise and tenon. Pine is used throughout, except for the plywood back (part G and H).

Begin by making the bottom (A), top (C), and two shelves (B). As shown in the detail, all four parts are identical. An eight foot length of 1 x 12 stock (¾ inch by 11¼ inch actual) will provide enough material. It's important that the angles be cut accurately, so check your saw before starting. Also, make sure the dimensions are cut exactly as shown.

To make part D, rip 1 inch stock (¾ inch actual) to a width of about 3⅜ inches, then set the table or radial arm

saw blade to a 22½ degree angle and cut a bevel along one edge. Return the blade to the zero degree position and with the beveled edge against the fence, rip the piece to its finish width of 3 inches.

Cut part E to the dimensions shown in the Bill of Materials. Be sure both ends are square. Referring to the detail, drill parts E and D for ⅜ inch diameter by 2 inch long dowel pins. If you have one, a doweling jig will be helpful here. Drill the holes slightly more than 1 inch deep to allow room for any excess glue in the hole.

Parts D and E can now be joined to form the outer frame. Apply glue to the mating surfaces of both parts and also to the dowel pins. Keep in mind that the dowel pins must have a lengthwise groove to allow trapped air and glue to escape, otherwise you may not be able to close the joint. Assemble parts D and E and clamp securely with bar or pipe clamps. Apply only enough pressure to bring the mating surfaces in firm contact - too much pressure will squeeze most of the glue out of the joint. Use small scraps of wood as clamp pads to protect the frame. It's important that the frame be square, so check this before setting aside to dry. Make adjustments as necessary.

Make the two back pieces (parts G & H) next. We recommend that plywood be used here. Note that part H is wider than part G. Also, part H has a ¼ inch deep by ½ inch wide rabbet along one edge.

The cabinet can now be partially assembled. Sand thoroughly parts A, B, C, frame parts D and E, and back parts G and H. If there are deep scratches or dents, you may need to start with 80 grit aluminum oxide paper, otherwise start with 100 grit. For a proper sanding job you also need to remove all planer marks (the marks made at the mill by the cutter blades of a surface planer). Follow the first sanding with a second sanding using 120 grit. A third and fourth sanding with 150, then 220 grit will result in a smooth finish that will take a stain nicely.

(continued on page 70)

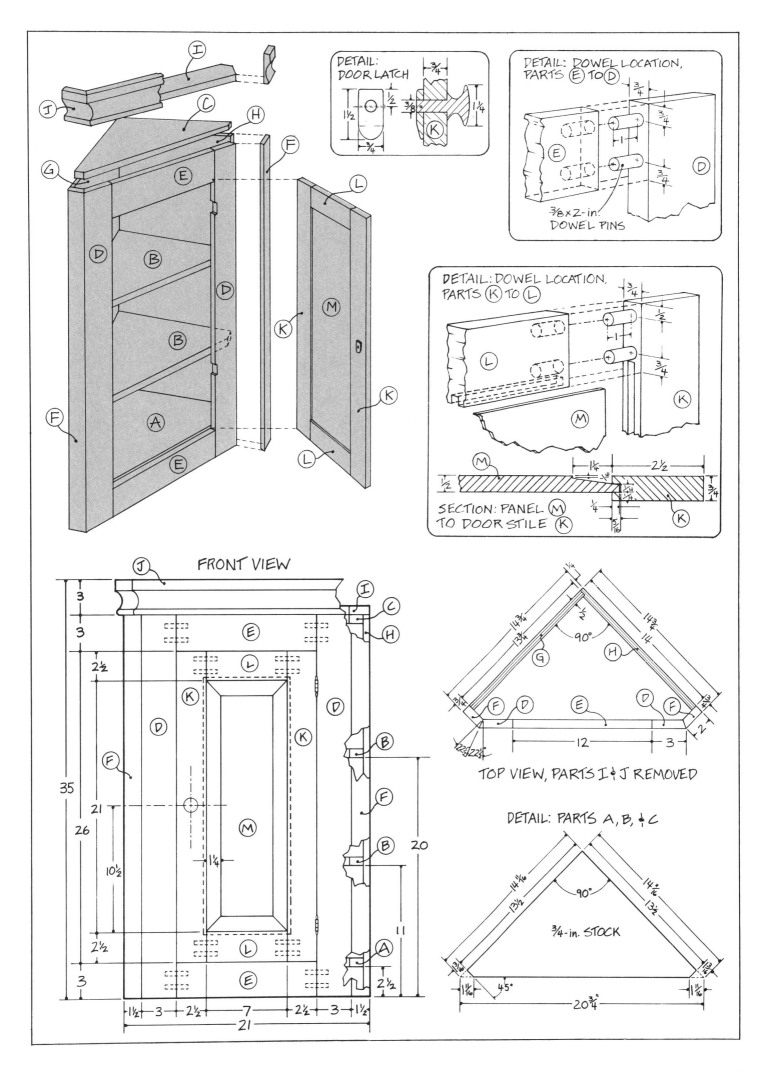

DETAIL:
DOOR LATCH

DETAIL: DOWEL LOCATION,
PARTS E TO D

³⁄₈ × 2-in.
DOWEL PINS

DETAIL: DOWEL LOCATION,
PARTS K TO L

SECTION: PANEL M
TO DOOR STILE K

FRONT VIEW

TOP VIEW, PARTS I & J REMOVED

DETAIL: PARTS A, B, & C

³⁄₄-in. STOCK

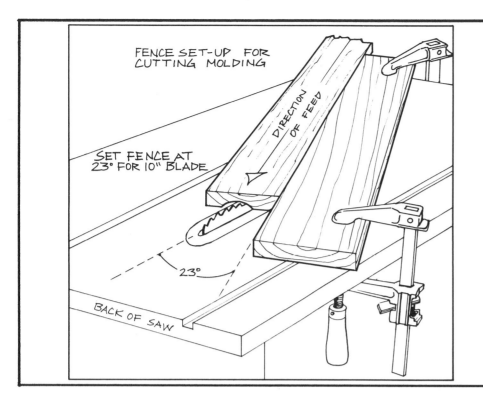

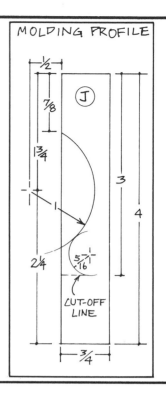

If you plan to paint or stain the cabinet, now is the best time to do it - before the parts are assembled. These cabinets often had painted interiors (in this case, parts B, the top of A, the bottom of C, and inside of G & H) with all other parts stained. If you use paint, choose one of the early American colors available at many paint stores. If you can't get one locally, several attractive colors can be ordered from Cohasset Colonials, Cohasset, MA 02025.

After the stain and/or paint has dried, the back parts (G & H) can be assembled to parts A, B, and C. Lay out and mark the location of parts A, B, and C, then join to the back parts with 1¼ inch x #8 countersunk wood screws. The front frame (parts D and E) can also be added at this time. I used square nails to give the piece a more authentic look. Before driving the nails through, I first drilled pilot holes in order to prevent the wood from splitting. The general locations of the nails are shown in the photo. A good source for old-fashioned cut and decorative nails is the Tremont Nail Company, P.O. Box 111, Wareham, MA 02571.

The two sides (part F) can now be made. Rip the stock to about 2½ inches, then cut a 22½ degree bevel along one edge. Now measure the actual opening on the cabinet and rip the stock so that it has an exact fit. Drill pilot holes, then secure with cut nails.

To make the molding (J), the table saw is set up as shown above. A 23 degree angle is used for a 10 inch blade. Other size blades will require some experimentation to get the correct angle.

Lower the blade so that it is barely (about 1/32 inch) above the table. When properly set up, just the very top of the highest tooth should contact the board at a point 2¼ inch from the edge. Make the first cut with the blade set at a height of 1/32 inch. Use two push sticks, one to hold the workpiece against the fence, the other to feed the stock. After each pass raise the blade another 1/32 inch. It will take around a dozen passes to complete the cove cut.

Rip the stock to three inches (see above), then round off at the cut-off line using a sharp plane followed by a good sanding. The plate (I) is cut to shape and glued to the top as shown. The molding is mitered at 22½ degrees, then attached to the plate with glue and finishing nails, countersunk and filled.

With the cabinet completed, the frame and panel door can be made next (parts K, L, and M). Cut parts K and L to size as shown. At this point, it's best to use actual measurements from the cabinet to determine dimensions. The 5/16 inch deep by ¼ inch wide groove can best be cut with a router. Note that the groove must be stopped short of the ends on part K.

The center panel (M) is the visual highlight of this piece, so try to select stock that has a pleasing wood figure. The tapered edge can be cut on the table saw, radial arm saw, or with a panel raising cutter on the shaper.

Sand all parts thoroughly, then stain or paint as desired. Assemble the door as shown. Use glue to join parts K and L, but do not glue the panel (M) in place. It must be free to expand and contract in the frame.

Various kinds of commercial door latches are available but the one shown is most authentic. The door hangs on a pair of 1¼ inch brass butt hinges which are mortised into parts D and K.

Stained surfaces can be finished with two coats of Minwax Antique Oil Finish. Painted surfaces can be left as is.

Bill of Materials (All Dimensions Actual)			
Part	Description	Size	No. Req'd
A	Bottom	See Detail	1
B	Shelf	See Detail	2
C	Top	See Detail	1
D	Cabinet Stile	¾ x 3 x 32	2
E	Cabinet Rail	¾ x 3 x 12	2
F	Side	¾ x 2 x 32	2
G	Left Back	½ x 13¾ x 32	1
H	Right Back	½ x 14 x 32	1
I	Plate	¾ x 2 x 21	1
J	Molding	See Detail	
K	Door Stile	¾ x 2½ x 26	2
L	Door Rail	¾ x 2½ x 7	2
M	Panel	½ x 7½ x 21½	1

Chest Of Drawers

This small chest of drawers, made from pine, is a fairly typical example of Danish country furniture from the early part of this century.

Begin by making the two front legs (part A). Cut each to 1⅝ inch square x 28¼ inch long, then lay out the locations of the four mortises for parts D and E. Use a sharp chisel to cut to the dimensions shown. The ¼ inch wide x ⅜ inch deep x 19 inch long groove is best cut with a router equipped with a ¼ inch straight bit. Note that it is stopped 9¼ inches from the bottom.

The two back legs (B) are cut to the same overall dimensions as the front legs. Two, ¼ inch wide by ⅜ inch deep by 19 inch long grooves are cut on each back leg, and again the grooves are stopped 9¼ inches from the bottom. Also, to accept the inside tenon on part G, part B has a short (¼ inch wide by ⅜ inch deep by ¾ inch long) groove cut at its top. A sharp chisel will make this groove in short order.

Refer to the step-by-step illustrations to make the curve shape on all four legs. Once the template is made, the profile can be quickly traced to the

stock, and all four legs can be cut in surprisingly little time.

The two sides (part C) are next. Since part C measures 13 inches wide (including the front and back tongue), it will be necessary to edge-glue two pieces of stock in order to get enough width. Two, 42 inch lengths of 1 x 8 stock (which actually measures ¾ inch x 7¼ inch) will provide enough material to make both sides and still allow for some final trimming. Locate and drill about three dowel pin holes along the mating edges of the 42 inch long boards. These dowel pins will primarily serve to align the boards as they are glued and clamped. Apply glue to both mating surfaces, then clamp securely with bar or pipe clamps. Allow to dry overnight. When dry, rip the board to a width of 13 inches. The ¼ inch wide by ⅜ inch long tongue can best be cut using a dado head cutter although repeated passes with a regular table or radial-arm saw will yield the same results. Check for a comfortable fit in the leg grooves. After the tongues have been made, the board can be crosscut into 19 inch lengths.

The three dividers (part D) and the

top divider (part E) are cut to the length and width shown in the Bill of Materials. The tenons are cut to the dimensions specified in the details. A tenon jig will be helpful here, but the joint can also be cut with a dado head cutter, or by hand with a back saw.

Next, the lower back frame (F), and the upper back frame (G) are cut to length and width. The tenons, shown in the details, are cut in the same manner as the dividers. Note that both parts have a ¼ inch wide by ⅜ inch deep groove along the entire length to accept the back (J).

After cutting the ¼ inch thick plywood back to length and width, the chest frame is ready for assembly. Sand all parts thoroughly, then assemble as shown using glue and bar or pipe clamps. Allow to dry thoroughly.

The drawer supports (H) are joined to the sides (C) with 1½ x #8 wood screws. Four screws are required for each support. The screw holes through part H should be slightly slotted so that part C will be free to expand and contract with changes in humidity. No glue should be used, except perhaps for a 2 inch long area at the middle. The drawer guide (I) can now be cut and glued to part H, but it should not be glued to part C.

The three drawers are made as shown on the drawing. Drawer pulls can be made as shown, although a number of ready-made commercial pulls would also look good.

The molding (L) is carved from ⅜ inch stock, then glued to the front legs. Drawer stops (K) are cut to size and glued in place.

Like the sides, the top (M) is made of edge-glued stock, and it is joined in the same manner. To add the molded edge, use a router equipped with a piloted 5/32 inch Roman ogee bit, then use sandpaper to round-off the lower edge. The top is joined to the rest of the cabinet with 1¼ x #10 round head wood screws (and washers) driven up through slotted holes in parts E and G, and also through a slotted block screwed and glued to the center of each side (C).

A stain like Minwax's Special Walnut looks good on a project like this. When dry, add several coats of their Antique Oil Finish for a soft, low luster final finish.

Bill of Materials (All Dimensions Actual)			
Part	Description	Size	No. Req'd
A	Front Leg	1⅝ x 1⅝ x 28¼	2
B	Back Leg	1⅝ x 1⅝ x 28¼	2
C	Side	¾ x 13 x 19	2
D	Divider	¾ x 1⅝ x 22½	3
E	Top Divider	¾ x 1⅝ x 22½	1
F	Lower Back Frame	¾ x 1½ x 21¾	1
G	Upper Back Frame	¾ x 1⅝ x 21¾	1
H	Drawer Support	¾ x 1½ x 10	6
I	Drawer Guide	¾ x ⅞ x 10	6
J	Back	¼ x 21-11/16 x 17-7/16	1
K	Drawer Stops	¼ x 1 x 2	6
L	Applied Molding	See Detail	2
M	Top	¾ x 16¾ x 26¾	1
N	Drawer	See Detail	3

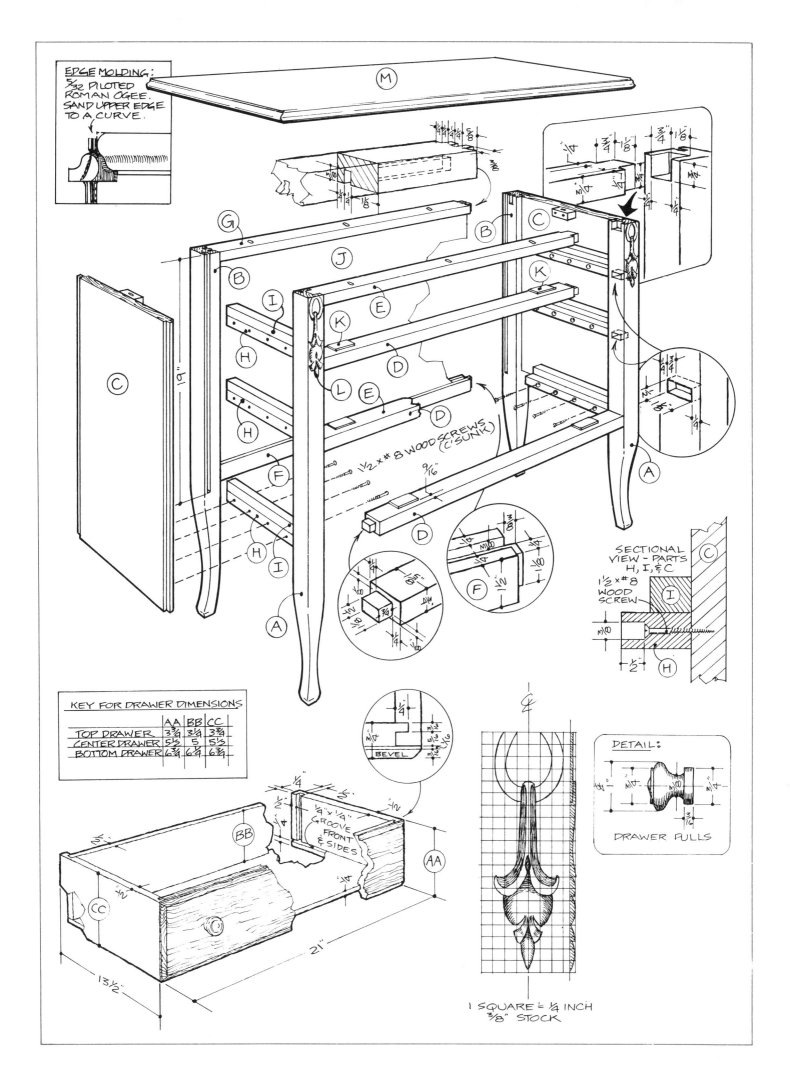

EDGE MOLDING:
⁵/₃₂ PILOTED
ROMAN OGEE.
SAND UPPER EDGE
TO A CURVE.

M

G

B

J

C

B

C

I

K

E

H

K

D

L

E

H

D

½ x #8 WOOD SCREWS (C'SUNK)

9/16

F

A

H

I

D

F

A

SECTIONAL
VIEW - PARTS
H, I, & C

C

1½ x #8
WOOD
SCREW

I

H

½

KEY FOR DRAWER DIMENSIONS

	AA	BB	CC
TOP DRAWER	3¾	3¾	3¾
CENTER DRAWER	5½	5	5½
BOTTOM DRAWER	6¾	6¾	6¾

BEVEL

BB

¼" x ¼"
GROOVE
FRONT
& SIDES

AA

CC

½

21"

13½"

DETAIL:

DRAWER PULLS

1 SQUARE = ¼ INCH
3/8" STOCK

Cutting Leg Curves

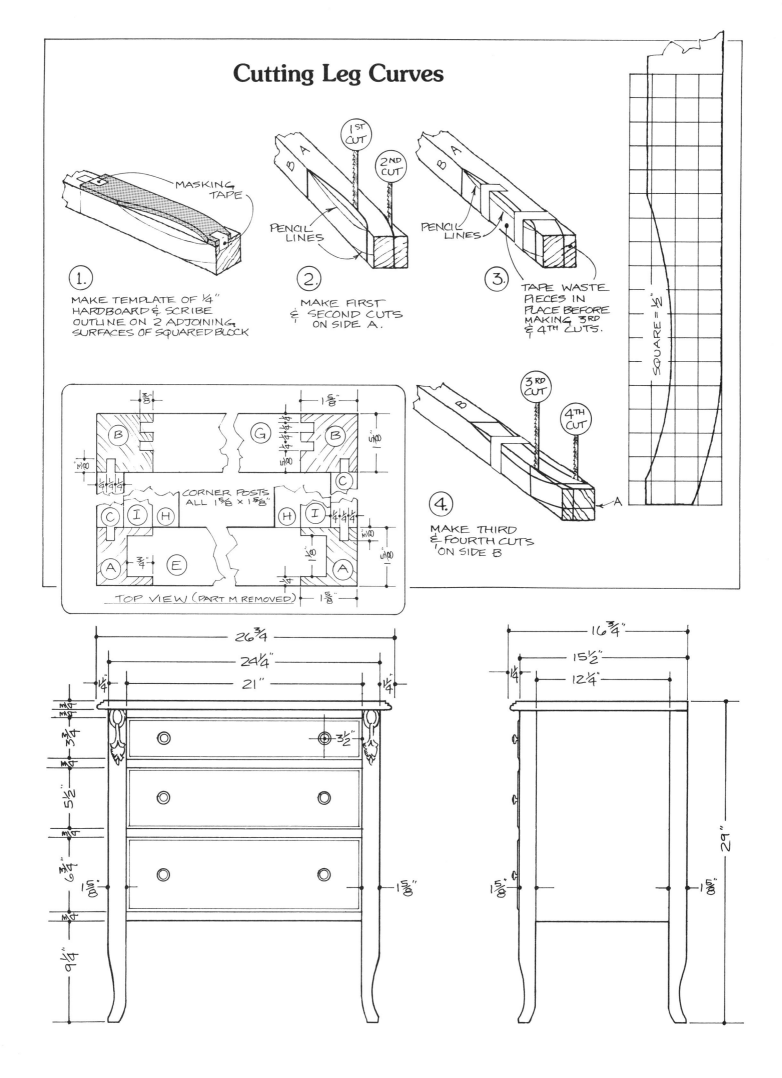

1. MAKE TEMPLATE OF ¼" HARDBOARD & SCRIBE OUTLINE ON 2 ADJOINING SURFACES OF SQUARED BLOCK

MASKING TAPE

2. MAKE FIRST & SECOND CUTS ON SIDE A.

1ST CUT
2ND CUT
PENCIL LINES

3. TAPE WASTE PIECES IN PLACE BEFORE MAKING 3RD & 4TH CUTS.

PENCIL LINES

4. MAKE THIRD & FOURTH CUTS ON SIDE B

3RD CUT
4TH CUT

SQUARE = ½"

CORNER POSTS ALL 1⅝ x 1⅝"

TOP VIEW (PART M REMOVED)

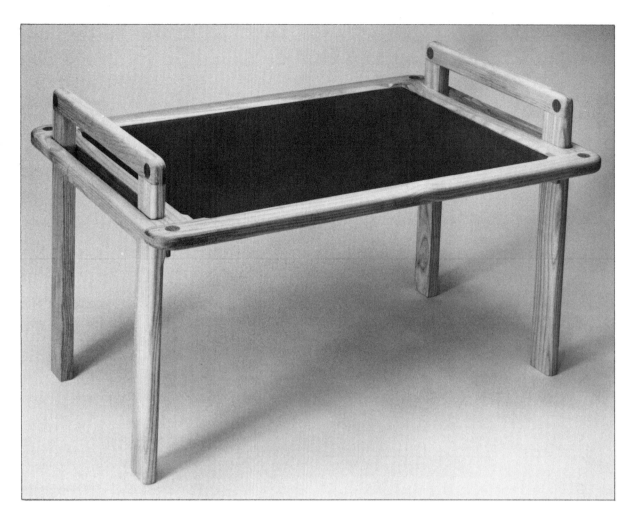

Breakfast Tray

What a luxurious way to start the day - breakfast in bed. This attractive contemporary styled serving tray features a Formica® top and legs that pull out of the tray to permit easy storage. Once disassembled, the three parts can be conveniently hung on a kitchen wall or stored flat in a cabinet.

Ours is made from ash, since this wood takes well to washing and scrubbing, although we think oak would also look good with this piece. The open mortise and tenon joints are both strong and attractive. A ⅝ inch diameter teak pin in each joint adds further to the strength and appearance.

The four legs (part A) can be made first. Cut each one to a width of 1½ inches and a length of 14 inches. The through tenon can best be cut using a tenon jig in conjunction with the table saw. With the saw blade adjusted for a 1 inch depth of cut, set the tenon jig to cut the ¼ inch wide by 1 inch long tenon.

The handle (part B) can now be cut to length and width. Again, the tenon jig can be used, this time to cut the open mortise. In order for this joint to look good, the parts must be close fitting, so make the mortise cuts carefully, removing a little at a time, and always checking the fit with the leg

tenon.

Part C, the tray support, serves to add strength to the unit while also acting as a stop for the removable tray. Cut this part to length and width, then add the notch on each end.

The tray frame members, parts D and E, also incorporate the through mortise and tenon, and are made in the same manner as parts A and B. As with parts A and B, make sure the joints are well fitted. The slot is cut by drilling a ¾ inch diameter hole at a point centered 2⅜ inches from each end of part E. Use a ruler to draw guide lines connecting the two holes, then cut out the waste material with a saber saw. Work carefully to make the cut a straight one. Keep in mind that if parts A and B are slightly thicker than ¾ inch, the width of the slot should be adjusted accordingly. A round file will expand the hole if needed.

The tray (part F) is made from ¼ inch birch plywood. Cut it to length and width, then apply Formica® to both the top and bottom. Since the tray is reversible, we used a rust colored Formica® on one side and plain white Formica® on the other.

The grooves in parts E and D can now be cut. Use a router to cut the groove ⅜ inch deep with a width that allows for a slip fit of the Formica®

top. Note that the groove must be stopped on each end.

Sand all parts (except the Formica® top) before assembly. Join with glue and clamps. Use a plug cutter to cut ½ or ⅝ inch diameter pins. We used teak, but any wood of contrasting color will look good, and of course, it adds strength to the joint.

Final sand all parts. The leg unit (parts A, B, and C) should slip easily into the slot in part E. Before applying the final finish, try the tray out by sitting with it in bed. Some readers may want to shorten the legs a bit, it depends on how tall you are and how soft your bed is. An application of Watco Danish Oil will complete the project.

Bill of Materials (All Dimensions Actual)			
Part	Description	Size	No. Req'd
A	Leg	¾ x 1½ x 14	4
B	Handle	¾ x 1 x 12	2
C	Table Support	¾ x 1 x 12	2
D	Front & Back Frame	¾ x 1¼ x 24	2
E	Side Frame	¾ x 2¼ x 16	2
F	Tray	¼ x 14⅛ x 20⅛	1
G	Formica®	As Req'd	

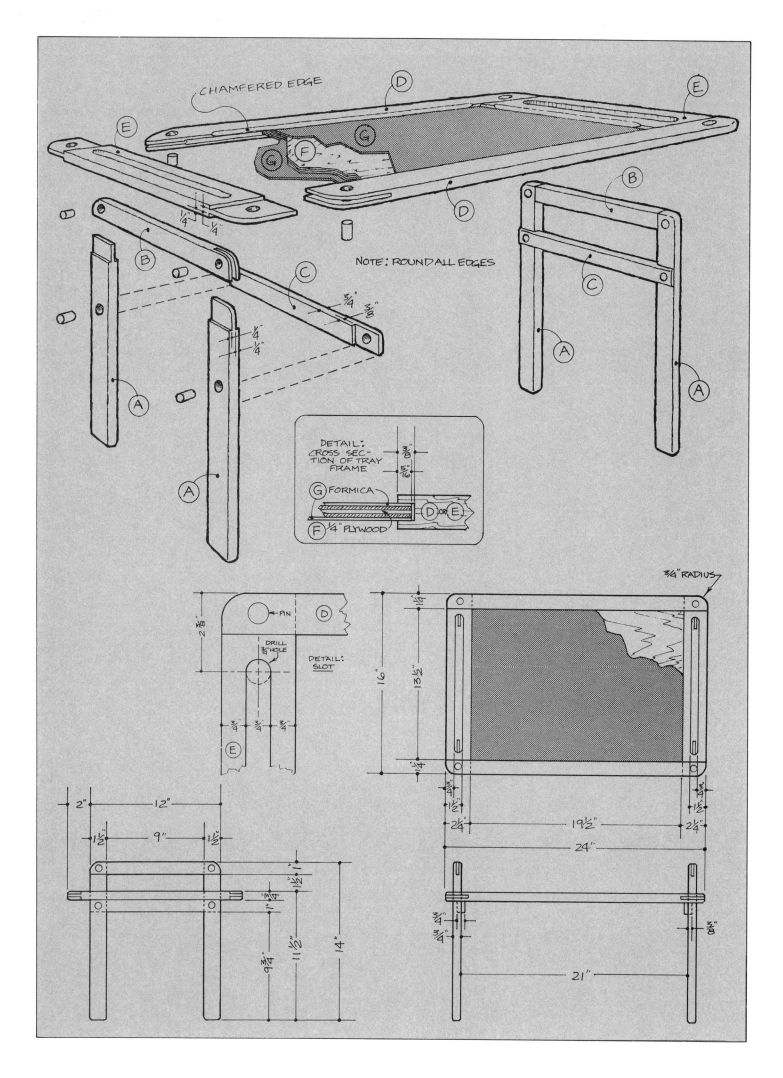

CHAMFERED EDGE

NOTE: ROUND ALL EDGES

DETAIL:
CROSS SEC-
TION OF TRAY
FRAME
G FORMICA
F ¼" PLYWOOD

DETAIL:
SLOT

PIN
DRILL
¾" HOLE

¾" RADIUS

next. Cut the groove for the veneer inlay using the router table and a straight bit. The miters are cut after the inlay is glued in place. The ¼ inch wide by ⅜ inch deep groove is cut by making repeated passes over the table saw blade. Holes are drilled at the miters to take ⅜ inch diameter by 1½ inch long dowel pins. Glue and clamp parts J and K to the top and allow to dry overnight.

The remaining parts are made to the dimensions shown. The leg (part A) will probably require edge-gluing two boards to get the 9⅜ inch width that is required.

On this project it is best to finish the individual pieces before assembly. Any good quality finish that is water and alcohol resistant is suitable. Polyurethane is suggested, although Watco Danish Oil Finish is also a good choice. Shellac is not suitable.

If a stain is to be used, it should be done after final sanding. Try a sample on scrap wood, including a coat of final finish. A filler may be required on open grain woods.

When polyurethane finish is used, three or four coats are required. Each coat should dry overnight followed by a light sanding with a fine paper. Do not use steel wool between coats as it is nearly impossible to remove all of the particles. The last coat should be sanded smooth using a 280 grit paper followed by a good rubbing using 0000 steel wool. This may be followed by a coat of good wax.

The assembly process is simple. With the top face down on a pad to prevent scratching, locate one cleat on the top, attach with screws and mount one leg as shown. Use a depth stop when drilling pilot holes so that you do not drill through the top. Place stretcher in slots and locate other leg so that the end is square with the top. Fasten the other cleat with screws as indicated and then mound the other leg. Turn table upright and insert pegs in slots. Thumb pressure or a light tap on the pegs is all that is required.

Veneered End Table

A curly birch veneer adds an especially distinctive look to this trestle style end table. Adding further to its visual appeal is a border or veneer inlay and a mitered birch frame.

All other parts are made of birch solid stock, although as usual, just about any kind of hardwood is also suitable.

For those who would like to avoid veneering, an alternate method is to make the entire top from solid stock, edge-gluing to obtain the required 15 in. width. The frame parts (J, K) would of course be eliminated.

Readers who enjoy veneering will probably choose to have a veneered top as shown in the exploded view. Cut the top (G) from ½ inch plywood to overall length and width. Make sure the corners are square. Both the top

and bottom of the plywood will require veneer in order to equalize stresses, although the veneer used on the bottom can be an inexpensive type. Poplar is often used here. Be sure the veneer runs at right angles to the grain direction of the face veneer on the plywood. And use birch plywood — not fir. The grain of fir plywood will eventually telegraph through. For more information on veneering, there is an excellent book called *Veneering Simplified* by Harry J. Hobbs. It's available by mail-order from Constantine, 2050 Eastchester Road, Bronx, NY 10461.

After applying the veneer, use a dado head cutter to cut the 5/16 inch by 5/16 inch rabbet around the perimeter of the top. Work carefully to avoid splintering the veneer.

The frame parts (J and K) are made

Bill of Materials

(All Dimensions Actual)			
Part	Description	Size	No. Req'd
A	Leg	¾ x 9⅜ x 18¹⁵⁄₁₆	2
B	Foot	1⅝ x 1⅝ x 11	2
C	Support	1⅜ x 1⅜ x 9¾	2
D	Cleat	¾ x ¾ x 8	2
E	Stretcher	½ x 2 x 19¾	1
F	Peg	¾ x ¾ x 2½	2
G	Top	½ x 10⅝ x 19⅝	1
H	Veneer	As Req'd	
I	Inlay	As Req'd	
J	Short Top Frame	¾ x 2½ x 15	2
K	Long Top Frame	¾ x 2½ x 24	2

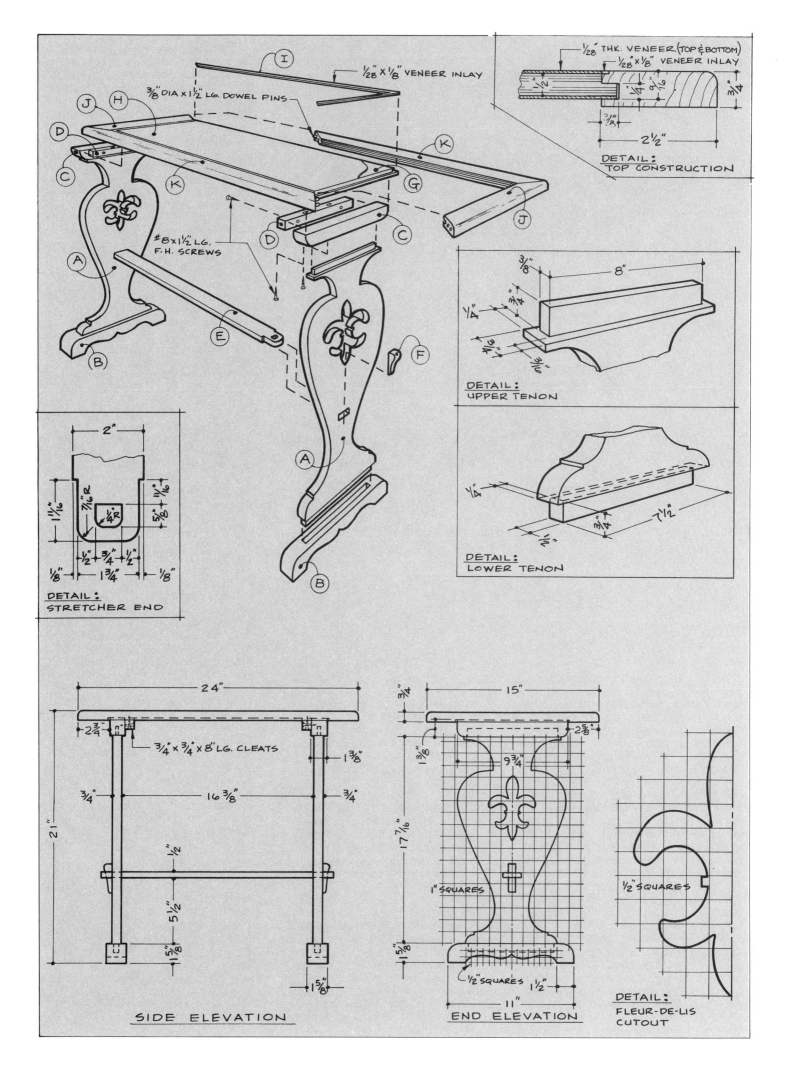

1/28" THK. VENEER (TOP & BOTTOM)

1/28" X 1/8" VENEER INLAY

DETAIL:
TOP CONSTRUCTION

I

1/28" X 1/8" VENEER INLAY

3/8" DIA X 1 1/2" LG. DOWEL PINS

J H
D
C
K
K
G
J

#8 X 1 1/2" LG.
F. H. SCREWS

A
B
D
C
E
F
A
B

DETAIL:
UPPER TENON

8"
3/8"
3/4"
1/4"
3/16"
3/4"

DETAIL:
LOWER TENON

1/4"
3/4"
7 1/2"
1/2"

DETAIL:
STRETCHER END

2"
7/16" R
1/4" R
1 1/16"
1 1/16"
5/8"
1/2" 3/4" 1/2"
1/8" 1 3/4" 1/8"

SIDE ELEVATION

24"
2 3/4"
3/4" X 3/4" X 8" LG. CLEATS
1 3/8"
3/4" 16 3/8" 3/4"
1/2"
21"
5 1/2"
1 5/8"
1 5/8"

END ELEVATION

3/4"
15"
2 5/8"
3/8"
1 3/8"
9 3/4"
17 7/16"
5/8"
1" SQUARES
1/2" SQUARES 1 1/2"
11"

DETAIL:
FLEUR-DE-LIS
CUTOUT

1/2" SQUARES

77

Chess Table

A chess table can be a popular addition to a den or living room, especially since it offers a pleasant alternative to the seemingly endless nonsense coming from the television set. The table can also be used to play the game of checkers, since chessboards and checkerboards are identical.

The one shown was made using an oak pedestal and a pine top, with mahogany and pine for the chess squares. As is generally the case though, the choice of wood is a matter of personal preference - just keep in mind that it is necessary to use woods of contrasting color for the board squares. Pine, maple, birch, ash, or holly can be used for the light-colored squares. For the dark squares consider mahogany, walnut, butternut, or rosewood.

Begin construction with the post (part A), which is made from five pieces of 1 inch nominal (¾ inch actual) stock, face-glued to form a 3¾ inch by 3¾ inch turning square. Since most 1 inch nominal hardwood measures about 13/16 inches thick, it will be necessary to surface plane the stock down to ¾ inch thickness before face gluing. Apply a thin coat of glue to both surfaces and clamp securely, allowing to dry overnight.

Lathe-turn part A to the dimensions shown, including the 1½ inch diameter by 1½ inch long tenon, then lay out and mark the location of the ¾ inch wide by 3¾ inch long foot mortise. Note that the mortise begins at a point ½ inch from the bottom of part A. Use a ¾ inch diameter drill bit to cut most of the mortise, then clean up using a sharp chisel. Make the mortise slightly deeper than the foot (part B) tenon to allow for any excess glue or loose chips that might prevent the joint from closing.

The four feet (B) are made from 2 inch nominal (1¾ inch actual) thick stock, cut to a width of 6¾ inches and a length of 12¼ inches. Transfer the grid pattern from the drawing, then cut out with a band or saber saw. The tenon can be cut with a tenon jig or a fine-tooth backsaw. The completed tenon should fit snugly in the post (part A) mortise.

The two cleats (part C) are made from 2 inch nominal stock (1¾ inch actual) that has been planed down to 1½ inch thickness. The middle is half-lapped as shown and a hole is drilled through both pieces to accept the post tenon.

To make the chessboard (part D), cut two, ½ inch thick boards to a width of 8¾ inches and a length of 20 inches. (The length and width allows for saw kerf waste.) Use a light-colored wood for one board, a dark-colored wood for the other. Rip each board into four pieces, with each piece 2 inches wide by 20 inches long, then alternate the dark and light strips and edge-glue all eight pieces. Before clamping, check to make sure the ends are reasonably close to being flush.

When the glue has dried, rip 2 inch wide strips *across the grain*. To create the alternating chessboard pattern, reverse every other strip, then once again glue and clamp.

The chessboard base (part E) consists of two pieces of ½ inch plywood glued together. The plywood should be cut to about 16¼ inches square to allow for later trimming.

After determining the best side of the chessboard (D), the opposite side can be glued to the plywood base. Apply glue to both surfaces and clamp securely. When dry, trim to 16 inches square.

To make the two short top boards (F), it will probably be necessary to edge-join two or more boards to get the 16 inch width. To be on the safe side, make the boards about 16¼ inches wide, then edge-join them to the top with three, ⅜ by 2 inch long dowels as shown. Clamp firmly, allow to dry, then trim to the exact width of the chessboard (part D). Next, the long top boards (B) can be joined in the same manner. Note that when all top parts are joined the grain all runs in one direction.

Sand the top smooth, then cut out the 30 inch diameter top with a band or saber saw. A router equipped with a ⅜ inch rounding-over bit can be used to round the top and bottom edges.

On the table shown, the chessboard surface was left natural while the rest of the table was finished with two coats of Minwax Special Walnut stain. Two coats of satin polyurethane varnish completed the project.

Bill of Materials
(All Dimensions Actual)

Part	Description	Size	No. Req'd
A	Post	3¾ x 3¾ x 26¼	1
B	Foot	1¾ x 6¾ x 12¼	4
C	Cleats	1½ x 4 x 24	2
D	Chessboard	½ x 16 x 16	1
E	Chessboard Base	½ x 16 x 16	2
F	Short Top Boards	1½ x 16 x 8	2
G	Long Top Boards	1½ x 8 x 27	2

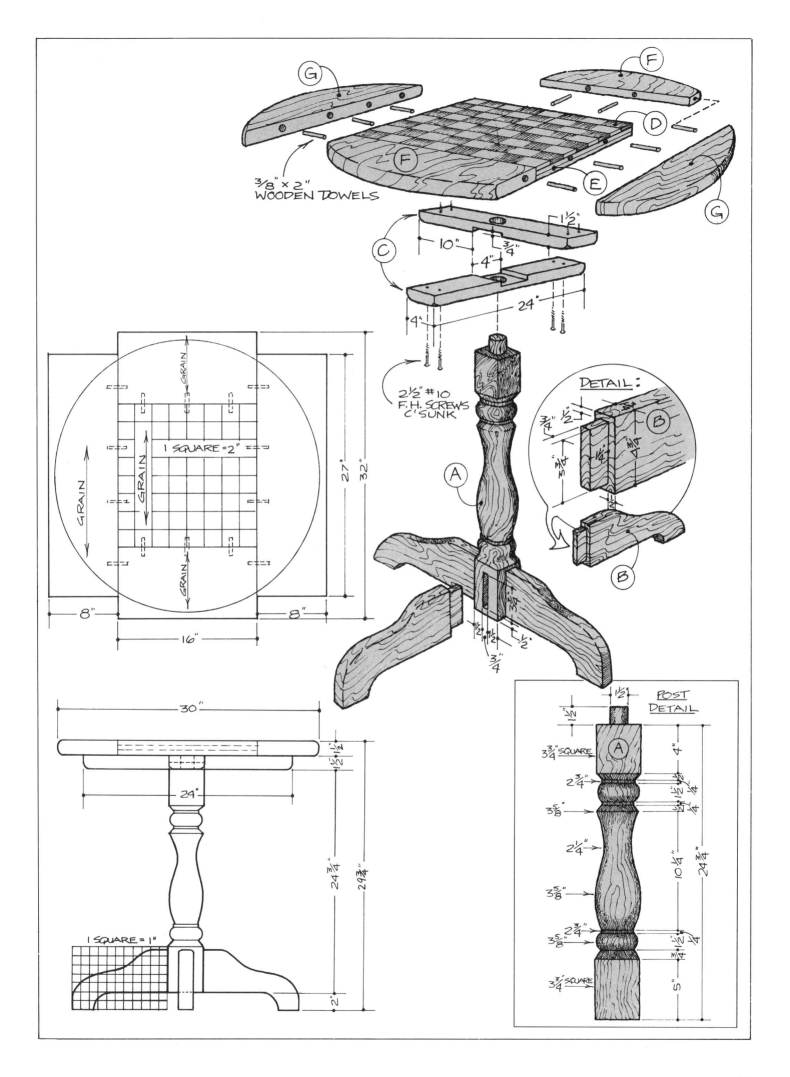

G

F

⅜" × 2"
WOODEN DOWELS

D

F

E

G

C

10"

1½"

¾"

4"

4"

24"

2½" #10
F.H. SCREWS
C'SUNK

A

DETAIL:

¾" ½"

¾"

3"

1¼"

¾"

B

B

GRAIN

GRAIN

GRAIN

1 SQUARE = 2"

GRAIN

GRAIN

27"

32"

8"

8"

16"

½" 1½"

¾"

½"

1½"

3"
4

½" ½"

1½"

¾"

30"

24"

24¾"

29¾"

1 SQUARE = 1"

2"

POST
DETAIL

1½"

½"

½"

3¾" SQUARE

A

4"

2¾"

3⅝"

2¼"

3⅝"

2¾"

10¼"

24¾"

3⅝"

3¾" SQUARE

5"

Contemporary Writing Desk

I designed and built this elegant writing desk for my daughter. With the top "pigeon-hole" cabinet removed, it also serves as an occasional table. Solid cherry lumber and some ¼" cherry plywood was used but walnut would be an excellent substitute.

Construction begins with the top which is made up of four solid cherry boards planed to ¾" thickness. After arranging the boards for the most interesting grain patterns, the mating edges are jointed and the boards are glued together and clamped. No dowels or splines are necessary to reinforce the edge-joints.

The legs are made up by face gluing and clamping two ¾" x 8" x 30" boards together. This lamination is then ripped into four 1½" square legs. While the legs are still square the stopped grooves which hold the rail tenons are laid out and cut. A router with a ⅜" straight bit can be used to cut the grooves a bit short of their full lengths. Use a ⅜" mortising chisel to square off the groove ends.

The legs are then tapered with a bandsaw or by using a taper jig with the tablesaw. Starting from a point 5" down from the leg top, each leg is tapered on four sides to ⅞" at the foot.

When making the tapering cuts, plan on leaving a little extra stock to allow for finish planing to remove the saw marks.

Next, lay out and cut the mortise in each leg to hold the ⅜" x ½" x 1¼" tenons of the lower leg rails (F). These mortises can be cut by first drilling out most of the waste, then cleaning up with a ⅜" mortising chisel. Two upper end rails (C) are then cut to length and rabbeted at each end to form tenons to fit snugly in the leg grooves. Using a router cut a ⅜" x ⅜" groove the full length of each rail and ⅝" up from the bottom edge. This groove houses the tongues on the drawer supports (H).

The back rail (D) is then cut and tenoned in the same manner as the end rails. A stopped groove is routed ⅜" below the top edge to take the ⅜" x ⅜" tongue of part L. This groove, as shown in the detail drawing is 2" long and centered on the rail.

To maintain a continuous grain pattern running the length of the front rail (E) and across both drawer fronts, it's necessary to cut the drawer fronts from the rail itself rather than from a separate board. While it's possible to cut starting slots with the tablesaw and then use a handsaw to finish cutting

out the large notches for the drawer fronts, it's safer and easier to simply rip a 1" strip off the rail bottom and then make the four crosscuts needed to separate the drawer fronts.

Choose a piece of fairly straight-grained stock for rail E and cut it oversize in length and width to allow for the kerf width of the ripping cut and the crosscuts. After the cuts are completed, set aside the drawer fronts for later work. The three remaining upright pieces and the bottom strip are then sanded, glued and clamped together so that drawer openings of 17⅞" across are established.

The glue joint between the four parts of rail (E) consists of long grain being joined and these joints should not require reinforcement, but you may find it helpful to run dowel pins into the joints up through the bottom rail just to keep the parts from sliding under clamp pressure. Allow ample time for the glue to cure before clamping the assembled rail to the bench and routing the tenons on each end. Also rout the groove in the center divider section of part E which takes the tongue of brace (L). This should align with the stopped groove cut in the rear apron.

The leg rails (F) are then cut from ⅝" stock and the tenons are formed at each end. To determine the exact length of these rails, temporarily assemble two legs and an end rail, clamp the assembly square and measure up 9" from the foot of each leg to mark the bottom edge of the rail. The tenons on each end of the rail are ½" long. Note that the shoulders on each side must be cut at an angle that matches the taper of the legs. With the clamped up assembly, the legs themselves can be used to mark these angles on the rail stock. The tenon cheek and shoulder cuts are best done with a fine toothed dovetail saw. Use the same saw to cut the notches centered on each rail to hold the long stretcher (G). Cut this stretcher ½" overlong so that the ends can be trimmed flush with the rails after assembly.

Part L, which braces the frame and provides a means of fastening the top, is cut and tongued to fit front and rear rails. The leg-frame assembly can now be glued and clamped together. Use a slow setting glue such as liquid hide glue and first glue and clamp together each leg and upper and lower rail using a pipe clamp and scrap stock to prevent marring the legs. When both leg-rail assemblies have dried, join them with the back rail D. If you don't have a pipe clamp long enough to span the full length, make and attach the slotted blocks shown in the detail for fastening the top and run pipe clamps from each block to the legs.

The front rail and brace L is then added, clamping from front to back at L. Two clamps are also used from the

(continued on page 82)

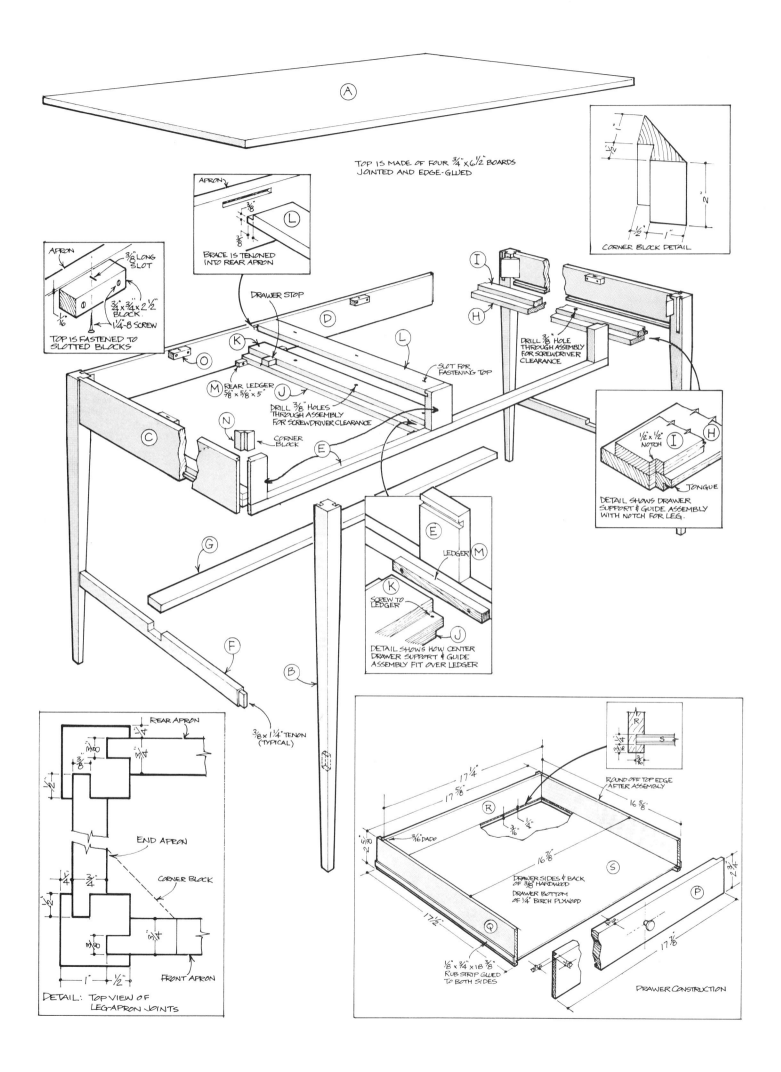

TOP IS MADE OF FOUR ³⁄₄" x 6¹⁄₂" BOARDS
JOINTED AND EDGE-GLUED

CORNER BLOCK DETAIL

Ⓐ

APRON

³⁄₈
³⁄₈
Ⓛ
BRACE IS TENONED
INTO REAR APRON

APRON
³⁄₈" LONG
SLOT
³⁄₄" x ³⁄₄" x 2¹⁄₂"
BLOCK
¹⁄₄-8 SCREW
¹⁄₁₆
TOP IS FASTENED TO
SLOTTED BLOCKS

DRAWER STOP

Ⓓ

Ⓘ
Ⓗ
DRILL ³⁄₈" HOLE
THROUGH ASSEMBLY
FOR SCREWDRIVER
CLEARANCE

Ⓚ
Ⓞ

Ⓛ
SLOT FOR
FASTENING TOP

Ⓜ REAR LEDGER
⁵⁄₈" x ⁵⁄₈" x 5" Ⓙ

Ⓝ
DRILL ³⁄₈" HOLES
THROUGH ASSEMBLY
FOR SCREWDRIVER CLEARANCE
CORNER
BLOCK

Ⓒ
Ⓔ

¹⁄₂" x ¹⁄₂"
NOTCH Ⓘ Ⓗ
TONGUE
DETAIL SHOWS DRAWER
SUPPORT & GUIDE ASSEMBLY
WITH NOTCH FOR LEG.

Ⓔ
LEDGER Ⓜ
Ⓚ
SCREW TO
LEDGER
Ⓙ
DETAIL SHOWS HOW CENTER
DRAWER SUPPORT & GUIDE
ASSEMBLY FIT OVER LEDGER

Ⓖ

Ⓕ
Ⓑ
³⁄₈" x 1¹⁄₄" TENON
(TYPICAL)

REAR APRON
¹⁄₄"
¹⁄₄"
³⁄₈"
³⁄₈"
¹⁄₂"

END APRON

CORNER BLOCK

¹⁄₄"
³⁄₄"
¹⁄₂"
³⁄₈"
³⁄₄"
1" ¹⁄₂"
FRONT APRON

DETAIL: TOP VIEW OF
LEG-APRON JOINTS

Ⓡ
Ⓢ
¹⁄₄"
³⁄₃₂"
³⁄₈"
ROUND OFF TOP EDGE
AFTER ASSEMBLY

17¹⁄₄"
17⁵⁄₈"
Ⓡ
16⁵⁄₈"
³⁄₁₆" DADO
¹⁄₄"
³⁄₁₆"
2⁵⁄₈"
16³⁄₈"
Ⓢ
DRAWER SIDES & BACK
OF ³⁄₈" HARDWOOD
DRAWER BOTTOM
OF ¹⁄₄" BIRCH PLYWOOD
Ⓟ
2³⁄₄"
17¹⁄₂" Ⓠ
¹⁄₈" x ³⁄₄" x 18³⁄₈"
RUB STRIP GLUED
TO BOTH SIDES
17⁷⁄₈"

DRAWER CONSTRUCTION

Writing Desk (cont'd)

front legs to each side of the center divider. The stretcher G can also be added at this point. Needless to say, you should constantly check the assembly for squareness during all clamping operations so that minor adjustments can be made before the glue sets.

Referring to the bill of materials, cut the required stock for the two end drawer supports (H) and the center support (J). Cut a ⅜" x ⅜" tongue the length of each end support to fit the end rails. A ⅜" x ⅝" rabbet is cut at each end of the center support to fit over front and rear ledger strips (M) which are screwed centered on the front and rear rails.

The end supports (H) are notched at each end to fit around the legs. Temporarily fit these supports into their grooves, then cut and fit end drawer guides (I) in place on top of the supports and tight against end rails (C). Run a pencil along the inboard edge of the guides to mark their location on the supports, then remove the parts and glue and nail or screw them together. The support-guide assemblies are then glued to the end rails using C-clamps and pads to protect the end rails.

The center support (J) and drawer guide (K) are glued together so that the guide is centered on the support. Three ⅜" dia. holes are then drilled through this assembly as shown and the assembly is fastened to the ledgers with four 1" screws.

Make up eight corner blocks (N) from scrap stock and glue and clamp them in place using the four extra as clamping pads on the outside corner of

each leg. After making and attaching the remaining slotted blocks (with all slots running across the table), the top is laid bottom side up on a rug. The frame is then adjusted for an equal overhang at each leg and fastened to the top with 1¼" No. 8 round head screws through the blocks and brace L. To get at the end screws you'll have to drill ⅜" access holes through the drawer support assemblies.

Drawer parts are next cut and assembled as shown. When gluing drawers together, take care to keep them square and flat until dry. The rabbet joints between the drawer fronts and sides are best reinforced with three small finishing nails or glue covered ⅛" dowel pins driven into holes drilled through the sides and into the front. The rub strips glued to each drawer side are cut to a thickness that allows the drawers to be centered in their openings.

The upper cabinet top, bottom and ends are cut from ⅜" stock so that the grain runs lengthwise of the top, down the sides and lengthwise of the bottom. This looks good and keeps shrinkage and swelling problems to a minimum. It will probably be necessary to edge-join two or more boards to get the 8¾" width of these parts. The original case was joined at the corners with screwed butt joints but the joinery shown in the drawing is preferable.

The top (T1) and bottom (T2) are identical so the various rabbets and dadoes should be laid out with the boards aligned side by side and taped together. The same situation applies to the ends (U). Except for the doors

which are ⅜" thick, the remaining parts are of ¼" cherry plywood. Although not shown in the drawing, all front edges of these plywood parts except the back (V) are faced with ⅛" thick strips of solid cherry to hide the laminations. Thus, all front to back plywood dimensions should be reduced by the thickness of the facing strips which are glued in place.

Before assembly, hinge pin holes are drilled through the top and bottom while they are aligned and clamped together. When drilling remember that the doors are inset ¼". The pins are driven in far enough to leave room for matching plugs to be glued in place to trap the pins and conceal the holes.

I added a brass gallery to the cabinet top and since the gallery posts were fastened by screws from underneath the top, it was necessary to locate and drill these screw holes before final assembly. Later a stubby screwdriver is used to screw the gallery posts in place. The original cabinet as seen in the photo used six brass posts but I would change the spacing and add one more post so that the gallery rails will be more rigid.

Editor's Note: We have been unable to locate a source for gallery hardware that is both small in size and contemporary in style. Assuming you do not want to omit the gallery one suggestion is that posts can be cut from ⅜" dia. brass rod. The top ends will need to be polished and the posts drilled to take 3/16" brass rod for rails. You can either drill and tap the lower ends for mounting screws or simply epoxy the

(continued on page 83)

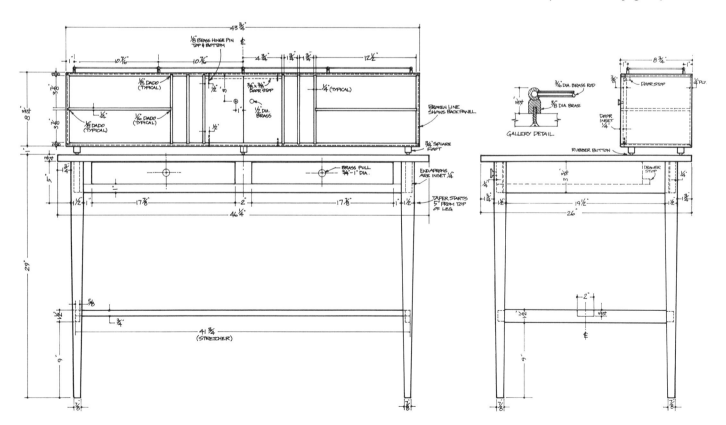

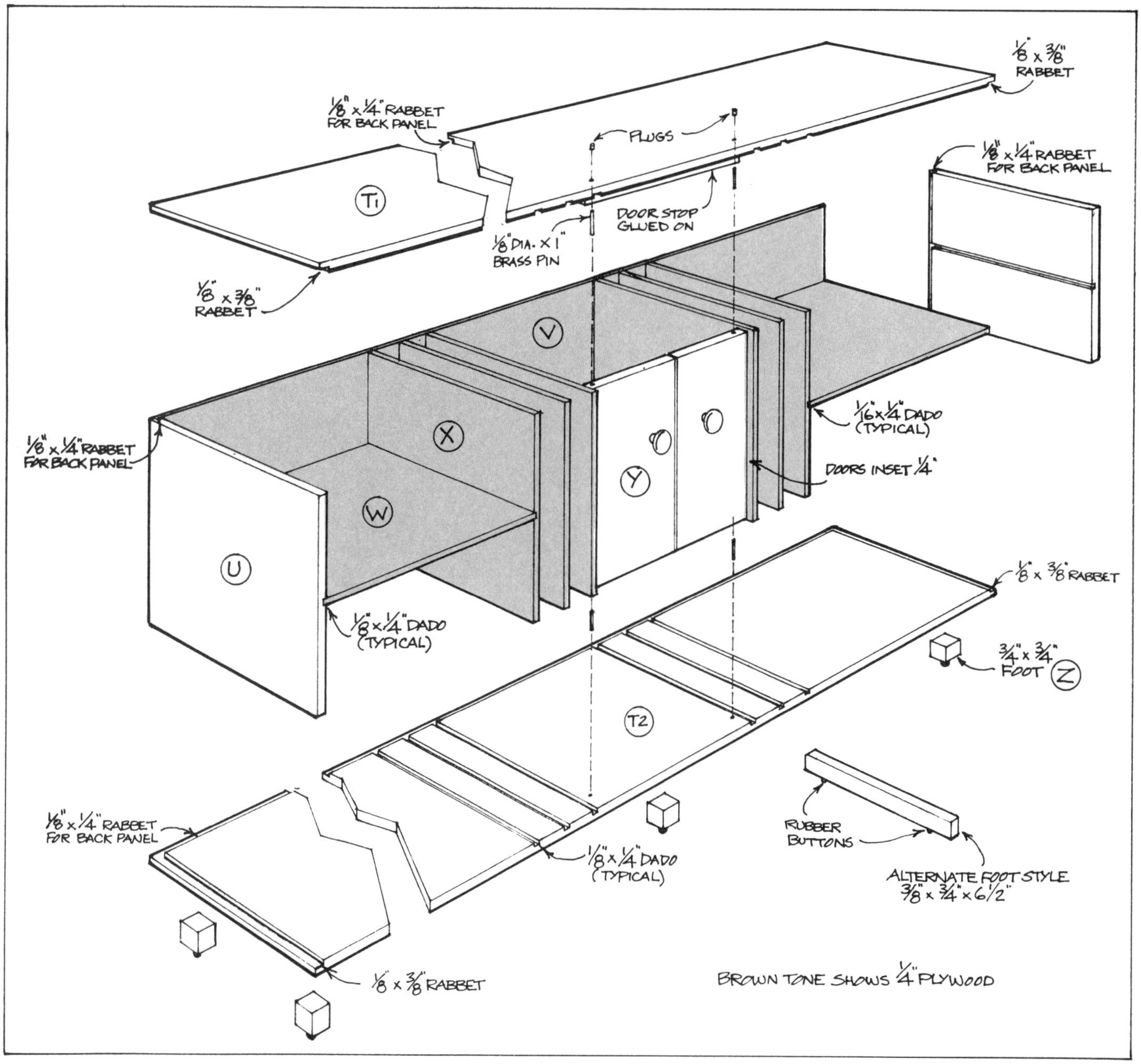
1/8" x 3/8" RABBET
1/8" x 1/4" RABBET FOR BACK PANEL
PLUGS
1/8" x 1/4" RABBET FOR BACK PANEL
T1
DOOR STOP GLUED ON
1/8" DIA. x 1" BRASS PIN
1/8" x 3/8" RABBET
V
X
1/8" x 1/4" RABBET FOR BACK PANEL
1/16" x 1/4" DADO (TYPICAL)
Y
DOORS INSET 1/4"
W
U
1/8" x 3/8" RABBET
1/8" x 1/4" DADO (TYPICAL)
3/4" x 3/4" FOOT Z
T2
1/8" x 1/4" RABBET FOR BACK PANEL
RUBBER BUTTONS
1/8" x 1/4" DADO (TYPICAL)
ALTERNATE FOOT STYLE 3/8" x 3/4" x 6 1/2"
1/8" x 3/8" RABBET
BROWN TONE SHOWS 1/4" PLYWOOD

ends into ⅜" dia. x ¼" deep sockets bored into the top. These plain cylindrical posts should look attractive on the cabinet.

After all parts have been tried for fit in a dry run, the cabinet is assembled with glue and clamped. Lacking enough clamps, heavy weights can be used on the top to clamp the corner joints and dadoed dividers. Either of the foot styles shown can be glued to the case bottom. Rubber or thick felt buttons are added to prevent marring of the top.

The finish to be applied is really a matter of personal preference. Generally, contemporary pieces of cherry or walnut look good unstained and finished with penetrating oil such as Watco Danish Oil or tung oil. This finish is very easy to apply, resists water or alcohol damage and is easy to repair. The insides of drawers however should be finished with shellac or varnish.

Bill of Materials
(All Dimensions Actual)

Part	Size	Quantity	Part	Size	Quantity
A	¾ x 26 x 46¼	1	N	1½ x 1½ x 2	4
B	1½ x 1½ x 28¼	4	O	¾ x ¾ x 2½	4
C	¾ x 3¾ x 20½	2	P	¾ x 2¾ x 17⅞	2
D	¾ x 3¾ x 40¾	1	Q	⅜ x 2⅝ x 17½	4
E	¾ x 3¾ x 40¾	1	R	⅜ x 2 ⅝ x 17¼	2
F	⅝ x 1½ x 21⅛	2	S	¼ x 16⅝ x 17¼	2
G	¾ x 2 x 41¾	1	T1, T2	⅜ x 8¾ x 43¾	1 ea.
H	¾ x 2⅝ x 20½	2	U	⅜ x 8¾ x 8¼	2
I	¾ x 1½ x 20½	2	V	¼ x 8¼ x 43¼	1
J	¾ x 3½ x 20½	1	W*	¼ x 8½ x 12 11/16	2
K	¾ x 2 x 20½	1	X*	¼ x 8½ x 8¼	6
L	¾ x 2 x 21¼	1	Y	⅜ x 4¾ x 8	2
M	⅝ x ⅝ x 5	2	Z	¾ x ¾ x ¾	6

*Adjust dimensions as needed to accommodate edging (not shown) on the front edge.

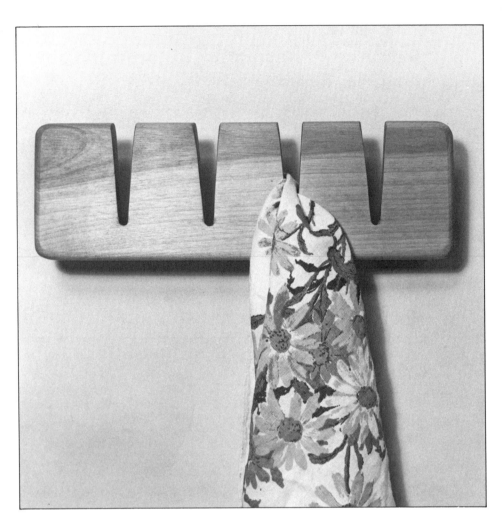

Here's a departure from the usual peg on the wall method of hanging dishtowels. Simply slip the towel end into one of the "V" slots and it will stay securely in place until it's time to face that pile of wet dishes. It's also not a bad idea to tie a knot on the end of one towel and keep it in the rack just for drying hands. The rack shown is made from birch, but maple and oak are also good choices.

The tapered and pinned blocks (A&B) provide a rather unique hanging method, resulting in a board that appears to have no visible means of support.

To make the blocks, cut two pieces of ¾ inch thick stock to 3⅛ inches (allows for saw kerf) wide by 2 inches long, then face glue and clamp the pieces together. For maximum glue strength, it's important that the grain run in the direction shown.

When dry, locate and drill the two ¼ inch dowel pin holes, then use a back saw to cut the block at an angle as shown. The front (C) is now made, then part A is glued and firmly clamped in place at a point ½ inch down from the top and centered across the length.

Secure part B to wall with screws. Position part A over part B so that the holes line up, then insert unglued dowel pins. An application of Deftco Danish Oil completes the project.

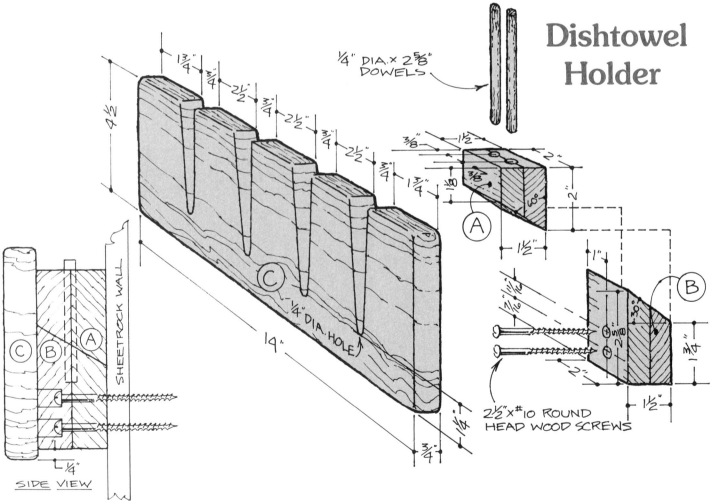

Dishtowel Holder

¼" DIA. x 2⅝" DOWELS

¼" DIA. HOLE

14"

SIDE VIEW

SHEETROCK WALL

2½" x #10 ROUND HEAD WOOD SCREWS

Whale Toy

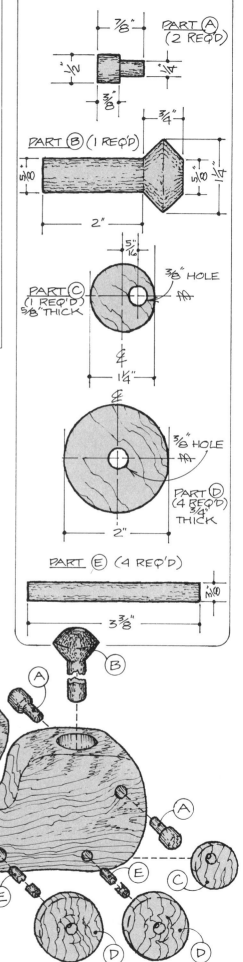

LIST OF PARTS WITH DIMENSIONS

PART A (2 REQ'D)

PART B (1 REQ'D)

PART C (1 REQ'D) 5/8" THICK — 3/8" HOLE

PART D (4 REQ'D) 3/4" THICK — 3/8" HOLE

PART E (4 REQ'D)

Although this friendly leviathan rolls rather than swims, it still "spouts" just like a real one. Actually, the "spout" is a shaped pin (part B) that moves up and down on a cam (part C) as the whale rolls along.

The company Cherry Tree Toys provided us with plans for the project. For a copy of their catalog, which lists many other toy plans plus various parts and wheels, send $1.00 to Cherry Tree Toys, P.O. Box 369, Belmont, OH 43718.

The whale can be made from just about any wood species, including pine, but for maximum durability maple is your best choice.

Make the body (part F) first. Cut a piece of 2 inch stock (1¾ inch actual) to 5 inches wide by 8 inches long, then transfer the profile shown on the grid pattern to the stock. Also, lay out the location of the two 7/16 inch diameter axle holes and the ¼ inch diameter eye holes. Use a drill press to bore these holes before cutting part F to shape with a band or saber saw. Next, use the drill press to bore the 1¼ inch diameter by ¾ inch deep countersunk hole for the spout (part B). Also, at this

time, drill the 11/16 inch diameter hole through the center of the countersunk hole.

The 11/16 inch wide slot is cut by hand with a back saw or dovetail saw, making two parallel cuts to establish the width. The scrap is then removed using a sharp chisel.

The remaining parts are made to the dimensions shown, although if desired, parts A, B, C, and D can be purchased from Cherry Tree Toys.

Sand thoroughly, taking care to remove all sharp edges. Assemble as shown, making sure that all parts (except part B) are glued securely. Keep in mind that a small part that falls off a toy presents a potential choking hazard to a young child. Also, when building toys, it's best to use a glue that's non-toxic such as Elmer's Glue-All. And the safest final finish is no finish at all.

1 SQUARE = ½ INCH

1¾" STOCK

1¼" HOLE DRILLED INTO CNTR OF STOCK

¼" HOLE

11/16" HOLE DRILLED & CENTERED FROM TOP

11/16" WIDE SLOT CUT INTO CENTER OF STOCK TO THIS LINE.

7/16" HOLE

7/16" HOLE

GRAIN

Laminated Shoehorn

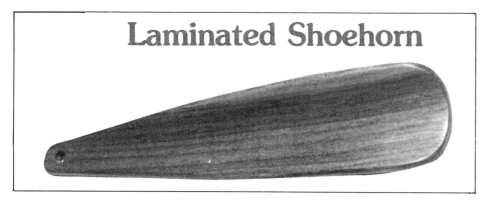

This laminated shoehorn not only makes a nice gift, it's a great way to use up those postcard size scraps of veneer left over from your last project.

The laminating form is made from 1½ inch PVC water pipe with a wall thickness of approximately 3/32 inch. Although it is called 1½ inch pipe, the actual outside diameter is closer to 2 inches. Because of the thin wall thickness and the inherent spring of PVC, the same size pipe is used for both the male and female parts of the form.

Start making the form by cutting two 8 inch lengths of the pipe. Next, cut one piece in half, lengthwise. Use sandpaper to smooth out any irregular-ities in the surface of the pipe. By using both halves of the form, you can laminate two shoehorns at once. Three worm-gear hose clamps (the type used on automobile radiator hoses) provide the clamping power (see Photo 1).

One shoehorn requires three or four pieces of veneer approximately 2 inch x 7 inch. The number of pieces depends on the veneer thickness; try for a finished thickness of around ⅛ inch. Spread liquid-hide glue evenly on each piece of veneer and stack them in one of the half-pieces of pipe. Press the piece of pipe that was not cut in half into the form that contains the veneer. If you are only making one shoehorn, snap the other half of the pipe on opposite the half containing the veneer so that the clamping pressure will be uniform. If you're making two at a time, load the second half with veneer and place it opposite the first half.

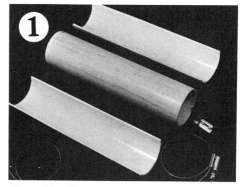

Now slip the three worm-gear clamps over the form and tighten them until the veneer is uniformly pressed into the form (see Photo 2).

After the glue has cured, remove the lamination from the form and cut it to shape. Round the edges and drill a ⅛ inch hole in the small end. Give the project a thorough sanding, then apply an oil finish.

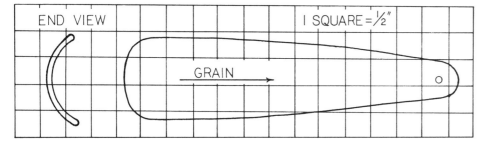

END VIEW — I SQUARE = ½"

GRAIN

Spaghetti Measure

Trying to judge how much spaghetti to prepare for the family dinner is usually a guessing game at best, and more often than not the cook makes much more than anybody can ever hope to eat. Now here's help - a gauge that tells exactly how much spaghetti to serve for one, two, three, or four portions.

Ours is made from red oak, but just about any wood from your scrap box can be used. It's an easy project to make, so if you are looking for something to sell at craft fairs or gift shops, you may want to consider this one.

You'll need a piece of ½ inch thick stock that measures about 3½ inches wide by 15 inches long. If you don't have ½ inch material, resaw ¾ inch stock on the table or band saw. Transfer the profile from the grid pattern to the stock, then cut out with a band or saber saw. Lay out the hole location before drilling the holes to the diameters shown. We used a spade bit to

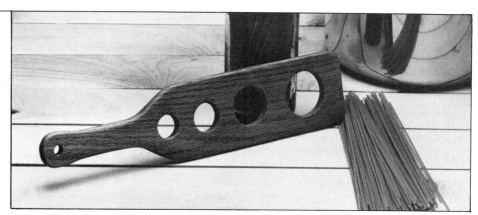

cut the ⅞ inch hole, an expandable bit to cut the 1⅛ and 1½ inch holes, and a hole cutter for the 1¾ inch hole. Also add a ⅜ inch hanger hole.

Sand thoroughly, rounding all cor-ners and edges. An application of Behlen Salad Bowl Finish (available from Wood Finishing Supply Co., 1267 Mary Drive, Macedon, NY 14502) provides an attractive non-toxic finish.

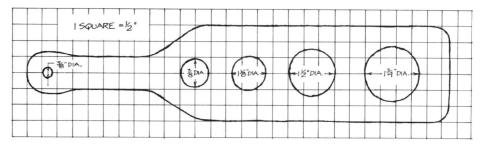

I SQUARE = ½"

⅜" DIA. ⅞" DIA. 1⅛" DIA. 1½" DIA. 1¾" DIA.

Candles will often make lovely additions to a festive occasion, especially if attractive holders are used. The one shown is made from walnut, although any hardwood that's suitable for turning can also be used. With a little practice this becomes a fairly easy turning job, making it a good item to consider for sale at craft fairs and gift shops.

Note that the project consists of three separate parts, a base, stem, and bowl. The stem is spindle turned and should present no special problems. The base is faceplate turned, and again no special problems should be encountered. For the bowl though, there are a few suggested procedures.

We used 2 inch nominal (1¾ inch actual) stock to make the bowl. Secure the stock to the faceplate, then turn the top half of the bowl, including the 5/16 inch deep by 3-3/16 inch candle well. This includes a ⅛ inch diameter pilot hole for the bottom of the spike. Sand thoroughly before removing from the faceplate. Carefully center a small faceplate in the candle well and fasten with short screws. The bottom half of the bowl can now be turned and sanded. After removing the faceplate, the screw holes in the well are filled with a mixture of sawdust and glue.

A center spike will add some stability to the candle and can be made using a 1 inch x #7 brass wood screw. Turn the screw into the pilot hole, then remove. Cut off the screw head and file this end to a point. Now, with a pair of pliers holding the pointed end, turn the screw into the bowl.

Apply glue to the spindle tenons and assemble the three parts. Several coats of Watco Danish Oil will provide an attractive final finish.

Candle Holder

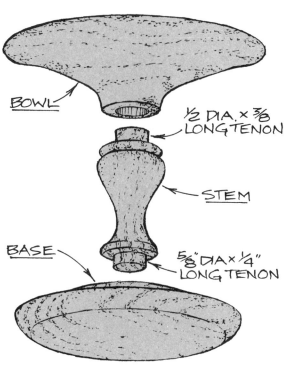

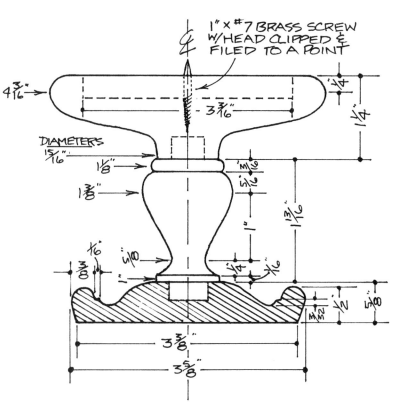

Lyre Clock

The basic design of this lyre clock is attributed to the famous clockmaker, Aaron Willard Jr., who was born in the late 1700's and lived most of his life in Boston.

The clock I built is made entirely from scrap wood that consisted of maple, Honduras and African mahoganies, pine from a turn-of-the-century pew, mahogany from a broken-up antique sewing table I found on a neighbor's wood pile, and striped mahogany and crotch veneers. It measures nearly 38 inches from finial to finial, is 12 inches wide and 5½ inches deep.

Begin this project with the sides, parts A. I chose pine because it would reduce the weight of the clock, and since the mechanism case would be bolted into the end grains of the sides, the strength offered by a hardwood wasn't a critical factor.

Two pieces of 1¾" x 3" x 14" long pine, glued face to face, will provide the 3½" width required for each part A. A cardboard template will help so that each half can be roughed out on a bandsaw before gluing. Be sure to leave extra wood at the top and bottom. A drum sander on a radial arm saw or drill press will finish shaping the contours. Since the sides will be veneered, imperfections can be filled in with wood filler. A smooth surface is necessary, so the final sanding should be done by hand.

The bottoms of parts A will have to be cut at 10 degree angles, and rabbets ⅜" wide by ¼" deep for the back panel, part B, can be made with a router.

The back panel, made from cabinet-grade birch plywood, will have its sides tapered 10 degrees from a base that measures 7¾ inches wide. To do this, I set my taper jig at 10 degrees, starting with a piece of plywood at least 8 inches wide by 13 inches long. I then ripped the panel on one side. My taper jig goes only to 15 degrees, however. When cutting symmetrical sides, the angle has to be doubled for the jig when the panel is turned over. So I taped the waste piece from the first cut to one side and ran it through the saw again. When finished, I screwed panel B, using ¾ inch #5 flathead brass screws, to parts A and set the assembly aside.

Start on the mechanism case, part C. This too is going to be veneered, so solid mahogany is not necessary, but a hardwood should be used since it has to hold a fair amount of weight. I would recommend two pieces of 1¾" thick maple glued face to face with a ½" thick piece of mahogany glued to the front. The mahogany will eliminate veneering the front. Be sure to run the grains in the same direction.

I glued the three laminated pieces to a piece of ¾ inch plywood, newspaper between, and attached the wood to a face plate. Once I turned the wood to a 7½ inch diameter, I used a parting tool to take out the center, leaving the walls of the case about 1⅛" thick.

To get a nicely fitting back panel, part D, I again used a parting tool and cut a rabbet ¼" deep x ⅞" wide into the back of C. Removing it from the lathe, I replaced it with a ¼" piece of birch plywood glued to a piece of ¾" plywood, newspaper between. This I turned to a diameter slightly larger than the diameter of the recess I made in the back of C, and, checking it with C, finished turning it down until I got a snug fit.

The front panel, part E, a piece of ⅜" plywood that holds the mechanism, does not need as accurate a fit as D, as the bezel will cover it, so the rabbet for it can be made with a router and a ⅜ inch rabbet bit. But E should be turned round on a lathe so its exact center can be located. This will determine where the handshaft of the movement will be. E is held to C with 1" #5 flathead screws.

A hole will have to be made in C for the pendulum to fit through. This I made 2 inches wide by 2 inches deep. Drawing the outline on the outside diameter, I drilled holes into the four corners and cut out the recess with a jigsaw.

Part C can be set aside so work can begin on the carved front, part F. A piece ½" thick x 11" wide x 13" long will be needed. A solid piece of lumber instead of a laminated one will be more stable and will not show the glue lines. I'd recommend Honduras mahogany since its grain is excellent for carving.

Take the waist of the clock, parts A, B and C, turn them panel side down on the mahogany board, and draw the outline for part F. What you must add, however, are the flares at the bottom.

When you cut F to shape, don't go inside the outline. Using 1¼" wire brads spaced about every 3" along the outline and ½" in, attach F to the front of parts A. But don't drive the nails all the way in as you'll want to remove F for carving.

Take the assembly to the drum sander and flow in F with the sides, using a fine grit sanding sleeve. I taped the lower portion of the sleeve with masking tape so it would not cut into the sides of parts A.

Next comes the joining of the mechanism case and the clock waist. Determine the vertical centerline of F and place the lowest portion of C at a point 11½" from the bottom of F on that line. Outline the diameter of C with a pencil. Bandsaw along the line, leaving a little extra wood.

What I discovered was this: hand tools and repeated passes with the sanding drum could not insure a good fit between the case and waist. What I did was lathe turn a piece of glued-up pine 4 inches thick to the same diameter as the housing, which is 7½ inches. Using contact cement, I glued a 4 by 24 inch sanding belt to the pine. I then had a sanding drum the same size as the case. The drum had a tendency to kick back the work, but with practice on a thick piece of scrap wood, I was able to get a good fit by holding the waist assembly to the drum.

The next problem was joining part C to the waist. This was solved with ¼" x 3" long lag screws. I chose them because they're stronger than wood screws and can be tightened with a ratchet wrench. To determine part C's position, I drilled shallow ¼" dia. holes into the tops of parts A and put ¼" dowel centers into them. Once the holes were located on C, I drilled slightly enlarged holes (oversized holes will allow for better positioning so long as they aren't bigger than the heads of the bolts) for the lag bolts and continued the holes into parts A, counterboring as needed to prevent the lags from splitting out the stock.

The next section to be tackled is the pendulum cabinet. Because of the weight of parts L and M, I chose dovetail joinery for the cabinet parts. First, dovetails are extremely strong; second, the cabinet sides will be veneered, so the dovetails won't take away from the clean lines of the clock.

Dovetails are not as difficult to make as they seem. And if you are not experienced and don't make them fit perfectly, wood filler will fill in the imperfections and the veneer will cover them.

In my scrap pile were pieces of old ½ inch African mahogany. I used this wood so I would have to veneer only the outside of the case. But another hardwood such as maple or poplar can be substituted.

Before gluing up the sides, parts H, and the top and bottom, parts G and I, you'll have to cut a hole into G for the pendulum rod. Into part I you should make countersunk holes for the 2¼" #8 flathead wood screws that will hold the lower shelf section that comprises parts L, M, N and O.

Part J, the back panel, is made after parts G, H, and I are joined and glued together. The groove for this ¼" thick piece of birch plywood is made with a ¼ inch rabbet bit in the back of the case with the corners squared with a chisel. The panel is held with ⅝" #3 brass flathead wood screws.

Part L is a ¾" thick piece of solid mahogany. The front and side edges can be rounded with a ⅜" beading bit. Part M can be made from any wood either solid or glued-up since it will be entirely veneered. A bandsaw can probably make all the curves, but since I used a hardwood, I ran the front over a table saw, making repeated passes over the blade and finished it up with a cove plane and sandpaper.

Part N is a piece of ⅛" thick mahogany. This can be ripped from the edge of a thick piece of mahogany. The front and side edges are rounded on a sanding disc.

Part O was made from two pieces of 5/4 mahogany glued together with newspaper between. After turning the block on a lathe with a 1-inch diameter tenon, I separated the pieces with a sharp chisel, clamped one half in a vise and cut a dovetail on the tenon with a dovetail saw. After M is veneered and N is glued to the bottom of M, the dovetail can be outlined on the back of M and N and cut out. Attach L to the top of M with four 1¼ inch #8 flathead wood screws countersunk into the wood. This entire shelf assembly is attached to the bottom of the pendulum case after the veneering is done, with 2¼ inch #8 flathead wood screws countersunk into the bottom of part I.

Before carving the front, part F, and before assembling the various component sections, be sure to veneer the sides, the pendulum cabinet, the mechanism case, the door and the shelf, part M. At a local lumber company I purchased matching striped mahogany veneer, a package that had five pieces, each measuring 5 inches by 36 inches. This was more than enough for the entire project.

The secret of veneering is a very smooth surface and lots of contact cement, Weldwood Cement being the best I've used. Start with the sides, parts A, and give at least two coats to both the wood and the veneer. When the surfaces have dried to the touch (at the very least, a half hour), put a newspaper between the wood and the veneer and slowly pull the newspaper out while pressing down on the veneer. I found a length of 1½" dia. dowel served well as a veneer roller. The veneer should overlap the edges of the wood being veneered since it can easily be trimmed with a razor knife. For the case, part C, I began the veneer at the exact bottom and rolled the case over a length of veneer that was a

little over 24 inches long. The veneer will stop adhering when it reaches the beginning. All I needed to do was trim the overlap with the knife.

Part M can be veneered on all sides, even over the sharp horizontal edges. The veneer should be glued with the grain running horizontally, and where it must fold over the sharp edges it will crack but won't separate. The veneer can then be trimmed and sanded flush.

Once the pendulum cabinet is veneered, you can put together the shelf assembly with glue and screws and cut out for the dovetailed lower finial, part O. The pendulum cabinet is then attached to the wast with ¼ inch by 2 inch lag bolts. Dowel centers will help position these two sections.

At this stage I built a stand out of 5/4 lumber to stand the clock upright while I worked on the door and fitted the mechanism.

The door of the pendulum cabinet (K) is next to be constructed. The one on my clock was also ½" African mahogany. But if you choose another wood it should be fairly stable and warp free. This you can tell be the end grain. If the growth rings are seen as arcs on the edge of the board, it's more likely to warp than a board on which the rings appear as lines that run up and down from top to bottom.

(continued on next page)

Photo shows back of clock case with cover removed. Note the 2 x 2 inch cut-out for the pendulum shaft and the four lag screws joining the lower case.

With the pendulum cabinet door open, the opening in the top of the cabinet can be seen. Note also the lag screws joining the cabinet to the upper case assembly.

If you veneer the door as I did, you must do both sides to equalize the absorption of moisture from the air. Veneering only one side will cause the board to warp. I used mahogany crotch veneer at least 7″ wide by at least 12″ long. Crotch veneers tend to be thicker and stiffer than other veneers, so once the door was veneered, I clamped it between plywood boards.

Cutting the ellipse in the door is next. A 1″ diameter sanding drum will effectively smooth the walls of the cutout. A ⅜″ rabbet bit will make the ⅛″ deep rabbet on the back for the glass. I first tried plywood for the retainer (part Q) but found it kept breaking. I finally settled on ⅛″ thick hardboard that I veneered. Two brass escutcheon nails will hold it and the glass on the door.

Before fitting the door with hinges, the molding, part P, will have to be made. This is much like a picture frame molding on a small scale. It should be made from a mahogany board ¾″ thick by at least 48″ long and several inches wide. I made the door slightly bigger than the dimensions shown so the door plus the molding would be bigger than the pendulum cabinet front. I was then able to run the door and molding over a jointer until it fit perfectly. The four-foot long board has to be stood on one edge and passed over a table saw blade set at 25 degrees. It may take some trial passes to get the same profile I got, but the results will be worth it. I then used the table saw and dado head to establish the ½″ deep x 5/16″ wide rabbet, before ripping the molding off the wider stock, and mitering it to length. Instead of nailing the mitered molding to the veneered door, I glued and clamped the pieces to part K. The hinges that hold the door are 1½″ long and made of brass. The flat hook that holds the door to the cabinet is also brass.

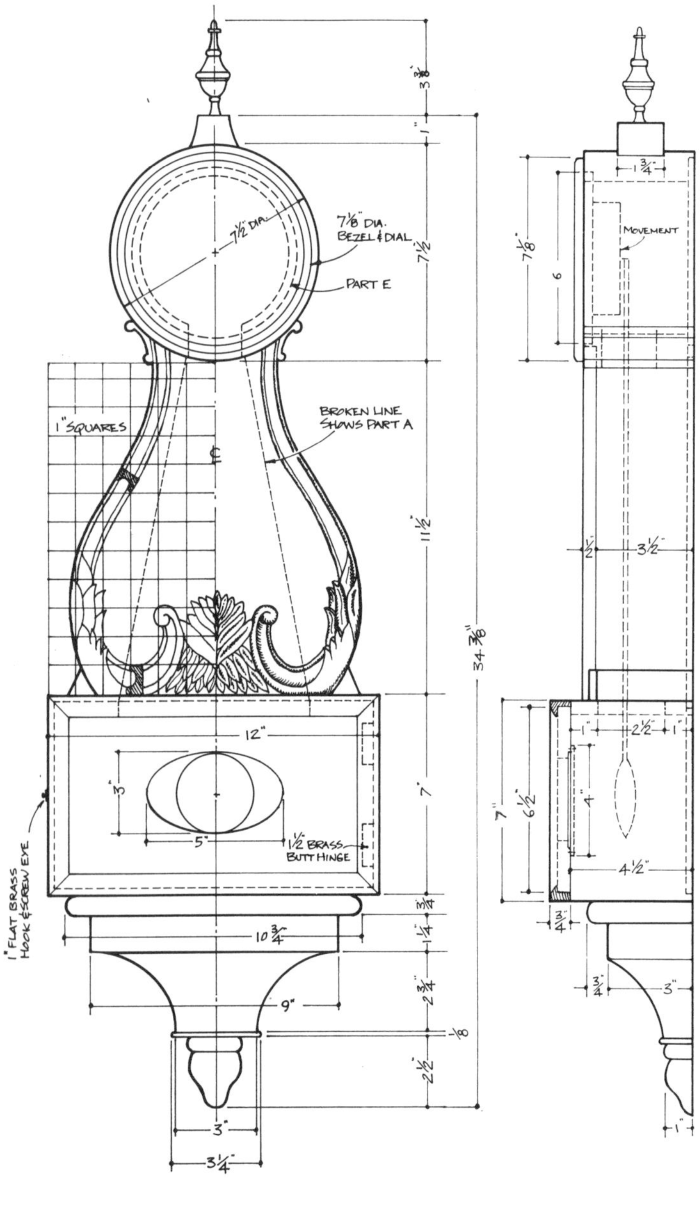

Now comes what may be the most difficult task for you, the carving of part F. If carving is not within your realm, Craftsman Wood Service, 1735 West Cortland Court, Addison, IL 60101 offers embossed carvings that can be applied. I'd recommend H2528 and H2514. If you are willing to carve the front, the best advice I can give is use a router with a ⅜ inch carbide straight bit and remove as much of the background, ¼″ deep, as you can. I would also glue part F to a slightly larger piece of ¾ inch plywood, newspaper between, that can be clamped to a bench. The margins, about 1 inch wide, that run along the sides are slightly hollowed, and these can be made with a veiner. Much of the rest of the detail can be put in with a parting tool. To get as smooth a background as possible, I raised the grain with a paint remover and went over it with a well-sharpened cabinet scraper.

For the finial base, part R, I again used my 7½″ diameter sanding drum and held a long piece of 8/4 mahogany to it to get a concave underside. It would help, however, to bandsaw the outline first. Notice that the sides are slightly flared outward. This can be done on a bandsaw before crosscutting to separate part R from the longer piece. Once sanded smooth, this part was attached to the top of C with contact cement.

To make the molding, part S, as shown in photo below, clamp a ¾″ thick piece of mahogany to your workbench. The board should be a little over 8″ long and at least 2″ wide. Draw parallel lines 1¾″ apart along the length of the board. On both ends within these lines draw the molding profile. Next draw parallel lines ⅜ inches in from the first lines to represent the beads. Along these lines I took a dovetail saw and cut a kerf about ¼″ deep. Then taking a wide no. 5 gouge, I scooped out the cove. After sanding the cove smooth, I ripped the outer edges of the molding profile at a 45 degree angle. This I clamped in a wood vise, shaping the back with the same no. 5 gouge. A sanding disc helped

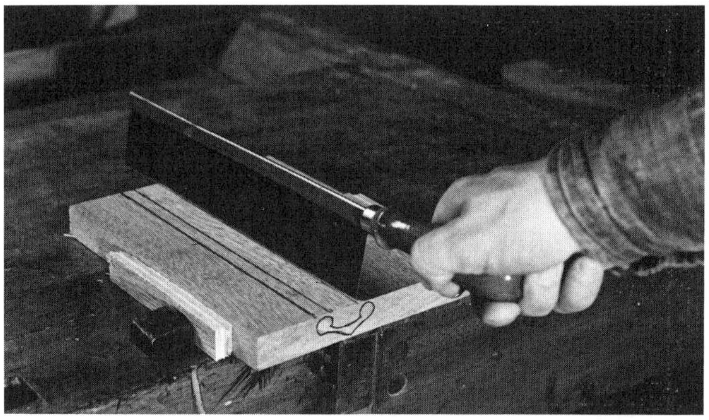

round the beads. One inch long wire brads will hold the molding to the clock sides.

The last pieces to be fitted are the wedges, parts T. These can be ripped from a 5/4 or 8/4 board of any wood since they will be veneered with the same striped mahogany used for the rest of the clock. The flares at the bottom of part F may have to be filed a bit so they flow flush with the wedges. Contact cement will hold these pieces to the top of the pendulum case.

To finish the case, I used a mahogany paste filler mixed with a dark walnut stain. Where contact cement had gotten on the veneer, I was able to remove it with a paint thinner and steel wool. Over the stain I applied several coats of satin polyurethane.

As if this project wasn't challenging enough, I made the clock case before I purchased the pendulum movement, one I had never used before. Happily, I found everything fit according to plan.

Mason & Sullivan Co., 586 Higgins Crowell Rd., West Yarmouth, Cape Cod, MA 02673 is the source for the eight-day spring driven movement (part no. 3340X), the bezel and dial combination (part no. 3403X), and the solid brass urn finial (part no. 3901B).

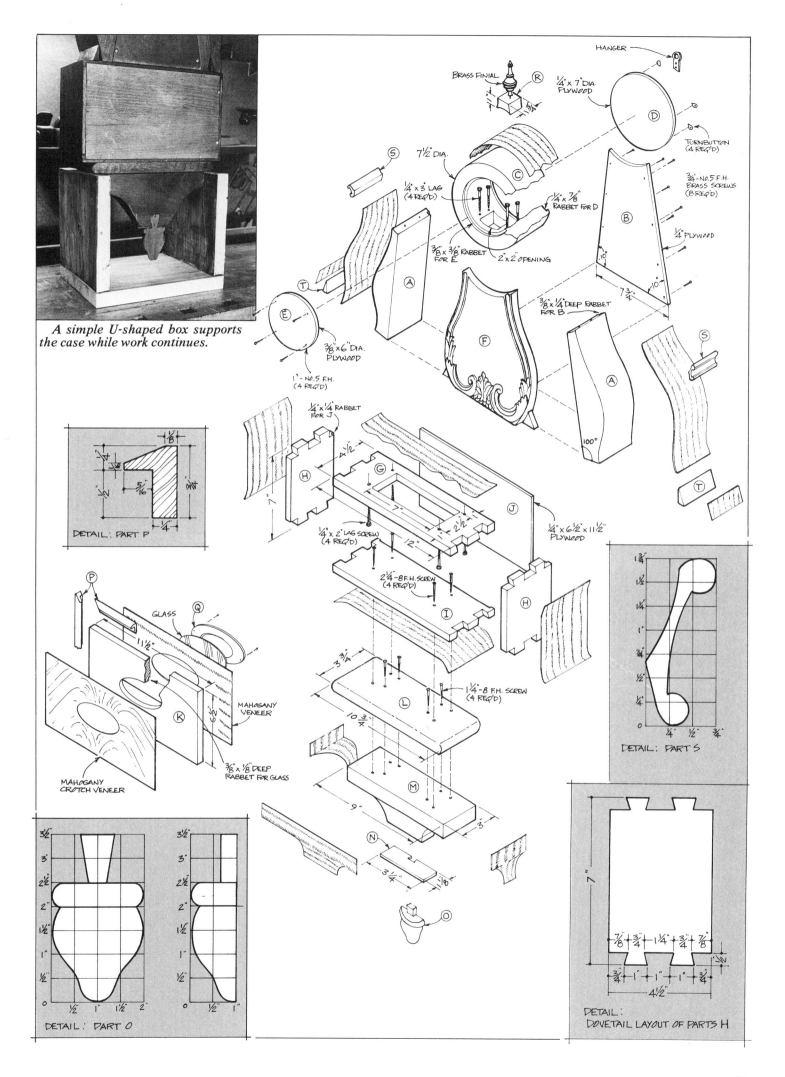

A simple U-shaped box supports the case while work continues.

DETAIL: PART P

DETAIL: PART O

DETAIL: PART S

DETAIL: DOVETAIL LAYOUT OF PARTS H

Geodesic Lighting Fixture

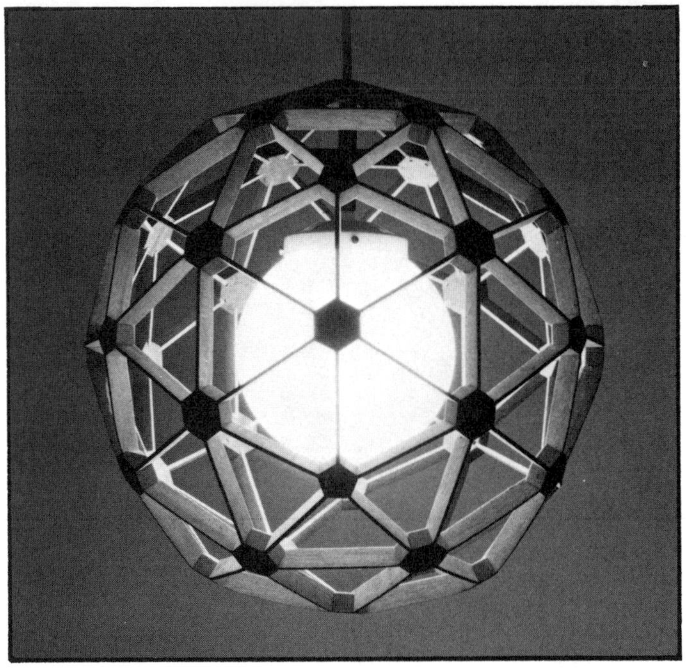

This intricate network of connectors and chords is fascinating to look at and equally fascinating to build. The completed sphere is quite rigid, yet light in weight, and lends itself admirably to a hanging fixture, with or without an enclosed lamp. We made ours of mahogany, but most clear cabinet woods can be used including pine.

Begin by making the hexagonal connectors (part A). Using glued up or solid stock, cut a workpiece of 1½" x 2" x 32". Set your tablesaw blade at 30 degrees. Don't depend on the machine tilt scale but instead use a drafting triangle or a carefully cut cardboard or plywood gauge to set the blade. Use a flat (not hollow-ground) saw blade that cuts a kerf close to ⅛" in width.

With a 2" wide side of the stock riding on the table as a base, cut both corners off leaving at least ⅞" at the base. Use a push stick to feed the workpiece and another notched stick to hold it down and against the fence. Flip the stock over onto the other 2" side and repeat. Trim both left-hand side cuts (or right side cuts) until all sides of the hexagon are an equal ⅞" in width.

With the blade still set at 30 degrees, rip a beveled strip off a straight piece of scrap and tack this to an auxiliary fence as shown. Use the regular fence to rip a slight bevel off the corner of the strip as shown in the sectional views. Attach the auxiliary fence to the regular fence with screws and lower the saw blade (still set at 30 degrees), to cut a 3/16" deep groove along each corner of the hex stock. The fence must be carefully set so that the grooves will be centered exactly on the hex corners for the full length of the workpiece.

After grooving, set the blade at 0 degrees and use the miter gauge to crosscut the hex stock, like a loaf of bread, into 30 pieces, each ¾" thick. When crosscutting, do not trap the pieces between the fence and the blade. Set a stop block against the fence, well ahead of the blade and ride off this. After cutting 30 pieces, you should have about 6" of waste left. Less than this would be unsafe to hold.

The pentagonal connectors (part B) are next. Cut a workpiece to 1½" x 1⅝" x 18". Again, use a prepared gauge to accurately set your tablesaw blade to 18 degrees. With a 1⅝" side as a base, cut off two base corners leaving a base width of ⅞". Tilt the workpiece counter-clockwise so that one newly formed side is a base. Adjust the fence for the next cut to make the base ⅞" wide. Using the same fence setting, rotate the piece counter-clockwise and make your last cut to form the pentagon.

Pull the 30 degree beveled strip off the auxiliary fence and replace it with one beveled at 18 degrees. This strip must also be slightly trimmed to clear the sawblade. Tilt the sawblade to 36 degrees and run grooves centered along the five corners of the stock, then set the blade at 0 degrees and crosscut 12 slices, each ¾" thick.

From ¾" stock, rip strips just thick enough to fit snugly in the grooves after sanding. You will need 60 pieces cut to a full length of 4⅜", mitered at each end at 18 degrees (part C), and 60 pieces cut to a full length of 3⅞", with ends mitered at 16 degrees (part D). Use a stop block on the fence to prevent binding the pieces when the ends are mitered and make test cuts with scrap to set the fence for the proper length of each part.

To assemble the sphere, mark a 16¾" dia. circle on a flat surface and with the hex connectors (A) and 10 long chords (C), form a circle on top of this template (photo 2). The 16¾" diameter represents the inside diameter of the sphere, and the hex connector and long chords are arranged around it. Only a small dot of glue such as TiteBond is needed in the slots. When the circle is complete, take one hex connector and two C chords and form a triangle using two of the hexes on the base circle. Continue until five triangles are built off the base (photo 3).

Using two hexes and three long chords, form an arc and connect two of the base triangles with this arc. Once added, you will see two connections to be completed between the last two hexes added (marked A in photo 4) and the top of one of the triangles on the base circle. Making these two connections, you will then see voids in the sphere that are pentagonal. These voids will later be filled in using the part B connectors, and the short chords (part D). Continue with your long chords and hexes until all have been attached, and then turn the dome over on a suitable support (I used an old towel in a doughnut shape). Build a mirror image dome on this side of the base circle, but rotate it one hex connector. In order to insert the globe and change burned-out bulbs, one *hex* connector at the bottom of the sphere should have its 6 chords glued to it but not glued to the surrounding connectors. At this point you will have a sphere with a series of pentagonal voids. Assemble the 60 short chords to the 12 pentagonal connectors, and mount in the voids to complete the sphere. Don't forget that the hexagonal connector at the bottom of the sphere, and the 4 long and 2 short chords that connect it must be removable. It's best to mark these connectors before final assembly to avoid confusion. To pull the joints together, use a tourniquet technique with a length of string and a pencil. Use enough string and pencils to evenly distribute clamping pressure. When all joints are dry,

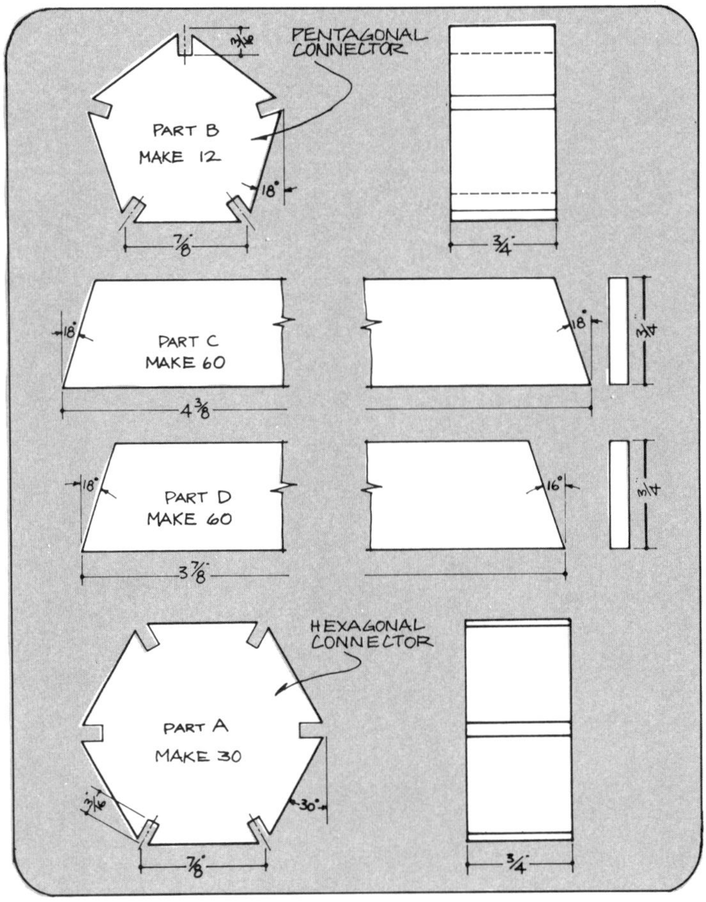

sand or chisel the tips of the chords flush with the tops of the connectors.

We used a white 8″ dia. globe and ceiling canopy. This unit is model no. 8496 by Thomas Industries and was purchased at a local electrical supply store. The fixture included a white line cord and all necessary hardware except the ½″ dia. x 3½″ tube which acts as a spacer between the globe and the underside of the top hex. The 8496 fixture is identical to that shown in the illustrations, except that the 8″ diameter globe is spring-mounted to the globe cover, rather than with 3 screws, as illustrated.

If desired, the sphere can be finished with a coat of penetrating oil such as Watco, applied to all surfaces with a small brush.

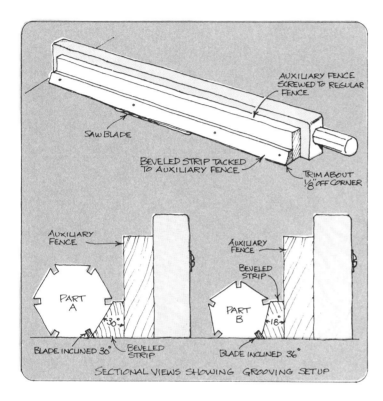

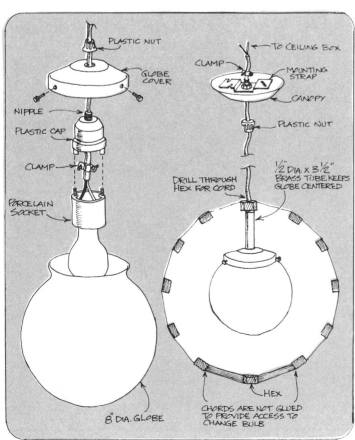

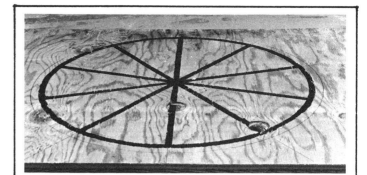

Photo 1: Draw a circle with a diameter of 16¾″ on plywood and divide it into 10 equal segments.

Photo 2: Using the circle as a template, join 10 hex connectors (A) with long chords (C) as shown.

Photo 3: With one hex and two long chords, form triangles off the hexes on the base.

Photo 4: Connect two base triangles by spanning them with two hexes and three long chords. These are marked A and C in the above photo. Next add two more parts C to join the part A connectors labled above with the part A connector at the top of the base triangle, as shown.

Oak Desk Clock

This compact oak clock will make an eye-catching addition to any desk and its small size insures that it won't take up much space while keeping you on schedule.

Begin by making the mitered case (parts A & B). As the case provides much of the visual appeal of the clock, try to select stock that has an interesting figure. It's also important that it be flat. Not much stock is required, in fact a piece measuring 2¼ inches wide by 23 inches long will take care of the entire case (the length allows for some scrap when cutting).

As shown in the cross-sectional view, the case stock requires two rabbets, one that's ¼ inch deep (for the back) and another that's 1⅞ inches deep (for the glass, spacers and dial board). Using the tablesaw, and referring to the drawings, you'll find that the rabbets can be cut with little difficulty.

Step 1 shows the sawblade making the first cut which establishes the width and depth of the rabbet for back (H). Note that the tablesaw rip fence is fixed at a point 2 inches from the right-hand side of the blade. Also, the blade is set to a height of 9/16 inches. After making this first cut, the fence is moved about ⅛ inch to the right, then a second cut is made. The process is repeated until the rabbet is completed.

Step 2 shows the sawblade making the cut which establishes the location of the rabbet for parts C,D,E and F. Note that the fence is now fixed at a point ⅜ inch from the right-hand side of the blade and the blade height is now ¼ inch.

Step 3 shows the final cut. The fence is fixed at a point ½ in. from the *right-hand* side of the blade with its height set at 1-13/16 in. The stock is passed over the blade on edge as shown.

To make the miters, set the sawblade to 45 degrees. For a good miter joint, the angle must be exact so it's best not to rely on the crude gauges that most tablesaws have. We like to use a draftman's 45 degree triangle which offers accuracy at a reasonably low cost. Also, before starting, be sure that the miter gauge is exactly square to the blade.

With the ¾ inch edge against the miter gauge, miter one end of the stock. Next, lay out the length of the piece, mark the location of the miter, then flip the stock over (so the opposite edge is against the fence), and cut the piece to length. Make all cuts accurately. Repeat this process until all four case sides are mitered.

Apply glue to the miters, then clamp securely with a strap clamp. The oak really soaks up the glue so it's a good idea to apply one coat, let it soak in, then add a second coat. Allow to dry overnight.

Next, a router equipped with a ⅜ inch piloted cove bit is used to cut a ⅛ inch deep cove around the inside of the front. Some router bit pilots have a tendency to burn into the stock, so use a light touch here. After routing, give all outside surfaces a thorough sanding, finishing with at least 220 grit. Lightly round over the edges. Finish with Deft Danish Oil.

The dial board (F) is made from a piece of ¼ inch plywood with veneer added to both sides. It's not a good practice to veneer just one side as uneven stresses could cause the plywood to warp at some point in the future. We chose walnut although rosewood, ebony or any other dark wood veneer would also be attractive. A less expensive veneer, such as poplar, can be used for the back of the board. For a small job like this, contact cement is probably the best way to apply the veneer. Finish with a light coat of oil.

Locate the center of part F, then use a compass to lightly scribe a 2⅞ inch diameter circle. At the center, drill a ⅜ inch diameter hole for the movement shaft. The black dots between numerals are made from ⅛ inch dowel rod cut to ⅛ inch lengths with a fine tooth dovetail saw. The ⅝ inch Arabic numerals (made of brass finished plastic), were purchased from Craft Products Company, 2200 Dean Street, St. Charles, IL 60174. Order their part no. 43765. Mark the location of the dots and numerals, then epoxy them to the board.

Cut the glass (C) to size. We chose a bronze tinted glass but clear also looks good. It's held in the case by the spacer strips (parts D & E) which are secured with a spot of glue at each center. This makes for easy removal should the glass ever need to be replaced.

The quartz battery powered movement, along with the minute and hour hands and the sweep second hand were also purchased from Craft Products. The movement is P/N 2325-X01, the minute and hour hands P/N 2450-K44 and the second hand P/N 2459-544.

The movement (G) is assembled as shown, with the brass locknut holding it in place. The hands are trimmed to fit within the dial face, then added to the movement shaft.

The dial face is inserted into the case and held in place with a glazier's (triangular) point at each side. A plywood back is secured to the case with four small brass screws. Another light coat of Deft Oil completes the project.

Bill of Materials
(All Dimensions Actual)

Part	Description	Size	No. Req'd
A	Case Side	¾ x 2¼ x 4¾	2
B	Case Top & Bottom	¾ x 2¼ x 5½	2
C	Glass	⅛ x 4-7/16 x 3-11/16	1
D	Side Spacer	3/16 x ½ x 3⅜	2
E	Top and Bottom Spacer	3/16 x ½ x 4½	2
F	Dial Board	¼ x 4-7/16 x 3-11/16	1
G	Movement	Craft p/n 2325-X01	1
H	Back	¼ x 5-1/16 x 4-5/16	1

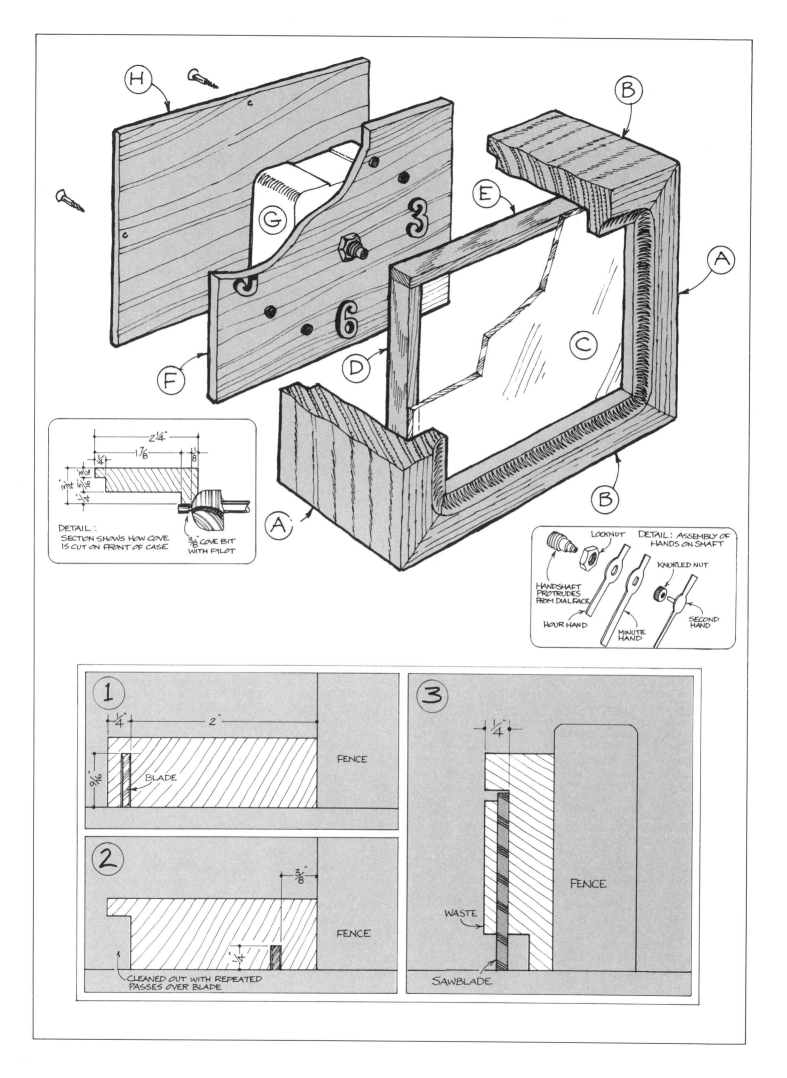

DETAIL:
SECTION SHOWS HOW COVE
IS CUT ON FRONT OF CASE

2¼"
1⅞"
¼"
⅛"
¾"
5/16" 3/16"
¼"

⅜" COVE BIT
WITH PILOT

DETAIL: ASSEMBLY OF
HANDS ON SHAFT

LOCKNUT
KNURLED NUT

HANDSHAFT
PROTRUDES
FROM DIAL FACE

HOUR HAND
MINUTE HAND
SECOND HAND

1
¼"
2"
9/16"
BLADE
FENCE

2
⅜"
¼"
FENCE
CLEANED OUT WITH REPEATED
PASSES OVER BLADE

3
¼"
FENCE
WASTE
SAWBLADE

Old-Time Radio Case

If you're a nostalgia buff, radio from the 30's and 40's holds a special place in your heart. Here's a project to help you relive that golden age of radio.

This reproduction of a cathedral radio case can serve many purposes. I originally intended it for use as a speaker enclosure. You can mount a speaker inside and then plug it into the earphone jack of a portable radio or tape player. A lot of today's small portables are equipped with tiny 2" to 3" speakers that can't handle all the sound the amplifier is capable of producing. You'll be amazed how good a small portable can sound when connected to a 6" to 8" extension speaker.

If you're really into nostalgia, you probably have tapes of old radio programs. Now you can really get the feel of sitting around watching the radio by playing your tapes through a speaker mounted in this old-time case.

By building two cases you can use them as extension speakers for your stereo. You can also mount a modern radio inside the case. There is ample room for most transistorized units with room left over for the addition of an oversized speaker. Even if you don't have any electronics experience, you can use the case to camouflage a modern piece of equipment by simply leaving the back off the case and putting the equipment inside.

The empty case can even be used to add a touch of nostalgia to a room's decor. Add a door in the back panel and use the case as a hidden storage space. Add a lock to the door and a slot in the top and it's a giant piggy bank.

Except for parts C and F, the case is made of ¼" 3-ply birch plywood. Start construction by making the front (A). Cut a slightly oversize piece of plywood and transfer the full size pattern to it. The pattern is symmetrical so only one half is shown.

Drill a small hole in the center of each of the outlined openings to allow a jig saw or coping saw blade to be inserted, then proceed to cut out all the openings. Smooth the edges with a rat-tail file and sandpaper wrapped around a dowel. Use part A as a pattern to make the back (part D).

The base (C) can be made of ½ inch or ¾ inch plywood or solid stock. Cut it to 9½ inches wide by 7½ inches long.

Now cut a piece of ¼" birch plywood to make the arched side (part B) and the two reinforcements (part E). The width of this piece should be cut about 1½" more than the finished width of the case (see Detail A). The grain should run lengthwise. Make saw cuts one-half way through the plywood, across the grain, every ⅜ inch as

shown in Detail A. After the kerfs have been made, rip two ½ inch wide strips to get parts E, then trim part B to the case width of 8 inches. Cut a ¼ inch wide x ⅛ inch deep rabbet on both of the long sides of part B to accept the front (A) and back (D).

Attach the front (A) to the base (C) with glue and two or three small brads. Also temporarily attach the back (D) with two small screws. Note that the front and back will extend beyond the base for ⅛ inch on each side. Apply glue to the sides of the base (C) and along the front rabbet of part B, but don't apply any glue to the rear rabbet. Secure one end of part B to the base with brads and then bend part B around the top curvature of the front (A) and back (D). The flexibility of plywood will vary depending on what type of core it has. A lauan core is very flexible and should be used if it is available. Plywood with a fir core will be harder to bend. If the plywood will not bend easily, it may be necessary to slightly dampen the kerfed side with water and preform the curve by working the plywood over a large diameter pipe before attaching it to the face. Pull part B tight and secure it with brads to the other side of the base. The dimensions given for part B include a small amount of overhang to compensate for any difference in the final dimensions of the front (A) and back (D) that might occur. Once part B is securely attached to the base, trim off the overhang.

Remove the back (D). The two strips (E) that were cut from part B are used as case reinforcements. Cut them to length so they will fit snugly inside the case. Glue the front reinforcement in place butted up against the inside of the front (A). The rear reinforcement should be positioned so its rear edge lines up with the edge of the rabbet.

Shape the two screw blocks (F) that the back attaches to so they will fit the contour of the arched top and glue them in place (see Detail B).

Now sand the case and round the front edge. What you do next depends on how you plan to use the case. If you're mounting some equipment in it, you'll need to drill the holes for the controls. If you'll be using it for an application that doesn't need controls, you'll need to make some dummy knobs (see Detail C). The dummy knobs are made of ½" dowel. Fold a piece of rag into a small pad and place a piece of 80 grit sandpaper on top. Put the pad and sandpaper in the palm of your hand and cup your hand. Now push the end of a dowel into the center of the pad and twist it back and forth. It won't take long before the end of the dowel will be nicely rounded.

Switch to finer sandpaper to smooth the dowels, then cut ½" off the end of the dowel to form the dummy knob. Repeat this procedure until you have made three knobs. Drill a blind pilot hole in the back of the knob for a #6 wood screw. Paint the knobs dark brown or black. Drill mounting holes for the knobs at the positions indicated on the plan.

Another part that will vary depending on your use of the case is the speaker board (G). Make part G out of a piece of ¼″ plywood. Cut the speaker board so it will fit inside the case butted against the inside of the front (A). If you're not installing a speaker, you don't need to cut any holes in part G. Just cover the front of part G with dark brown or black grill cloth from an electronics supply store. In the area of the speaker board that will be behind the station indicator window, cut away the grill cloth. Cut out the paper station indicator on the full-size pattern. (If you don't want to cut up your copy of *The Woodworker's Journal*, make a photocopy). Use rubber cement to glue the paper to the speaker board where it will show through the window. Cover the paper with a piece of clear contact paper to protect it. The speaker board is held in place with four #6 brass flat head wood screws as indicated on the full-size pattern.

To install a speaker, hold it in place on the board and trace around it. Position the speaker so it will not interfere with the speaker board screws. If the speaker is too large to miss the screw positions, leave a projection of wood in the speaker hole for the screw to attach to (see examples of 5 inch and 8 inch speaker cut-outs). Remove the speaker and draw a circle ¼″ inside the traced line. Use a saber saw to cut along the inside line. Drill holes in the speaker board that correspond to the mounting holes in the speaker. Countersink the holes on the side of part G that faces part A. The speaker is held in place by flat head machine screws and nuts. Cover the front of part G with grill cloth.

When all the holes are drilled and the speaker board is removed from the case, you can apply the finish. Since tastes have changed over the years, most modern finishes won't look very authentic on this project. The originals were usually finished with a dark varnish/stain. The closest thing I've found to the original is Super-Tex Britenal spray varnish/stain #B-804 which is marketed by Sprouse Reitz Co. Super-Tex Britenal #B-803 Walnut is also a close match. Some of the darker colors of Deft spray lacquer/stain also look similar to the original finish.

Once the finish is dry, install the speaker board and any other components. If you're using the dummy knobs, attach them with screws from the inside of the case. Screw the back in place and you're ready to enjoy Fibber Magee and Molly (if you have a tape!).

(continued on next page)

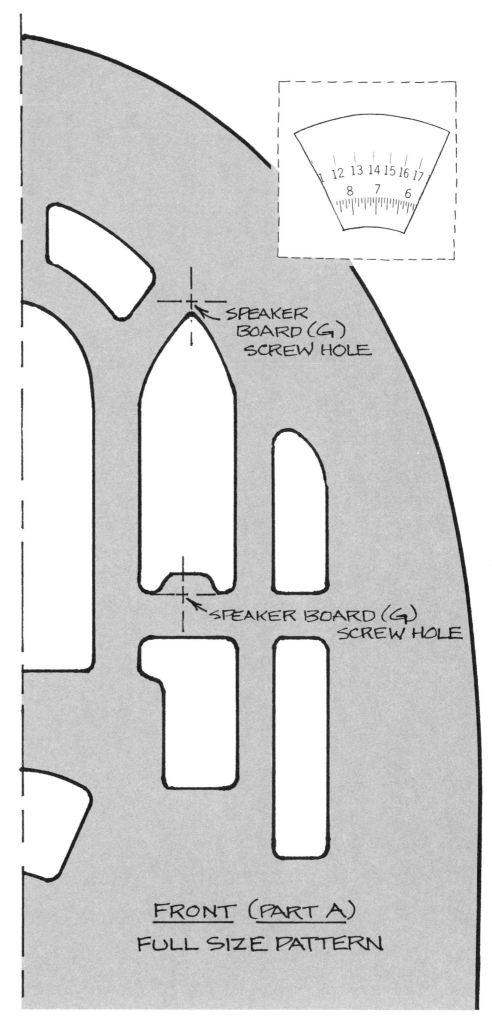

SPEAKER BOARD (G) SCREW HOLE

SPEAKER BOARD (G) SCREW HOLE

FRONT (PART A)
FULL SIZE PATTERN

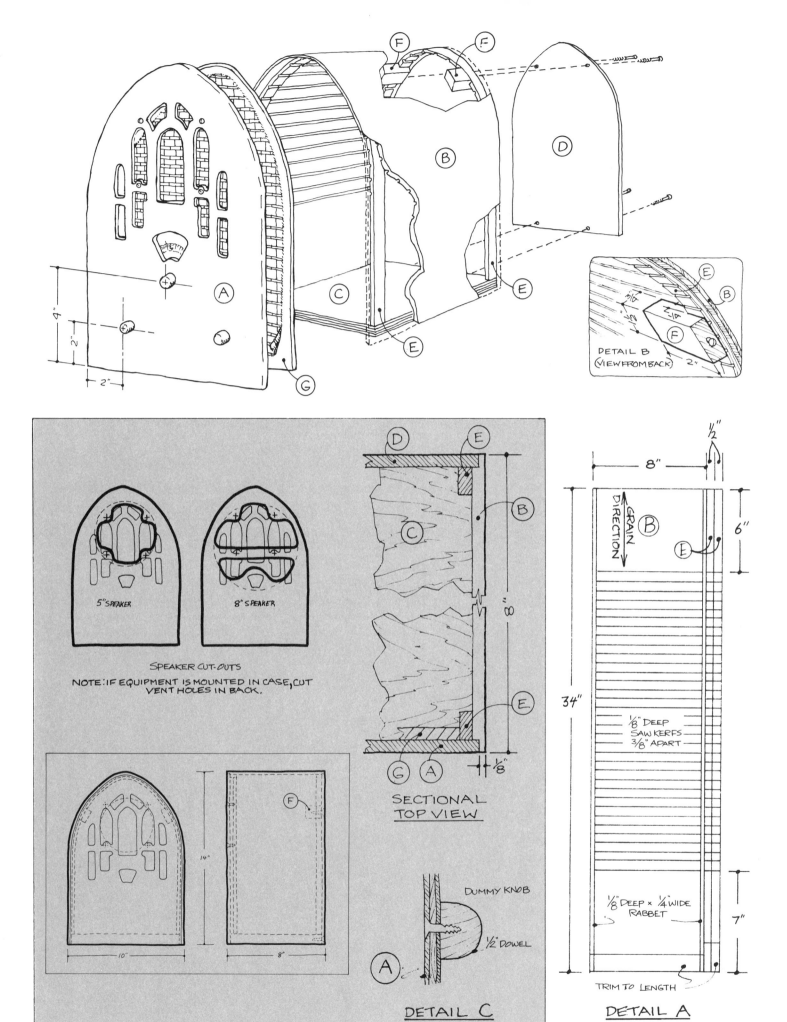

SPEAKER CUT-OUTS

5" SPEAKER

8" SPEAKER

NOTE: IF EQUIPMENT IS MOUNTED IN CASE, CUT VENT HOLES IN BACK.

SECTIONAL TOP VIEW

DUMMY KNOB

½" DOWEL

DETAIL C

DETAIL A

GRAIN DIRECTION

⅛" DEEP SAW KERFS ⅜" APART

⅛" DEEP × ¼" WIDE RABBET

TRIM TO LENGTH

DETAIL B (VIEW FROM BACK)

Avoid any with loose knots. Begin by cutting parts A, B, and C to the lengths shown. You'll need four pieces of each part. Set up a dado head cutter to make a ¾ inch deep cut, then proceed to cut the sixteen half-lap joints as shown in the exploded view. When cutting the joint in part A for the stretchers (C), make them slightly less than the width of the stretchers. Later when the stretchers are sanded, the slight reduction in width will make for a good snug fit.

Assemble the two frames (parts A & B) as shown. Use glue and clamp firmly with bar or pipe clamps to pull the edges in close contact. It's also a good idea to add a C-clamp at each corner to squeeze the lap joint faces together. Be sure to use clamp pads in conjunction with the clamps.

When dry, drill a 1 inch diameter hole through each joint to take a 1½ inch long dowel pin. Cut the pins so they protrude on each side about 1/32 of an inch. This allows them to be

sanded flush with the surface.

With a saber saw, apply the 1 inch radius to the corners, then use a router equipped with a ¼ inch piloted rounding over bit to round off all edges. Next, give all surfaces a complete sanding. Start with a grit that will remove planer marks with a minimum of effort. We started with 80 grit, then followed with 100, 150, and 220.

Use the router to round-over the outside edges of part C, but on the inside, stop the bit just short of the lap joint. Sand thoroughly, then joint to the frames with glue and clamps. Two ½ inch diameter dowel pins further secure the joint.

Final sand all parts, then stain to suit. Two coats of polyurethane varnish will provide a durable final finish. Four feet in the form of 1 inch diameter by ¾ inch long dowel pins, will help stabilize the rack on uneven floors. These feet are inserted in ⅜″ deep holes so they will extend ⅜″ from the bottom.

Firewood Rack

Readers in many parts of the country are no doubt starting to sample some of those uncomfortably chilly temperatures that come right along with the late fall season. It's a prelude to the long winter - one that many weather forecasters say will be unusually cold, not only here in New England, but also in most other areas of the country.

With those thoughts in mind, we decided a firewood rack was in order, so we designed one that could hold a pretty fair amount of wood, yet not take up the entire living room area. To save cost it's made using standard 2 by 4 construction lumber, although those who have access to oak or other hardwoods will want to consider putting them to use here. The lap joints and dowel pins make for very solid construction. Ours is sized for 18 inch logs. If you use shorter or longer logs, change dimensions to suit.

Select 2 by 4 stock that is well seasoned and free from any warp.

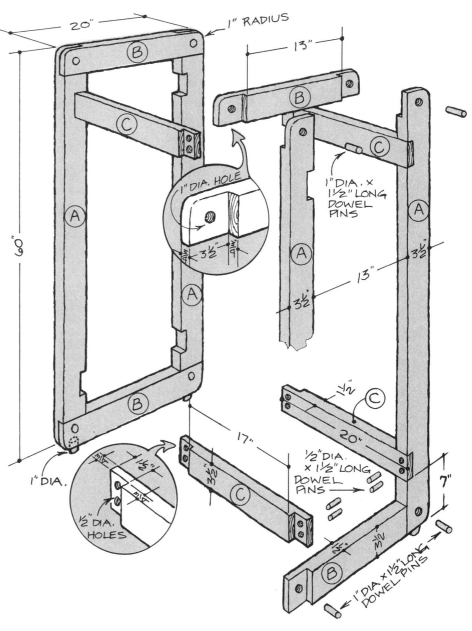

Cider Press Lamp

As I studied an antique cider press, it occurred to me that it could make a lovely lamp with just a few modifications. Basically, the modifications involved adding parts F and G (see Drawing) and some lamp hardware. However, if you'd rather have a working cider press, exclude parts F and G, but add plate (L) and cleat (M) as shown in the Detail.

Except for the press screw (K), all parts for the project can be obtained at most hardware stores. Part K can be ordered from Craftsman Wood Service Co., 1735 West Cortland Court, Addison, IL 60101. Order their part no. H0401.

The one shown is made from cherry, but most any other hardwood would be suitable. Softwoods should be avoided.

Begin by cutting the 1⅜ inch thick by 2¼ inch wide stock for the frame (parts A, B, and D), yoke (parts F and G), and feet (part C). You will need approximately nine linear feet. For the frame cut two pieces 12 inches long (for part A) and two pieces 13 inches long (for parts B and D). Apply a 9/16 inch wide by 7/16 inch deep lengthwise groove along the inside of parts A to accept the ⅜ inch threaded rod (I). Holding the uprights (A) in place on the bottom (B), mark where the inside of the groove falls. Drill a hole in the bottom to accept the rod. Also drill an angled hole for the lamp cord (see Front Elevation). Turn the uprights over onto the top (D) and repeat this.

Cut two 10 inch lengths of stock for the feet (C), chamfer as shown, then locate them under the bottom (B). Mark where the hole is to be drilled through the feet using the bottom as a template. First countersink the hole to a depth of ⅝ inch with a 1¼ inch spade bit, then drill a hole big enough to accept the threaded rod.

Cut two pieces of stock to 8⅞ inch (part F) and one piece 9½ inch (part G) for the yoke. Lay out and cut the dovetails (see Detail), and the tenons. Place the yoke assembly on the top frame

piece (D) and mark for the mortises. Groove part G and the right side part F to hide the wiring, then mortise the top of the frame (D). At this time drill and counterbore part G for the lamp nipple and locknut. The counterbore is 1 inch diameter by ⅝ inch deep. The through hole is ⅜ inch diameter.

Also, part D can now be drilled for the threaded nut of the press screw (K). It's held in place with a pair of wood screws. The frame (A, B, & D), yoke (F & G), and feet (C), along with the threaded rods (I), can now be assembled with glue. Use the threaded rods to help clamp the frame and feet. Use additional clamps for the yoke.

Next make the support plate (E) for the barrel. Cut 1 inch stock to 9⅞ inch square, and cut off the corners at 45 degrees to make the 4-1/16 octagonal sides. Mark the center, and using a router and a trammel, groove the top of the plate. A ½ inch core-box bit was used to remove the remaining stock in between the grooves. The outside diameter of the groove should measure 8¾ inches. The completed groove measures ¼ inch deep by 1½ inches wide. Groove out for the spout in the same fashion without the trammel. After sanding, attach the plate in place with two #10 x 2 inch flat head wood screws.

To make the barrel, buy two lengths of ¾ inch wide x ⅛ inch thick iron strapping (J). If your hardware store has galvanized straps, lightly sand the coating. You will be amazed how thin the coating is. Mark for eighteen holes, 1½ inches apart, starting ½ inch from one end of a three foot strap. From one inch stock cut eighteen strips (H), 1⅛ inch thick by 8 inches long. Line them up on a surface and draw lines one inch from the top and bottom, across all pieces. Drill the straps and lay one over the wood strips, lining up the top edge of the strap with the top pencil line. Attach with ¾ inch round or flat head wood screws. The other strap is attached to the bottom in the same manner.

Bend the assembly into the barrel shape, then remove the screw from the first strip. Overlay the strap so that the holes line up and screw the first strip back in place through both straps. Cut off the excess metal. Chamfer the tops of the strips with a router or a plane, and place in the groove of the support plate.

Refer to the drawing for the arrangement of the lamp parts. The cord is fed down through the nipple and into the groove in parts G & F. It then runs down the inside of part A (use double pointed tacks), and through the angled hole in part B. When installed, the shade should just cover the socket.

Give all parts a final sanding. Apply a coat of Watco Danish Oil and while wet rub on a coat of Minwax Ebony stain. The result is an attractive antique look.

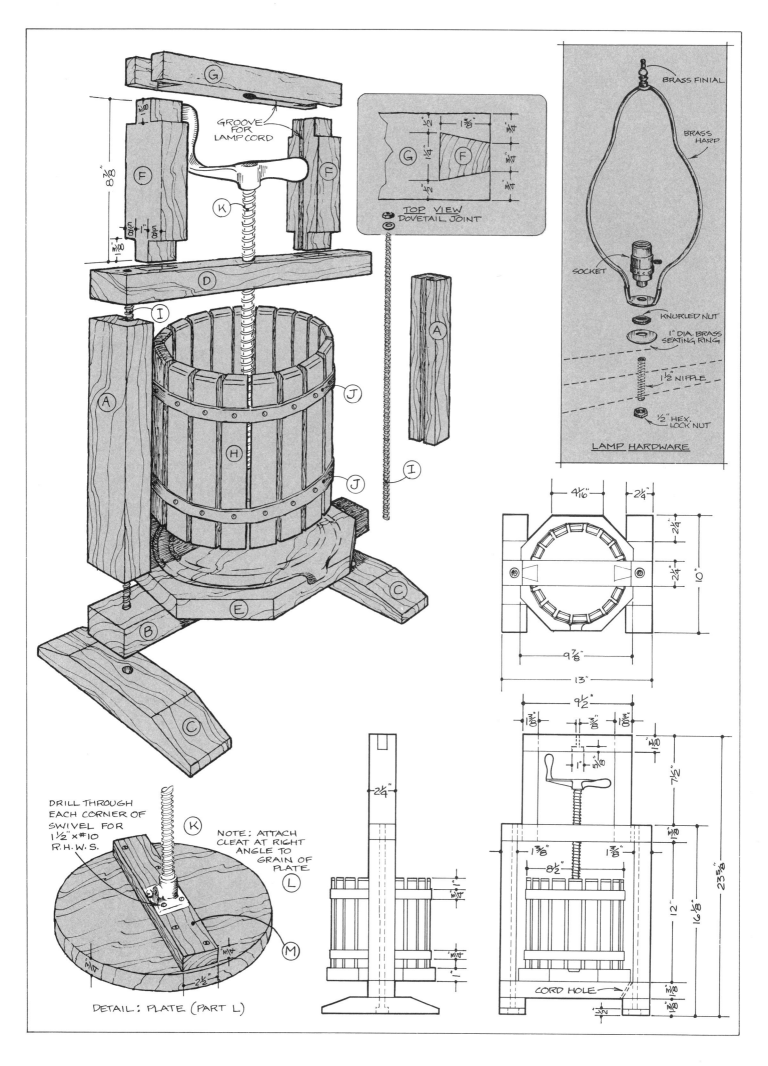

GROOVE FOR LAMP CORD

TOP VIEW
DOVETAIL JOINT

BRASS FINIAL

BRASS HARP

SOCKET

KNURLED NUT

1" DIA. BRASS SEATING RING

1½" NIPPLE

½" HEX. LOCK NUT

LAMP HARDWARE

DRILL THROUGH EACH CORNER OF SWIVEL FOR 1½" x #10 R.H.W.S.

NOTE: ATTACH CLEAT AT RIGHT ANGLE TO GRAIN OF PLATE

DETAIL: PLATE (PART L)

CORD HOLE

Oak Hanging Light Fixture

Anyone who has gone shopping for light fixtures knows that you can pay a small fortune for anything that is in the least decorative. We faced that problem recently when looking for a fixture with at least a little wood in it to go in our new dining room addition. The room has stained oak trim, much like our new kitchen cabinets which were part of the same project. We priced a few fixtures close to what we had in mind, and after recovering my composure, I decided to make my own.

This fixture also uses ordinary 60 watt household bulbs which are much cheaper to replace than the decorative ones required in so many light fixtures. All electrical parts and other materials are common hardware and lumber store items. Total cost should be around twenty dollars. When compared to the hundred dollars and up you'll pay for anything similar, this fixture is a real bargain.

Start by cutting out all the pieces. Grain should run horizontally around the arms and vertically up the main body of the fixture. Give each part a thorough sanding, taking particular care to remove any planer marks. Do not round corners or edges at this time.

Start assembly on the main body (parts A & B) of the fixture. Use a good quality woodworker's glue on all joints. Be careful not to smear any on the outside surfaces as that will seal the pores and the wood won't accept stain in that spot. After the bottom (part F) piece is mounted, the body is ready to be "bullnosed" or rounded at the edges. This can be done using a router or shaper with a ½″ radius bit. Round all except the top edges of this five-sided box.

Now determine which pieces of the arm assemblies (parts C, D, & E) go where and round all the lower edges, inside and out, using a ¼ inch radius bit. Also round the exposed ends of each side piece for the arms (part C). Be careful not to round edges that butt against other parts or the upper edges of the arms.

Before assembling the arms of the fixture you should mount the moldings (H) that go around the inside to hold the translucent plastic panels (G) in place. Miter each end to the correct length; mount one on the face of the fixture body and the other three on the inside surfaces of the arm pieces. Mount them ⅛ inch above the bottom edge of part D (⅜ inch above part C) using wood glue.

Part E, which provides a strong method for securing the arm assembly to the body, has two countersunk mounting holes for #8 by ¾ inch flat head wood screws. Add glue to one side, then secure part E to the body with the two wood screws. Later, all other parts of the arm assembly will be supported by part E, so make sure it's properly located on the body.

Locate and mount the porcelain sockets to part E as shown. It should be as high as possible without letting the bulb show over the arm side. With the bulb I used, the dimension to the centerline of the socket is 1½ inches (see drawing). This will allow room for circulation and prevent the bulb heat from damaging the plastic panels (G). To keep heat to a minimum, don't use a bulb larger than 60 watt.

Just above the wire terminals drill two ⅜ inch holes through parts E and the body (parts A and B). Using U.L. approved 16 gauge (heavy) lamp cord, pass the cord through these holes and wire the sockets as shown. Be sure to leave enough length to weave the wire through the fixture chain with at least 6 inches extra for the hook-up. Take your time and do a neat and careful job. Sloppy wiring causes fires. If you are not experienced in electrical work, have a licensed electrician do it for you.

Next, assemble part D to C. Use glue and clamp firmly. When dry, part C can be glued to part E, again using clamps. Be sure to add glue to the ends of part C and make sure there is good contact between C and the body. Allow to dry, then remove clamps and drill for 3/16 inch diameter dowel pins to reinforce parts D and E.

If you aren't ready to quit for the day, now would be a good time to cut your plastic panels. If you have the type that is widely used in flourescent light fixtures you will find that it is brittle and will chip and crack if not cut properly. The easiest way would be to use a band saw with a fine tooth blade. I cut mine on a table saw without too much difficulty. Set the blade height so it just barely cuts through, then hold a block of scrap wood on top of the material directly over the blade while pushing it through with the other hand. Do not place your hand directly over the blade, grasp the block a few inches before it, and don't forget your safety glasses. If you don't have a band saw or a table saw, you can cut the material with a circular saw. Just provide a solid backing, like a piece of scrap plywood, and set the blade to just cut through the plastic. Cut the panels a little smaller than the inside dimensions of the fixture arms so they go in easily.

Give the entire piece a final sanding before finishing. I used Tungseal Dark Oak oil base stain and spray lacquer.

Now connect the chain to the steel strip as shown. Weave the lampcord through the chain and run it through the center hole of the fixture plate. Get someone to help hold the fixture while you connect the wiring and screw the fixture plate into your ceiling box. Note the grounding instructions on the drawing. Install the plastic panels and the bulbs (maximum 60 watts). Stand back, admire a job well done and take someone out to dinner with the money you've saved.

Bill of Materials (All Dimensions Actual)			
Part	Description	Size	No. Req'd
A	Body End	½ x 6½ x 12	2
B	Body Side	½ x 5½ x 12	2
C	Arm Side	½ x 4¾ x 10	8
D	Arm End	½ x 4½ x 4½	4
E	Arm Support	½ x 3½ x 4½	4
F	Bottom	½ x 6½ x 6½	1
G	Panel	⅛ x 4-7/16 x 8-15/16	4
H	Molding	½″ quarter round	As req'd
I	Porcelain Socket	2″	4

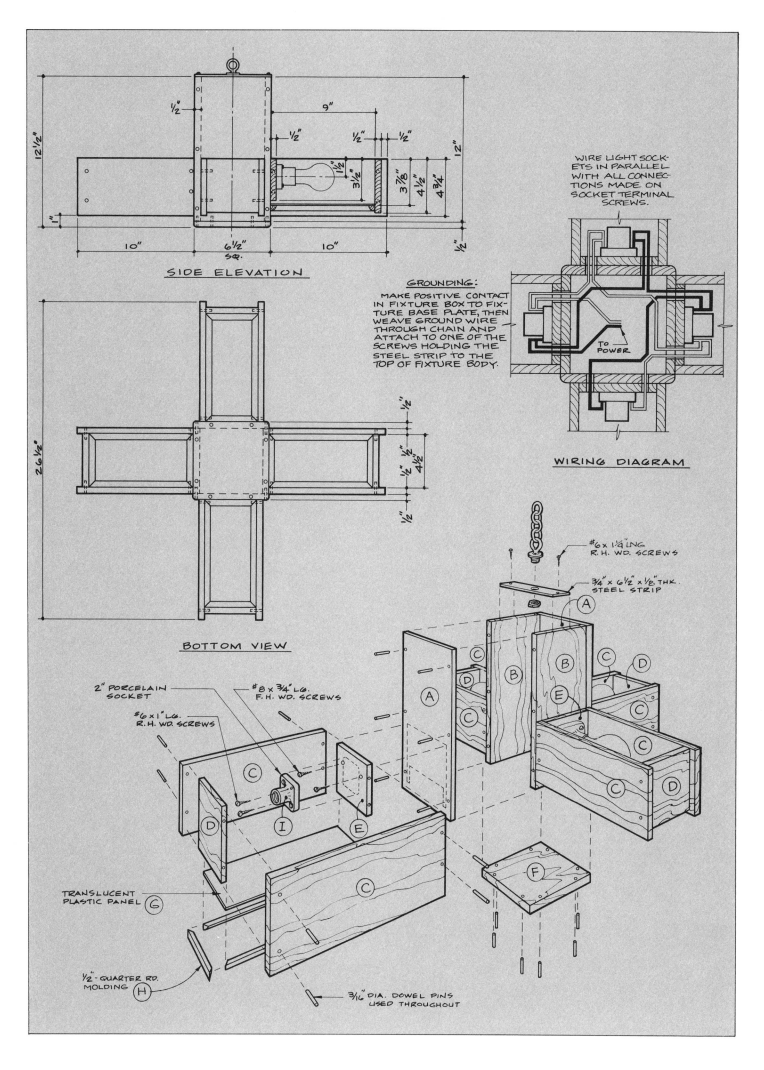

SIDE ELEVATION

BOTTOM VIEW

GROUNDING:
MAKE POSITIVE CONTACT IN FIXTURE BOX TO FIXTURE BASE PLATE, THEN WEAVE GROUND WIRE THROUGH CHAIN AND ATTACH TO ONE OF THE SCREWS HOLDING THE STEEL STRIP TO THE TOP OF FIXTURE BODY.

WIRE LIGHT SOCKETS IN PARALLEL WITH ALL CONNECTIONS MADE ON SOCKET TERMINAL SCREWS.

TO POWER

WIRING DIAGRAM

#6 x 1⅛" LNG
R.H. WD. SCREWS

¾" x 6½" x ⅛" THK.
STEEL STRIP

2" PORCELAIN SOCKET

#8 x ¾" LG.
F.H. WD. SCREWS

#6 x 1" LG.
R.H. WD. SCREWS

TRANSLUCENT PLASTIC PANEL Ⓖ

½"- QUARTER RD.
MOLDING Ⓗ

3/16" DIA. DOWEL PINS
USED THROUGHOUT

103

Tree Ornaments

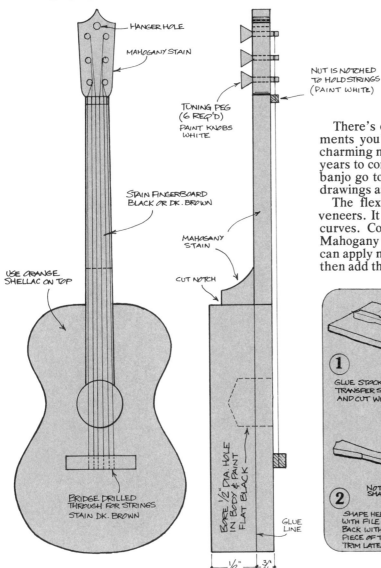

HANGER HOLE

MAHOGANY STAIN

TUNING PEG
(6 REQ'D)
PAINT KNOBS
WHITE

NUT IS NOTCHED
TO HOLD STRINGS
(PAINT WHITE)

STAIN FINGERBOARD
BLACK OR DK. BROWN

MAHOGANY
STAIN

CUT NOTCH

USE ORANGE
SHELLAC ON TOP

BRIDGE DRILLED
THROUGH FOR STRINGS
STAIN DK. BROWN

BORE ½" DIA. HOLE
IN BODY & PAINT
FLAT BLACK

GLUE
LINE

½"   3/16"

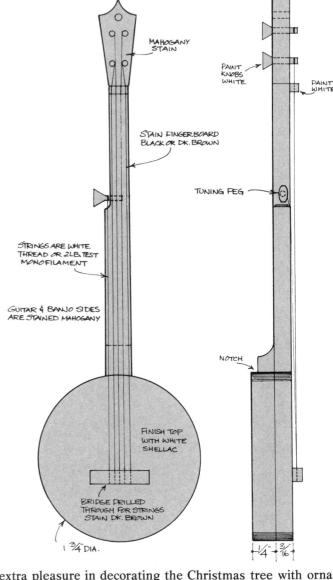

MAHOGANY
STAIN

PAINT KNOBS
WHITE

PAINT
WHITE

STAIN FINGERBOARD
BLACK OR DK. BROWN

TUNING PEG

STRINGS ARE WHITE
THREAD OR 2LB. TEST
MONOFILAMENT

GUITAR & BANJO SIDES
ARE STAINED MAHOGANY

NOTCH

FINISH TOP
WITH WHITE
SHELLAC

BRIDGE DRILLED
THROUGH FOR STRINGS
STAIN DK. BROWN

1 ¾" DIA.

¼"   3/16"

There's extra pleasure in decorating the Christmas tree with ornaments you've made yourself. Hung with slender red ribbon, these charming miniatures will add a unique decorative touch to your tree for years to come. The step-by-step drawings show how the parts for the banjo go together but the same procedure applies to the guitar. The drawings are full size for tracing.

The flexible veneer is available from mail-order firms that sell veneers. It has a thin backing and can be easily bent to the required curves. Contact cement makes the veneering job quick and easy. Mahogany veneer looks best but if you have scraps of other types, you can apply mahogany stain. Finish with a few coats of varnish or shellac then add the strings and red ribbon.

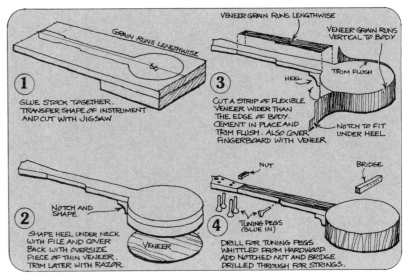

① GRAIN RUNS LENGTHWISE
GLUE STOCK TOGETHER. TRANSFER SHAPE OF INSTRUMENT AND CUT WITH JIGSAW

② NOTCH AND SHAPE
VENEER
SHAPE HEEL UNDER NECK WITH FILE AND COVER BACK WITH OVERSIZE PIECE OF THIN VENEER. TRIM LATER WITH RAZOR.

③ VENEER GRAIN RUNS LENGTHWISE
VENEER GRAIN RUNS VERTICAL TO BODY
HEEL
TRIM FLUSH
NOTCH TO FIT UNDER HEEL
CUT A STRIP OF FLEXIBLE VENEER WIDER THAN THE EDGE OF BODY. CEMENT IN PLACE AND TRIM FLUSH. ALSO COVER FINGERBOARD WITH VENEER

④ NUT
BRIDGE
TUNING PEGS (GLUE IN)
DRILL FOR TUNING PEGS WHITTLED FROM HARDWOOD. ADD NOTCHED NUT AND BRIDGE DRILLED THROUGH FOR STRINGS.

Willie & Tuna

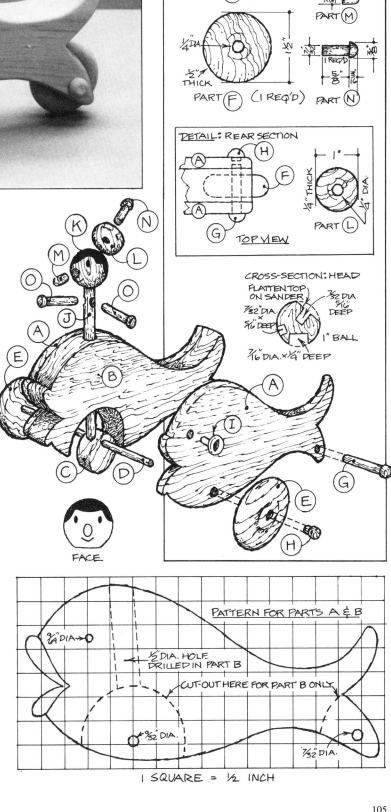

PARTS G+O

PART C (1 REQ'D)

PART E (2 REQ'D)

PART F (1 REQ'D)

PART H

PART M

PART N

DETAIL: REAR SECTION

TOP VIEW

PART L

CROSS-SECTION: HEAD
FLATTEN TOP ON SANDER
7/32 DIA.
5/16 DEEP
7/32 DIA. × 5/16 DEEP
1" BALL
7/16 DIA. × 1/4 DEEP

FACE

Push the tuna along and little Willie will move up and down — much to the delight of kids. Our thanks to Armor Products for providing us with plans for the toy. For a free copy of their toy brochure, which lists toy plans and parts, write to them at Box 445, East Northport, NY 11731. And if readers prefer not to make parts C, D, E, F, G, H, I, J, K, L, N, and O, they can be purchased ready-made from Armor.

Begin by making part A. Cut ¼ inch stock to a 3¾ inch width by 8 inches long. The ¼ inch stock can be cut from 4 inch lattice which is available at most lumber yards. Also, at this time, cut ¾ inch stock to the same width and length for part B. Sandwich part B between parts A and brad together without glue. Next, transfer the tuna profile from the grid pattern and cut out with a band or saber saw. Also drill the holes for the eye and front and rear axles.

Separate the ''sandwich'' and re-cut part B along the dotted lines (see grid pattern) to allow room for the cam (C) and rear wheel (F). The ½ inch diameter hole for Willie can now be drilled.

Next, insert part D (¼ inch diameter by 2⅜ inch long), through the cam, letting it protrude equally from both sides. The axle should fit snugly. If necessary, use glue.

Apply glue to the mating parts of A and B, then close the sandwich with the cam in place. Re-brad in the same holes, then clamp securely.

Willie is made from parts J (7/16 inch diameter by 4¼ inch long), K, L, M, N, and O. Assemble as shown using glue. If you intend to add Willie's face, do this before gluing the hat and nose in place. Use a felt-tipped pen to paint the features, using the drawing as a guide. To prevent the ink from running on the wood surface, apply a clear finish to the wood beforehand.

Add the rear wheel as shown. To make part H simply shorten an extra part N. Add the wheels (E), keeping in mind that it's a good idea to place a steel washer on the axle to prevent the wheels from rubbing against the sides of the fish.

The eye (I) can be purchased from Armor, although if necessary a simple drilled hole will suffice. No final finish is necessary.

PATTERN FOR PARTS A & B

3/8" DIA.

½" DIA. HOLE DRILLED IN PART B

CUT-OUT HERE FOR PART B ONLY

9/32" DIA.

7/32" DIA.

1 SQUARE = ½ INCH

Toy Tool Box

If you've been looking for Christmas gift ideas for a favorite little one, you may want to consider this cute toy box for your next project. It's a toy that will keep young hands pretty busy, and parents will be pleased to learn that it educates as well as entertains. Equipped with a sturdy wrench and screwdriver, the child assembles the screws, bolts, and washers to the box sides. And they all fit neatly in the box at the end of the day.

We used ½ inch thick maple for all parts except the wrench, which is made from ¾ inch plywood. If you choose to apply a finish, be sure to use one that's non-toxic.

After cutting parts A & B to size, set up a dado head cutter to cut a ¼ inch deep by ¼ inch wide groove for the plywood bottom (C). Also cut the ¼ inch deep by ½ inch wide rabbet on the end of each part B. Lay out the locations of the 1⅛ inch diameter holes, then bore out with a spade bit. Be sure to back up the workpiece with scrapstock to prevent splintering as the bit breaks through.

The 1 inch diameter by ¼ inch deep hole for the handle (D) is best cut with a Forstner bit, if you have one. Because they don't have a spur, Forstner bits drill a flat hole, making them ideal for drilling holes like this. With a spade or auger bit, the spur will begin to break through the other side and it will be necessary to fill or plug the hole after assembly.

Part A tapers to 1½ inches at the top. Use a pencil to lay out this taper, then cut out with a band or saber saw. The bottom (part C) is made from ¼ inch birch plywood cut to a width of 4-15/16 inches and a length of 11-7/16 inches. Check to make sure that it fits comfortably in the grooves cut in parts A and B, keeping in mind that sanding will reduce the thickness slightly.

All box parts can now be given a complete sanding. Counterbore and drill pilot holes for the ¾ inch by #8 flathead wood screws. If you choose to enamel part A, as we did, it should be applied at this time. We made ours a bright red. Allow to dry thoroughly. Assemble all parts as shown using wood glue. The plywood bottom (C) does not need to be glued in place.

The grid pattern shows the profile of the wrench (E). For maximum strength use plywood. Be sure to give the surfaces a good sanding and round off all edges.

To make the threaded nuts, bolts, and screws you'll need a threadbox and tap. They can be ordered from Constantine, 2050 Eastchester Road, Bronx, NY 10461.

The screw heads (J) are made from a piece of ¾ inch stock 2 inches wide by 12 inches long. Use the table saw blade to run an ⅛ inch kerf, ¼ inch deep, down the center. Lay out the 1¾ inch diameters, bandsaw, and then sand to smooth.

The washers (H) are made from ⅜ inch stock. A 2¼ inch holesaw is used to cut them out. A 1⅛ inch spade bit cuts the center hole.

To make the eight nuts (G), cut a piece of ¾ inch thick stock to a width of 2¼ inches and a length of 26 inches. The extra length and width is needed to prevent splitting when the thread is tapped. The extra length also makes it safer to do the crosscut operation. Lay out the location of the nuts along the stock, then drill and tap the holes. Now rip ¼ inch off each side of the stock (the stock is now 1¾ inches wide with the tapped holes in the middle). The tap will probably cause some splintering, so use a sharp plane to smooth the surface. This will reduce the thickness to about ⅝ inch. Next, use the miter gauge to crosscut the stock into 1¾ inch squares (with the hole at the center). Following this, the bandsaw is used to make the four 45 degree corner cuts. The four boltheads (I) are made in essentially the same manner except reduce the length of stock to 10 inches. And a 1 inch diameter by ⅜ inch deep hole is drilled rather than tapped.

Three feet of 1 inch birch dowel will be more than enough to make the threads for parts I and J. Most lumber yard dowel stock is out-of-round, and this sometimes causes threading problems. You may want to lathe turn your own, or you can purchase high quality dowel stock for threading from Conover. Sometimes the first two or three threads don't cut cleanly, so it's a good idea to run the thread a little long and cut off the first three. We've also found it helps to let the threads sit for three or four days, then rethread.

The threads can now be glued to parts I and J. When dry, apply a chamfer to the top of part I and round over part J. We spray coated ours with a light coat of enamel, red for the screws, blue for the bolts.

Make the screwdriver handle (F) from 1½ inch square stock cut four inches long. Use a sharp plane to cut the corners at 45 degrees. The ⅝ inch diameter "blade" fits into a hole drilled in the socket.

Bill of Materials - Toy Tool Box (All Dimensions Actual)			
Part	Description	Size	No. Req'd
A	Box End	½ x 5 x 7	2
B	Box Side	½ x 3 x 12	2
C	Bottom	¼ x 4-15/16 x 11-7/16	1
D	Handle	1 Dia. x 11½	1
E	Wrench	See Detail	1
F	Screwdriver	See Detail	1
G	Nut	See Detail	8
H	Washer	⅜ x 2¼ Dia.	8
I	Bolt	See Detail	4
J	Screw	See Detail	4

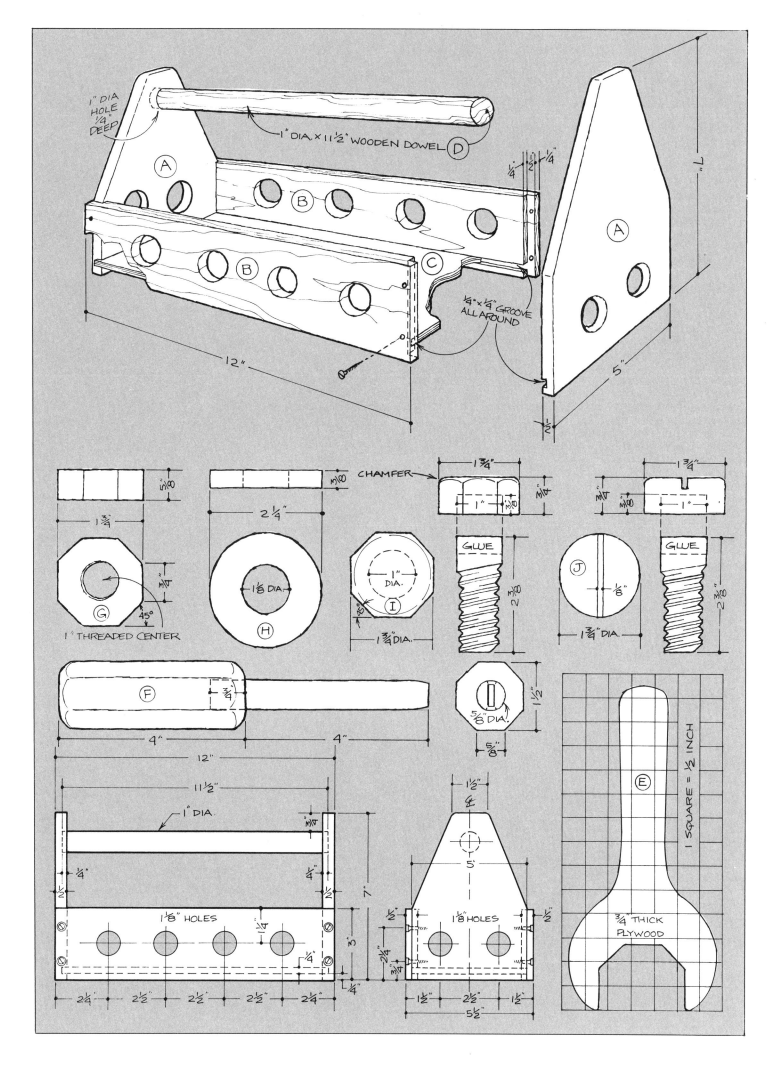

1" DIA HOLE ¼" DEEP

1" DIA. x 11½" WOODEN DOWEL D

A

B

B

C

1" DIA. x 11½" WOODEN DOWEL D

¼" x ¼" GROOVE ALL AROUND

A

12"

5"

½

"L"

¼ 2" ¼

CHAMFER

1¾"

1"

¾"

¾

3∕8

GLUE

2⅜"

1¾" DIA.

1¾"

¾

3∕10

1"

GLUE

J

1∕8"

1¾" DIA.

2⅜"

5∕8

1¾"

¾"

45°

G

1" THREADED CENTER

2¼"

3∕8

1⅛ DIA

H

1" DIA.

45°

I

1¾" DIA.

1½"

⅝ DIA.

⅝"

F

¾"

4"

4"

12"

11½"

1" DIA.

¾"

¼

½

¼

½

7"

1⅛" HOLES

¼

3"

¼

2¼" 2½" 2½" 2½" 2¼"

1½"

¢

5"

½

2¼

3∕4

½

1⅛" HOLES

¼

1½" 2½" 1½"

5½"

E

¾" THICK PLYWOOD

1 SQUARE = ½ INCH

107

The dimensions of these lovely pine shelves are nearly identical to a Shaker original that hangs at the Hancock Shaker Village in Hancock, Massachusetts. The only significant difference is in the thickness of the stock - ours is ¾ inch while the Hancock piece was made from ⅝ inch lumber. The Shaker pegs (F) can be turned to the profile shown or purchased from Shaker Workshops, P.O. Box 1028, Concord, MA 01742.

Cut the two sides (A) from 1 x 8 nominal stock, then use an adjustable dado head cutter to make the ¼ inch deep by ¾ inch wide rabbet for part B. The ¼ inch deep by ¾ inch wide dadoes for parts C and D can be cut at the same time. Next, lay out the curved profile (see grid pattern), before cutting with a band or saber saw.

After cutting shelves B, C, and D, and pegboard E to dimensions shown, give all parts a thorough sanding. Assemble with glue and clamp securely. When dry, remove clamps, then add the ¼ inch diameter by one inch long dowel pins as shown. Use a sharp plane to bevel the front edge of the two upper shelves. Glue pegs (F) in place, then give the entire project a final sanding. Ours was stained with Minwax's Fruitwood stain, followed by a final finish of Minwax's Antique Oil.

Two counterbored holes permit the pegboard to be secured to the wall. A pair of leather laces, tied in a loop, allows the shelf to be hung from the two pegs - a common practice of the Shakers.

Shaker Shelves

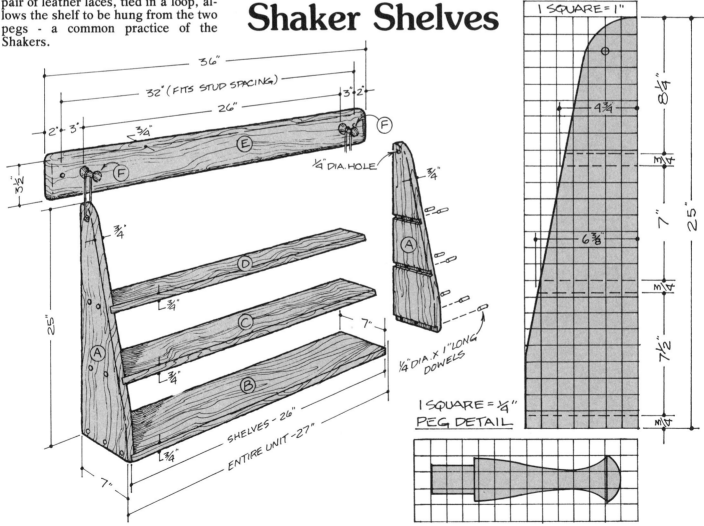

Woodpile Trivet

A firewood pile can often provide more than just BTU's on a bitter cold night. With a minimum of work, a short log can be transformed into an eye-catching trivet that's going to invite lots of compliments.

There's no hard and fast rule that dictates the size of the log, but we used one with a diameter of about 2¾ inches. Each disk was cut to a ½ inch thickness. You'll want the wood to have an interesting figure, so it may be necessary to slice a few logs to find one you like. However, be sure to use a log that's well seasoned or there will be splitting problems.

Locate the dowels 90 degrees apart, then drill 5/16 inch diameter by ⅜ inch deep holes for ¼ inch diameter dowel pins. The extra 1/16 inch hole diameter allows for any misalignment of the dowel pins. The pins are then secured in place with epoxy glue, which is fast setting and will fill any gaps in the hole. Sand both sides smooth, finishing with 220 grit, then final finish with an application of Watco Danish Oil.

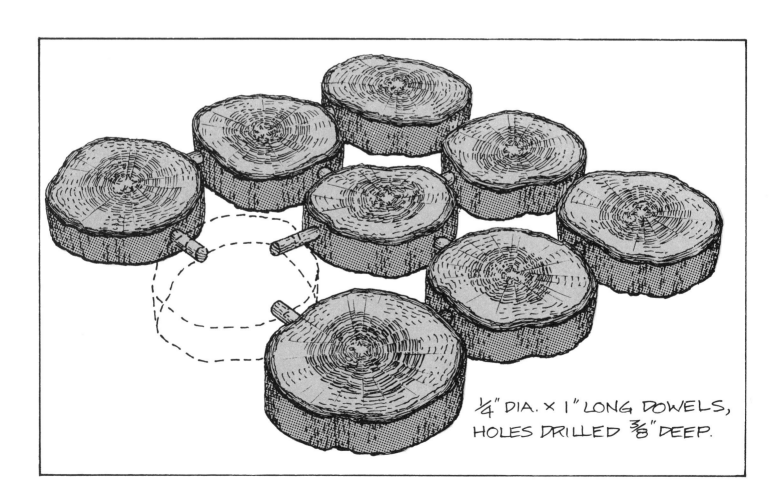

¼" DIA. × 1" LONG DOWELS, HOLES DRILLED ⅜" DEEP.

Sources of Supply

The following pages list companies that specialize in
mail-order sales of woodworking supplies.

United States

General Woodworking Suppliers

Constantine's
2050 Eastchester Rd.
Bronx, NY 10461

Craftsman Wood Service
1735 West Cortland Ct.
Addison, IL 60101

The Fine Tool Shops
170 West Road
Portsmouth, NH 03810

Frog Tool Co., Ltd.
700 W. Jackson Blvd.
Chicago, IL 60606

Garrett Wade
161 Avenue of the Americas
New York, NY 10013

Highland Hardware
1045 N. Highland Ave., N.E.
Atlanta, GA 30306

Seven Corners Ace Hardware
216 West 7th Street
St. Paul, MN 55102

Shopsmith, Inc.
6640 Poe Ave.
Dayton, OH 45414

Trend-Lines
375 Beacham St.
Chelsea, MA 02150-0999

Woodcraft Supply Corp.
41 Atlantic Ave.
Woburn, MA 01888

The Woodworkers' Store
21801 Industrial Blvd.
Rogers, MN 55374

Woodworker's Supply of New Mexico
5604 Alameda, N.E.
Albuquerque, NM 87113

W.S. Jenks and Son
1933 Montana Ave., N.E.
Washington, DC 20002

Hardware Suppliers

Allen Specialty Hardware
332 W. Bruceton Rd.
Pittsburgh, PA 15236

Anglo-American Brass Co.
Box 9487
4146 Mitzi Drive
San Jose, CA 95157

Horton Brasses
Nooks Hill Rd.
P.O. Box 120
Cromwell, CT 06416

Imported European Hardware
4320 W. Bell Dr.
Las Vegas, NV 89118

Meisel Hardware Specialties
P.O. Box 258
Mound, MN 55364

Paxton Hardware, Ltd.
7818 Bradshaw Rd.
Upper Falls, MD 21156

Period Furniture Hardware Co.
123 Charles St.
Box 314 Charles Street Station
Boston, MA 02114

Stanley Hardware
195 Lake Street
New Britain, CT 06050

The Wise Co.
6503 St. Claude
Arabi, LA 70032

Hardwood Suppliers

American Woodcrafters
905 S. Roosevelt Ave.
Piqua, OH 45356

Austin Hardwoods
2119 Goodrich
Austin, TX 78704

Bergers Hardwoods
Route 4, Box 195
Bedford, VA 24523

Berea Hardwoods Co.
125 Jacqueline Drive
Berea, OH 44017

Maurice L. Condon
250 Ferris Ave.
White Plains, NY 10603

Craftwoods
109 21 York Rd.
Cockeysville, MD 21030

Croy-Marietta Hardwoods, Inc.
121 Pike St., Box 643
Marietta, OH 45750

Dimension Hardwoods, Inc.
113 Canal Street
Shelton, CT 06484

Educational Lumber Co.
P.O. Box 5373
Asheville, NC 28813

General Woodcraft
531 Broad St.
New London, CT 06320

Hardwoods of Memphis
P.O. Box 12449
Memphis, TN 38182-0449

Kaymar Wood Products
4603 35th S.W.
Seattle, WA 98126

Kountry Kraft Hardwoods
R.R. No. 1
Lake City, IA 51449

Leonard Lumber Co.
P.O. Box 2396
Branford, CT 06405

McFeely's Hardwoods & Lumber
43 Cabell St.
Lynchburg, VA 24505

Native American Hardwoods
Route 1
West Valley, NY 14171

Sterling Hardwoods, Inc.
412 Pine St.
Burlington, VT 05401

(continued on next page)

Wood World
1719 Chestnut
Glenview, IL 60025

Woodworker's Dream
P.O. Box 329
Nazareth, PA 18064

Wood Finishing Supplies

Finishing Products and Supply Co.
4611 Macklind Ave.
St. Louis, MO 63109

Industrial Finishing Products
465 Logan St.
Brooklyn, NY 11208

The Wise Co.
P.O. Box 118
6503 St. Claude
Arabie, LA 70032

WoodFinishing Enterprises
Box 10017
Milwaukee, WI 53210

Watco-Dennis Corp.
1433 Santa Monica Blvd.
Santa Monica, CA 90401

Clock Parts

Craft Products Co.
2200 Dean St.
St. Charles, IL 60174

Klockit, Inc.
P.O. Box 542
Lake Geneva, WI 53147

S. LaRose
234 Commerce Place
Greensboro, NC 27420

Mason & Sullivan Co.
586 Higgins Crowell Rd.
West Yarmouth, MA 02655

Newport Enterprises
2313 West Burbank Blvd.
Burbank, CA 91506

Miscellaneous

DML, Inc. (Router Bits)
1350 S. 15th Street
Louisville, KY 40210

Formica Corporation (Plastic Laminate)
1 Stanford Road
Piscataway, NJ 08854

Freud (Saw Blades)
218 Feld Ave.
High Point, NC 27264

MLCS (Router Bits)
P.O. Box 53
Rydal, PA 19041

Homecraft Veneer (Veneer)
901 West Way
Latrobe, PA 15650

Sears, Roebuck and Co.
(Misc. Tools & Supplies)
925 S. Homan Ave.
Chicago, IL 60607

Wilson Art (Plastic Laminate)
600 General Bruce Drive
Temple, TX 76501

Canada

General Woodworking Suppliers

House of Tools Ltd.
131-12th Ave. S.E.
Calgary, Alberta T2G 0Z9

J. Philip Humfrey International
3241 Kennedy Rd., Unit 7
Scarborough, Ontario M1V 2J9

Lee Valley Tools
Unit 6, 5511 Steeles Ave. West
Weston, Ontario M9L 1S7

Stockade Woodworker's Supply
P.O. Box 1415
Salmon Arm, British Columbia V0E 2T0

Tool Trend Ltd.
3280 Steele's Ave. West
Concord, Ontario L4K 2Y2

Treen Heritage, Ltd.
P.O. Box 280
Merrickville, Ontario K0G 1N0

Hardware Suppliers

Home Workshop Supplies
RR 2
Arthur, Ontario N0G 1A0

Lee Valley Tools
Unit 6, 5511 Steeles Ave. West
Weston, Ontario M9L 1S7

Pacific Brass Hardware
1414 Monterey Ave.
Victoria, British Columbia V8S 4W1

Steve's Shop, Woodworking & Supplies
RR 3
Woodstock, Ontario M9V 5C3

Hardwood Suppliers

A & C Hutt Enterprises, Ltd.
15861 32nd Ave.
Surrey, British Columbia V4B 4Z5

Longstock Lumber & Veneer
440 Phillip St., Unit 21
Waterloo, Ontario N2L 5R9

Unicorn Universal Woods Ltd.
4190 Steeles Ave. West, Unit 4
Woodbridge, Ontario L4L 3S8

Clock Parts

Hurst Associates
151 Nashdene Rd., Unit 14
Scarborough, Ontario M1V 2T3

Kidder Klock
39 Glen Cameron Rd., Unit 3
Thornhill, Ontario L3T 1P1

Murray Clock Craft Ltd.
510 McNicoll Ave.
Willowdale, Ontario M2H 2E1

Miscellaneous

Freud (Saw Blades)
100 Westmore Dr., Unit 10
Rexdale, Ontario M9V 5C3

Index

(continued on next page)

Imperial to Metric Conversion Table

Feet	Inches — Centi-metres	1	2	3	4	5	6	7	8	9	10	11
		2.54	5.08	7.62	10.16	12.70	15.24	17.78	20.32	22.86	25.40	27.94
1	30.48	33.02	35.56	38.10	40.64	43.18	45.72	48.26	50.80	53.34	55.88	58.42
2	60.96	63.50	66.04	68.58	71.12	73.66	76.20	78.74	81.28	83.82	86.36	88.90
3	91.44	93.98	96.52	99.06	101.60	104.14	106.68	109.22	111.76	114.30	116.84	119.38
4	121.92	124.46	127.00	129.54	132.08	134.62	137.16	139.70	142.24	144.78	147.32	149.86
5	152.40	154.94	157.48	160.02	162.56	165.10	167.64	170.18	172.72	175.26	177.80	180.34
6	182.88	185.42	187.96	190.50	193.04	195.58	198.12	200.66	203.20	205.74	208.28	210.82
7	213.36	215.90	218.44	220.98	223.52	226.06	228.60	231.14	233.68	236.22	238.76	241.30
8	243.84	246.38	248.92	251.46	254.00	256.54	259.08	261.62	264.16	266.70	269.24	271.78
9	274.32	276.86	279.40	281.94	284.48	287.02	289.56	292.10	294.64	297.18	299.72	302.26
10	304.80	307.34	309.88	312.42	314.96	317.50	320.04	322.58	325.12	327.66	330.20	332.74
11	335.28	337.82	340.36	342.90	345.44	347.98	350.52	353.06	355.60	358.14	360.68	363.22
12	365.76	368.30	370.84	373.38	375.92	378.46	381.00	383.54	386.08	388.62	391.16	393.70
13	396.24	398.78	401.32	403.86	406.40	408.94	411.48	414.02	416.56	419.10	421.64	424.18
14	426.72	429.26	431.80	434.34	436.88	439.42	441.96	444.50	447.04	449.58	452.12	454.66
15	457.20	459.74	462.28	464.82	467.36	469.90	472.44	474.98	477.52	480.06	482.60	485.14
16	487.68	490.22	492.76	495.30	498.84	500.38	502.92	505.46	508.00	510.54	513.08	515.62
17	518.16	520.70	523.24	525.78	528.32	530.86	533.40	535.94	538.48	541.02	543.56	546.10
18	548.64	551.18	553.72	556.26	558.80	561.34	563.88	566.42	568.96	571.50	574.04	576.58
19	579.12	581.66	584.20	586.74	589.28	591.82	594.36	596.90	599.44	601.98	604.52	607.06
20	609.60	612.14	614.68	617.22	619.76	622.30	624.84	627.38	629.92	632.46	635.00	637.54

Fractional Equivalents

in.—cms.		in.—cms.	
1/16 = 0.15875		1/8 = 0.31700	
3/16 = 0.47625		1/4 = 0.63500	
5/16 = 0.79375		3/8 = 0.95250	
7/16 = 1.11125		1/2 = 1.27040	
9/16 = 1.42875		5/8 = 1.58730	
11/16 = 1.74625		3/4 = 1.90500	
13/16 = 2.06375		7/8 = 2.22250	
15/16 = 2.38125		1 = 2.54000	

Measures of Length—Basic S.I. Unit—
Metre = 100 Centimetres = 39.37 Inches

Example:

(1) To convert 13 feet 6 inches to centimetres, read along line 13 under feet and under column 6 inches read 411.48 cms. To reduce to metres move decimal point two spaces to left; thus, 4.1148 metres is the answer.

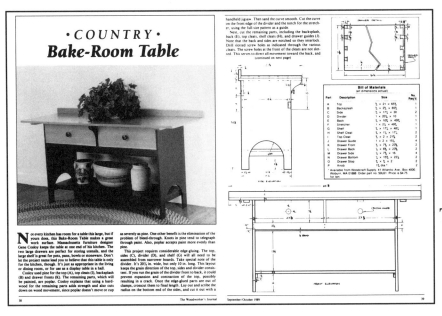